W9-BUY-158

LIFE AFTER LOSS

Conquering Grief and Finding Hope

Raymond A. Moody, Jr., M.D., Ph.D.
and Dianne Arcangel, M.S.

HarperSanFrancisco
A Division of HarperCollins*Publishers*

To you, the reader

ISBN 0-06-251729-5

Contents

Eight: Transcending Loss

Nine: The Blessings Received from Loss

Ten: We Will See Them Again

Supportive Resources

Foreword

When archaeologists recently examined a Neanderthal grave that was more than forty-four thousand years old, they found traces of ancient pollen from hyacinth and hollyhock flowers, apparently the remnant of a garland left by a mourner. It was a poignant reminder that grief, loss, and bereavement have been part of the human experience for a very long time.

Some say this will change. Experts are predicting a sensational increase in human longevity in the near future. There is heady talk about postponing death indefinitely, as scientists unravel the mysteries of aging. So far, however, the statistics are compelling—everyone dies, no exceptions—which means that the primal sense of loss is unlikely ever to be eradicated.

Although death remains a constant, our attitudes toward it are changing. One of the most significant developments in Western cultures during the twentieth century was our increased willingness to confront death openly. Books on death and dying are best-sellers. Courses in "death mentoring" and compassionate care for the dying have become standard fare in medical schools, hospitals, and secular institutions. Hospice care of the dying is helping medicine reestablish contact with its spiritual roots. Talk of a "natural," "good," "peaceful," and "graceful" death abounds. Baby boomers, now in their fifties, who once wrote their own wedding vows, are now writing their funeral scripts in an attempt to personalize their departure and ease the grief of those left behind.[1]

One reason for these developments is the recognition that painful emotional experiences such as grief and loss can best be dealt with by entering them fully instead of ignoring them or burying them in the unconscious mind. As Buddhism says, "Welcome everything, push nothing away." This is where Moody and Arcangel's *Life After Loss* excels. There is no better practical guide for confronting pain and loss than their fine book. They write from personal insight and experience, and they have immense wisdom to share.

During the reign of materialistic science in the past two centuries, it became fashionable to consider human consciousness the equivalent of the brain. This meant that, with the death of the brain and body, consciousness was annihilated and total personal destruction was assured. This view not only deepened the experience of grief and loss for survivors; it reminded them of their own impending destruction as well. Today, however, many lines of evidence suggest that we must rethink the assumption that mind equals brain. The reason, in a nutshell, is this: scientific evidence shows that consciousness can do things that brains cannot. Quite simply, brains and consciousness are not the same.

In his investigation of near-death experiences (NDEs), Raymond Moody, Jr., has illuminated some of the evidence suggesting that consciousness may transcend the physical brain and body. Like the academic philosopher that he is, Moody is careful not to overstate the case for the survival of consciousness. Yet hope for survival is clearly in the air.[2] As a team of British physicians recently put it, "The occurrence of NDE during cardiac arrest raises questions about the possible relationship between the mind and the brain."[3]

When we speak of grief and loss, what, actually, is lost? The physical body obviously dies, but what about consciousness? John Searle, one of the most distinguished philosophers in the field of consciousness studies, has said, "At our present state of the investigation of consciousness, we *don't know* how it works and we need to try all kinds of different ideas."[4] Philosopher Jerry A. Fodor has observed, "Nobody has the slightest idea how anything material could be conscious. Nobody even knows what it would be like to have the slightest idea about how anything material could be conscious. So much for the philosophy of consciousness."[5] Recently Sir John Maddox, the former editor of *Nature*, soberly stated, "The catalogue of our ignorance must . . . include the understanding of the human brain. . . . What consciousness consists of . . . is . . . a puzzle. Despite the marvelous success of neuroscience in the past century . . . , we seem as far away from understanding . . . as we were a century ago."[6] These observations show that we are appallingly ignorant about the nature of consciousness, the relationship of mind and brain, and the origin and destiny of consciousness. It is important to acknowledge our ignorance, because this permits a greater openness to the new views of consciousness and perhaps for survival.

We are entering a renaissance in which scholars are investigating how consciousness operates beyond the brain.[7] For example, the evidence for distant healing and intercessory prayer is compelling and continues to increase.[8] As a result of this and many other lines of evidence, we are beginning to realize that some aspect of consciousness transcends the physical brain and is apparently nonlocal or *infinite* in space and time, thus eternal and immortal.[9]

Why emphasize these developments? Nothing, I believe, could be more important in annulling the sting of death and the sense of loss and grief following the death of loved ones.

I love the ambiguity of this book's title, *Life After Loss.* Life for whom? For those who remain? For the deceased? My answer is: life for *both*.

Many people still believe that grief and loss are brute experiences that must be borne in isolation, solitude, and silence. *Life After Loss* demonstrates that this assumption is wrong. Practical steps can be taken to diminish the pain of grief, mourning, and bereavement, as the authors show.

This book is a work of love and caring, and only someone capable of deep compassion could have written it. The authors deserve our collective gratitude for nudging us toward the realization that, although we cannot annul death, that is not the final chapter for those who remain—nor, perhaps, for the departed as well.

—LARRY DOSSEY, M.D

Acknowledgments from Raymond Moody

I want to express my deep appreciation to all the special people who have come to me seeking solace for their losses, I thank them for what they have taught me about the process of grief, and about the importance of love.

And I so appreciate my friend Dianne Arcangel, and treasure our association and friendship through the years. Thanks so much, Dianne, for your kindness and forbearance during this project.

Many Thanks to my wonderful wife Cheryl, and our children Carter and Carol Ann, for providing time and inspiration for me to work on this project. And thanks to all the great people at HarperSanFrancisco, including David Hennessy and Terri Leonard, for their support and interest."

—RAYMOND A. MOODY PHD, M.D.

Acknowledgment from Dianne Arcangel

"Please put your words in writing," bereaved families have requested over the years. "I'd like to have them to read on difficult nights." To those who have waited so long—thank you for your patience and for being the catalysts for *Life After Loss*.

Acknowledgments go to Raymond Moody and his wife, Cheryl, for asking me to make this book a joint venture and for taking the initial steps that commenced the writing in October, 1997. I especially appreciate Raymond's willingness to share his personal life with our readers.

From the conception of this book, agent Nat Sobel believed in and contributed. His support graces every page. Appreciation also goes to Nat's remarkable staff Laura Nolan, Anna Bliss, and Catherine Crawford at SobelWeber, Inc.

Although this book lists two authors, many individuals joined ranks with one intention—to offer their loving support to you. I was humbled by the graciousness of many of my professional colleagues. Sonja Earthman and Charles

Novo enthusiastically jumped in from the very beginning and contributed every way they could. Their insight added depth throughout the project. Bruce Greyson unselfishly provided data, suggestions, editorial comments, and a great deal of emotional support. To list every professional would be daunting; however, certain others contributed in a special way: April Reckling, Cara McElhaney, Carmen Martinez, Colin Caffell, Diego De Leo, Donna Medford, Elaine Stillwell, Gary Rosen, Geri Colozzi Wiitala, Jarrett Huffman, Jerrod Daigle, Jim Monahan, Jo Ann Thomas and staff at the Gateway Center, Josephine Caragdine, Pam Kircher, Rhea White, Robert Neimeyer, Rupert Sheldrake, Ruth Landaur, Sally Feather, Sheldon Rubenfeld and his staff at The Thyroid Society for Education and Research, and Tom Golden. My colleagues at the Association for Death Education and Counseling, the American Association of Suicidology, American Cancer Society, and The Hospice at the Texas Medical Center immediately provided support every time they were asked, as did the staff at Earthman Funeral Homes, Scott and White Hospice, Pasadena Public Library, and World Health Organization.

Many friends, each in his or her unique way, offered their support to you as well: Billie Mackrill, Bob Bigelow, Carol Poole, Connie Carey, Luanne Valkner, Monica McCormick, Rick Kelly, Terry Huber, and Tod Steiner. To those who asked that their last names remain anonymous, thank you Betty, Elaine, Gail, Gary, Jerry, Jimmie, Joe, John Paul, Lottie, Pam, Ruth, and Tanya.

My heart-felt appreciation to the preview readers who critiqued the original manuscript: K'Anne Thompson, Sonja Earthman, Charles Novo, Leona Muckleroy, Rhea White, Carol Poole, Diane Bigelow, and Madeline Westbrook.

Thank you to Leona Muckleroy, my best friend, for her integrity, advice, personal story, and for many of the chapter quotes. Her daily support was monumental.

My deepest gratitude goes to the wonderfully supportive editors at HarperSanFrancisco. Their patience and expertise were beyond the call of duty: David Hennessy, Gideon Weil, Terri Leonard, and Anne Collins. Appreciation goes to all the staff at HarperSanFrancisco who diligently worked to create a work of art.

I never work alone. Elisabeth Kubler-Ross guides me as I care for the bereaved, Karlis Osis inspires my writing, and the Dalai Lama keeps me focused on my intentions. Eternal gratitude to them.

My daughter K'Anne, grandson Silas, and son-in-law Clark, provided numerous stories for this book, but more importantly, I appreciate the "book breaks" they gave me during my many consecutive days and nights of writing.

My husband, Joe, read every word of the many drafts of this book, and although he was its greatest literary critic, he remained a continuous cheerleader throughout. His only hope, like mine, is that *Life After Loss* will help someone else make it through the night.

—DIANNE ARCANGEL

Introduction

Ours is a grief-denying culture. After a loved one dies, most people escape their feelings of loss by indulging in mundane things: work, food, liquor, drugs, music, television, exercise, sex, books, shopping, the Internet—the list goes on and on. Why not escape? Who wants to feel pain? Who wants to feel anything even remotely related to mourning?

What if you were to look across a deep, forbidding valley to envision a perfect place, high atop a beautiful mountain. Not only is this place beyond anything you have ever imagined; it is surrounded by everything you hold dear. Only one connection exists between you and this wondrous place—a bridge. That mountaintop is your optimum self, the person you were born to potentially become. In the valley lies the gulf of grief, and the bridge is mourning. Mountainous growth does not develop through joy and splendor, but from sorrow.

Glimpses of the bridge appear many times—when friends move away, Grandma goes home, holidays are over, relationships end, opportunities are missed, seasons change, and so on. Crossing that bridge, however, can only be achieved by having loved, lost, and mourned for someone dear to your heart.

Loss can be heartbreaking. It can be devastating. It can seem like the end of everything. Our journey began forty years ago in classrooms, libraries, and churches while we were trying to understand and manage our own grief. Our personal losses became catalysts for our professional work in the fields of thanatology (the study of death and dying) and survival (life-after-death studies). As we were researching, counseling, and teaching, it became clear that others who were bereaved sought the same things we did: comfort, hope, and reassurance that our states of mind and emotions were "normal."

This book is our offering to others; however, we did not write as experts teaching people how to grieve. We believe that each person is the lone expert for his or her grief. Although some readers will discover their own paths for mourning within these pages, we present no formulas. Formulas are not applicable to something as individualized as grief. Our intention is similar to Tommy's.

Tommy's Story

Tommy, only six years old, had been wanting a wristwatch. When he finally received one on Christmas Day, he was eager to show it to his best friend, Billy. Tommy's mother approved and warned her son as he was leaving, "Now, Tommy, you are wearing your new watch and you know how to tell time. It takes two minutes for you to walk home from Billy's, so there will be no excuses for returning home late. Be here before six o'clock for supper."

"I will, Mom," Tommy assured her as he scurried out the door.

Six o'clock came and went, but no Tommy. At six-fifteen, when there was still no sign of him, his mother became irritated. Then at six-thirty and still no Tommy, she felt angry. At six-fifty, her anger turned to fear. Just as she stood to go search for her son, the front door eased open. Tommy quietly stepped inside.

"Oh, Tommy!" she scolded. "How could you be so inconsiderate? Didn't you know I'd be worried? Where have you been?"

"I've been helping Billy . . ." Tommy began.

"Helping Billy what?" his mother yelled.

Again the young child tried to explain. "Billy got a brand-new bike for Christmas, but it fell off the curb and broke and . . ."

"Oh, Tommy," she interrupted, "what does a six-year-old know about fixing a bike? For heaven's sake, you . . ."

This time, it was Tommy who interrupted, "No, Mom. I wasn't trying to help him fix it. I was sitting on the curb beside him helping him cry."

Our Purpose

Our intention, like Tommy's, is not to try to "fix" anything. Grief is far too profound for anyone to fix. Although we cannot sit on the curb beside all those who mourn, we can offer words of comfort, hope, and inspiration as you cross your own bridge, in your own way, and in your own time. In some way, we can be there with you.

For You, Personally

Life After Loss was written for individuals in the throes of grief; however, our reflections can be applied to other losses as well. Some of this material will be exactly what you need, and some will not. We invite you to use what will serve you and set the rest aside, perhaps returning to it at a later time. How you find comfort within these pages is up to you; however, this book should never be considered a substitute for treatment or professional counseling

Format

The text was designed to address the questions we are most frequently asked: How do some bereaved individuals grow stronger from their losses? How can sympathy be offered and received? What are the differences between functional grief and dysfunctional grief? When will my suffering end? How do survivors rebuild their lives after loss? How can stress be managed? We conclude by presenting some of the blessings that loss offers and then list available resources, including books, magazine articles, newsletters, journals, associations, organizations, bereavement centers, crisis hot lines, support-group affiliations, and Internet sites.

At the request of certain people whose stories are told in these pages, we altered their names and other identifying details to protect their privacy. The integrity of their stories, however, remains undiminished.

ONE

Early Grief Experiences

> The child's sobs in the silence curses deeper
> than the strong man in his wrath.
>
> —ELIZABETH BARRETT BROWNING

The death of a loved one reactivates our very first experiences with separation and grief. People who grow stronger during times of loss are willing to explore their early encounters. Therefore, in this chapter we will examine five events that continue to influence us into adulthood: prebirth sensations, the experience of birth, attachment and loss, the introduction to the concept of death, and, finally, beliefs about mortality that were formed during childhood.

PREBIRTH INFLUENCES

Early on, psychologists disregarded prebirth recollections, insisting that fetuses were too underdeveloped to carry repercussions from intrauterine events. Numerous claims, however, have brought the issue forward. Mothers who were grief-stricken during their pregnancies attest that their children were born sorrowing. Other family members, and sometimes the children themselves, have made similar claims. Jenni's case carries reliable evidence that prebirth sensations can extend well into adulthood.

"I feel myself in a deathly dark room"—Dianne's Story

For as long as she could remember, Jenni, a successful New York model, had carried deep-seated sorrow and fear, which she tried to resolve for many years.

It was midsummer, 1988, and everybody who could had deserted Manhattan—except Jenni. "I'm determined to resolve my emotional difficulties," she said when we met. "I've tried every kind of counseling, even hypnotherapy, but every time a therapist told me to go back in time I felt myself in a deathly dark room and became hysterical. I still feel this continuous nagging restlessness in my heart. I don't know where it belongs, and I'm tired of it complicating my relationships. I'm concerned about what I might uncover, but I have to do something. Dianne, will you help me?"

Our two hypnotherapy sessions produced the same results. "I'm in a completely blackened room," Jenni relayed. "I have no hint of light in here. Voices . . . I hear loud muffled voices outside. Now I hear someone screaming . . . it sounds like my mother's voice. I'm being tossed around. I'm so scared in here. Someone . . . Mother . . ."

Jenni was wincing and squirming; therefore, I reminded her, "We are in this together. You're safe." After she settled down, I asked, "What's going on now?"

She tried to identify what was happening outside her confine, saying, "I can't tell. I think . . . someone . . . someone is hurting my mother . . . now I'm . . . I'm in danger . . . all alone in here . . . in the dark . . . tossing around . . . everything is . . ." and, with that, Jenni's body collapsed into her chair. Her breathing slowed.

"What's going on now?" I asked.

"I'm just in here," she answered.

"How old are you?"

"I don't know. I'm little, very little."

"Who else is there?" I asked.

"I'm trying hard," she answered, "but I can't tell." Only vague, isolated noises penetrated her motionless boundary. Then stillness, quiet, and finally an eerie peacefulness comforted Jenni as she rested inside her small enclosure.

"Wow," she said, opening her eyes. "Whatever happened is stronger in my mind. I felt like I was a young child, maybe two or three years old, and hiding inside a closet. I was helpless, listening as someone was trying to hurt my mother. But how could I, inside a closet, have experienced jostling like that? It doesn't make sense. I have to find out what happened to me."

The following week Jenni flew home to Asia to ask her parents about her childhood, but when she began to inquire, her mother uncontrollably sobbed. Her father scolded, "Don't you ever bring that up again!" After that, she approached her maternal grandmother, who disapprovingly dismissed her as well.

"My trip ended in disappointment," reported Jenni, "because I had to leave without answers to my questions. But at least I know there must be a story." Haunted by her memories, Jenni was driven to uncover her past. Patiently, she waited for a family gathering.

Sometime thereafter, she was certain that her cousin's large wedding was the perfect place for her to approach family members. With the flow of alcohol-fueled reminiscences, her questions seemed part of the fun. Jenni's aunt, at last, revealed the troublesome event.

Many years ago, her father's jealous mistress had broken into their house, taken a butcher knife from the kitchen, and proceeded toward the bedroom with murderous intent. Jenni's mother, eight months pregnant with Jenni, awoke from a nap to see a figure creeping toward her. The mistress jumped onto the bed, cursing and lashing at the mother-to-be with the knife. Jenni's mother struggled desperately to defend herself and her unborn child, fending off her crazed attacker until her husband rushed into the room. A large muscular man, he grabbed the other woman from behind and was able to subdue her and drag her from the bedroom. Alone and too debilitated to move, Jenni's mother thanked God that the episode was over.

The attack explained the sensations Jenni had felt during her hypnotherapy sessions—her feeling of being tossed around while inside a dark enclosure, the loud and muffled voices, her sense of terror, and then, finally, a holy stillness.

"That was a miracle," Jenni wrote in an e-mail to me ten years after our sessions together. "I know that Divine Providence presented those events—my restlessness, the therapy, the vivid flashbacks, and then the family gathering. The experience taught me that God does not give us a spirit of fear, but one of power, love, and sound mind, and that has become my life theme. I went back to college and am now a licensed clinical social worker. I develop spiritually based programs for children in the United States and abroad. I've never before been this peaceful and happy."

Clinicians and researchers have gathered a great deal of evidence that suggests intrauterine events can leave impressions. This means that your first experience with grief could actually have occurred before you were born.

Birth Leaves an Imprint

The process of birth is intensely stressful for newborns, psychologically as well as physiologically. The initial separation may cause an anxiety that remains for life. Some psychologists believe that all human beings carry a deep-seated desire to return to the womb.

Other psychologists assert that life begins as a tabla rasa, or "clean slate," and that we form impressions of life and the world around us only from the moment of birth onward. Accordingly, they argue that infants are not developed enough for any complex emotion, such as separation anxiety, to be created during birth.

A combination of the contrasting opinions offers practical insight. It seems reasonable that separating from the comfort of the womb would be stressful. After months of living in a dark, warm, stable environment, infants are suddenly exposed to a very different world. They are startled by bright lights, loud noises, open space, and cold air. Then they are passed from hand to hand to be washed, poked, and prodded. Birth can also be physically painful, as Dianne's three-year-old grandson, Silas, recounted to her daughter and then to her.

"It hurt me"—Dianne's Story

A team of twenty doctors and nurses crammed into the delivery room. After nine months of a difficult pregnancy and sixteen hours of complicated labor, K'Anne underwent a cesarean section and Silas was finally born.

"Three years ago, at this very moment, you were being born," K'Anne told Silas, pointing to her watch.

"It hurt me," Silas said, bowing his head.

"What do you mean?" she asked.

"It hurt me real, real bad. I wanted to stay in there," he said, frowning.

Upon their arrival at my house, K'Anne (an occupational therapist with a second master's degree in psychology) pulled me into the kitchen. After repeating their conversation to me, she questioned, "He couldn't actually remember, could he?"

"I don't know," I said. "It sounds unbelievable. Do you want me to ask him about it?" After the family gathered for supper that evening, I posed the question to Silas, "Do you remember the day you were born?" at which time he made the same statements.

We must all endure leaving the womb, and whether consciously remembered or not, this first great loss plays a fundamental role in the development of our early psyches.

Early Attachment, Separation, and Grief

We are born into this world totally dependent. We all need nourishment, warmth, shelter, protection, and love. Attachment and mourning are as primary and instinctual. Studies of attachment and separation expose the undiminished misery of both grieving human beings and grieving animals.

Attachment, Separation, and Grief in Animals

Just like people, many animals become grief-stricken by separation. Pets sometimes grieve themselves to death after their owners have died. Even though the separation may be temporary, some are in such despair that they refuse life-sustaining care. Numerous veterans report that when they left for war, their pets refused water and food and starved themselves to death.

Certain animal communities (elephants, for instance) rally around their dying, never faltering from their side. Observing such a community has carried a lifelong effect for Joe.

"What have I done?"

When Joe was ten years old, his dad gave him a shotgun. By the time he was twelve, he often ventured into nearby fields and woods alone. When no game was available, he would shoot any creature that moved, just to improve his marksmanship. Joe sorrowfully recalled his last hunting experience.

Nothing was unusual about the day's expedition—that is, until Joe shot a seagull. As the beautiful white bird fell shrieking toward a nearby pond, dozens and dozens of seagulls rushed to its aid. They circled above their comrade lying mortally wounded at the water's edge. Their gentle flight was in contrast to their grievous cries. Soon, from every direction, many more seagulls joined overhead, until there seemed to be at least one hundred. High-pitched shrieks of mourning filled the air as they circled around and around in anguished protest.

Never had such an experience befallen Joe before. *What have I done . . . what have I done?* he thought. More birds than he had ever seen collected to fly vigil. The community of seagulls never wavered from its grieving flight, even after their comrade lay lifeless. Joe turned away, no longer able to tolerate the haunting sobs and forlorn circling of the graceful birds.

"I regretted what I had done," he explained, "so I began to run, thinking I would leave the aftermath behind. But I couldn't. The mourning flock made me realize that this one little seagull's life had been significant, and that *every* living thing had meaning and a right to live. I vowed never to harm another animal."

Although time and distance eventually separated Joe from the reverberating calls, the mourning he witnessed that day lingered in his memory. His experience catapulted him into a lifelong interest in attachment behaviors and loss. He verifies that all living species (human, nonhuman, wild, and domesticated) suffer grief. Grieving loss is as innate as eating when famished.

Early Attachment and Grief in Human Beings

Infants depend on attachment for survival.[1] Babies usually attach to their mothers first and cry out in grief when separated from her.

Even though their separation may be only temporary, or even imagined, it can be intensely devastating. No behaviors are powered by stronger emotions than grief, and they do not disappear with infancy. Adults carry the same feelings and behaviors they experienced during their first year of life, along with others that develop through the years.

Grief Patterns Develop

Infants are not developed enough to understand their feelings of separation or grief, and, even if they could, they would not have the necessary verbal skills to express how they feel. As a result, they bring all those emotions into their next stage of development.

During the next stage, the second and third years of life, children begin to understand their feelings, and they also begin to develop the ability to express them. At that point, grief responses become more obvious. Unfortunately, few people realize that children hold a genuine need for attachment and that they need to express their sorrow when separated. Most adults respond by saying, "Stop that bawling," "Big kids don't cry," "There's no reason to cry," or "Cry, and I'll give you something to cry about." The following examples chronicle how grief patterns can develop.

"We didn't want you kids to raise a big fuss"

Emily and her two sisters were parents of six children, all between the ages of one and four. Early on, the three mothers agreed to share baby-sitting duties. Wanting to avoid their children's crying episodes when being left behind, they devised a system for leaving them. Emily, for example, made no mention to her children that they would be staying with one of their aunts for a few hours. When they arrived at the aunt's home, everybody gathered in the living room. Then, when it was time for Emily to leave, one of the adults distracted all the children by taking them into the backyard to play. But every time Emily's children returned to the room where they had last seen her, they panicked. "Mommy . . . Mommy . . . Mommy," they screamed and cried, beating on the door for her to return. Their feelings of abandonment, betrayal, and grief were dismissed by their aunt's scolding, "What's the matter with you? You know she'll be back."

Now fully grown, Emily's children's deep-seated grief, abandonment, and betrayal resurface with every loss, yet they dismiss their feelings—just as they were taught to do during childhood. One niece, however, probed into her background after her mother died. "What were all of you thinking?" she asked her aunt.

"We just didn't want you kids to raise a big fuss," was the response.

After understanding how her feelings had developed, Emily's niece explained to us, "I prepare my kids. I kiss them good-bye and remind them that I'll be back in a few hours. They might grieve a little when I leave, but they won't feel abandoned and lost the way I did."

"Here comes the funeral procession again"—Dianne's Story

From the time I was very young, my grandmother stayed with me while my parents worked. On my fifth birthday, my parents, older sister, and I moved from Hot Springs, Arkansas, to Houston, Texas, leaving Grandma behind. Although we visited her often, our departure for the long drive back to Texas always ended the same.

My mother and sister said their good-byes to Grandma inside her house and then hastened to our sedan. That gave Grandma and me time for our private and emotional good-byes. During my last few moments inside, I grasped for every millisecond by absorbing the aroma of her freshly baked buttermilk cake, the drip-drip-drip of her leaky kitchen faucet, the faded floral wallpaper, and Grandma's tight embrace in which I was lovingly enveloped.

Mother, meanwhile, patiently sat behind the steering wheel, while my sister, perched on two puffy pillows, drummed her painted fingernails against the rear window. After some time, Mother revved the car's engine, a signal that it was time to leave. As Grandma and I emerged through the creaky screen door, sobbing and clinging together, my sister loudly voiced her complaint, "Oh God. Here comes the funeral procession again."

Sitting down in the front passenger seat, I hurriedly cranked my window down to eliminate the glass that stood between my grandma and me. As the car rolled forward, I threw one last kiss. Wiping the tears with her dainty hand-stitched apron, Grandma looked as if her heart was breaking; nevertheless, her wrinkled hand moved to her mouth to return my kiss. I craned my head and shoulders around, my eyes ever longing to keep me connected to the grandma I so adored. Finally, a blur of houses stood between us. Grandma was gone again. "Oh, honey, please don't cry. If you cry, you'll get sick," Mother pleaded.

Such a little girl not to be allowed to have her feelings, but that is the way it is for most children. My mind, however, took Mother's warning one step further. My grandfather had died from an undiagnosed illness; thus, I made up the equation as follows: *If I cry, I will get sick, and if I get sick, I will die. Cry = get sick = death.* Tears became a survival issue, with only one way to cope—to hold them in, no matter what.

Some thirty years later, after my parents died, I felt as if my heart was drowning in tears. In my memory, I revisited my early losses and my pattern for dealing with them. I investigated crying, its effects on the immune system, and other grief responses. On the one hand, I know that Mother wanted to protect my health, and I will always love her for that. On the other hand, I learned beyond what she knew. I discovered that bottled sorrow is not beneficial to anyone's well-being and that tears actually eliminate toxins from the body. I now carry numerous conscious choices for reacting to separation instead of the unconscious *one.*

"I have grieved all my life"

In a home for unwed mothers, a seventeen-year-old gave birth. "Baby girl" became the newborn's identity. That's the way illegitimacies were handled back then, on June 28, 1922, in Fort Worth, Texas.

After three days and a long train ride, "Baby girl's" twenty-year-old adoptive parents arrived. The tiny infant with thick dark hair and a button nose was finally given a loving mother, a wonderful home, and a name: Leona.

"I remember life being so sweet," Leona said, as she reflected on her early years. "But then my mother got sick and had to have an operation. She died during the surgery. At the age of three, I had been orphaned twice. But we never talked about it," Leona said with a sigh. "I just grieved and grieved all to myself. It was awful. And it was fresh grief all over again when I started school, graduated, got married, gave birth to each of my children, and became a grandmother. I cried myself to sleep many nights, and not just on special occasions. Now I realize that I have grieved every day of my life."

As Leona's story points out, repressed grief can be resurrected, and not only during bereavement. Any longing can initiate the original pain.

Introduction to the Concept of Death

Before the age of two, children have usually had an encounter with death. In premodern times, people were not sheltered from it; instead, death was a natural and intricate part of their lives. With the advent of our youth-focused culture, however, the subject of death has become verboten, and television is now the major introducing medium. Unfortunately, the violent scenes presented there teach nothing wholesome about dying. Death is not portrayed as real, nor is any sense of sorrow for the bereaved.

Children's first personal experiences with death are often the most vivid and color their perception for the rest of their lives. For many, it might be finding a dead bird or insect in the yard. Or perhaps a beloved pet or family member dies. Still others are introduced to the concept of death through a grandparent's mourning. Grief is so powerful that it can silently pass from one generation to another, as the following example illustrates.

Multigenerational Grief—Dianne's Story

Rays from the morning sun reflected rainbowlike patterns through my stained-glass goblet, a gift from a former hospice patient. I used it only when my spirits needed a lift, and I certainly needed it this day. My twenty-year-old cat, Cuddles, was not well, and the veterinarian had called to report that recent blood tests indicated that his kidneys were failing.

Cuddles was beginning to knead his snow-white paws on my robe when the telephone rang again. This time it was my daughter. "Hi! Let's have a birthday celebration!" she invited. "Silas is six months old today." But I did not feel festive, and I did not want to expose them to my sorrow. After some thought, I decided that an outing would give me a break and I would avoid mentioning my sickly cat. Like a clown preparing for a party, I threw on my most colorful outfit and happiest face.

As I stepped inside their front door, my usual cheerful greeting "Hi!" was met by my grandson's squeal of excitement. From across the room, his tiny outstretched arms were ready for his grandma. With his bright blue eyes and broad toothless grin, Silas prepared to leap from his mother to me. As the distance between us narrowed to a few feet, Silas's delighted baby face completely changed. By the time he reached my arms, his sparkling eyes and upturned lips had wilted into the deepest expression of sorrow. Simply and calmly, he cupped my face in his tiny hands and fixed his eyes on mine. Then he draped his arms around my shoulders and snuggled his face against my neck. As if that were not enough evidence for multigenerational grief, he moaned several times. "He knows . . . he knows," I said. Without Silas loosening his grip, I carried him to the sofa, where we sat nestled together in silence. Finally, I drew in a deep breath and explained Cuddles's grave diagnosis.

Many children experience their first loss by intuiting a parent's grief—grief that is silently passed from their grandparents to their parents, and then to them. In Silas's case, my grief was passed directly from me to him. His example also illustrates that even infants are capable of feeling and expressing grief. Although Silas may not be able to recall this early experience, it will probably influence the way he copes with his own losses in the future.

Other people not only recall their first introduction to the concept of death but are profoundly influenced by it. Instead of being the Father of Near-Death Experience, Raymond might be the father of several children along a U.S. mail route (his second choice for a career was to become a mail carrier) had he not had an exceptional introduction to the concept of death.

"Poor little Frisky died"—Raymond's Story

There were no neighborhoods in Porterdale, Georgia. With a population of only two thousand people, the town itself was a neighborhood. The townspeople could venture in one of two directions, downhill or uphill. Down led to Blackie's Drug Store, where fountain sodas, ice cream, comic books, and records were staples. Up the hill, giant oak trees and modest homes lined the narrow streets. From their front porches, people greeted neighbors who strolled by. Porterdale in 1945 was representative of the simplicity and innocence that inhabit Norman Rockwell paintings.

My uncle Fairley owned a dog that resembled a pocket-sized white Chihuahua. Frisky was such a free-spirited little canine that he basically belonged to everybody. He and I were as attached as any dog and toddler could be. When he saw Mother taking me for a walk, he yapped, jumped, and fetched his leash to join us. All along the way, he trotted beside my blue stroller with the big wheels, refusing to allow anyone near. Any glance toward the stroller's precious cargo was intercepted by Frisky's snarling teeth and throaty growl. His frozen stance added to his warning demeanor. Although tiny in stature, Frisky fancied himself a gargantuan, ferocious guard dog.

One morning, when I was about eighteen months old, the little dog was hit by a car and died soon after. Uncle Fairley carried Frisky's lifeless body to the town dump, which was the normal method for disposing of animals at that time in Georgia. It was a sad day in Porterdale. Although my family did not show any signs of sorrow (as usual), I overheard their stoic rumbling, "Poor little Frisky died."

Then, exactly three days later, much to everybody else's surprise, Frisky came trotting home. What exactly happened to him I'll never know for sure, but he went on to live for many years. My first companion's crossing the barrier and then coming back seemed normal to me.

That first encounter with death was, in effect, similar to the near-death experiences that I would grow up to study, but it was not until we began writing this book, more than fifty years later, that I realized the two were connected. Would I have coined the term *near-death experience* or be committed to the field if Frisky had not "returned from the dead"? The incident had a permeating impact on my life and still affects my attitude toward death in a powerful way. The entire event remains partly outside my whole conscious awareness, but my next memory is as distinctive as on the evening it occurred.

While waiting beside our ranch-style house in the suburbs for my father to return home from work, I peeked around the corner just as he appeared in the driveway. I can vividly recall Dad's white shirt and crew cut as he sauntered toward me. He knelt down and calmly explained, "I'm late because just as I was leaving the hospital a man had a cardiac arrest right in front of me. His heart stopped beating, so I had to cut his chest open and massage his heart to get it going again."

I was shocked. Wanting confirmation, I asked, "You mean he was dead and you brought him back to life?"

"That's right," he replied.

He was dead and now lives again, my mind raced.

Those introductory experiences initiated my curiosity about life after life and still influence the way I deal with loss. Unfortunately, however, my family's stoic pattern for mourning remains intact for me. Like links in a chain, connecting generation to generation, family attitudes endure—that is, until one person breaks the link.

I became fascinated with near-death experiences in 1965 and began interviewing people in our home. My wife and I were congenial hosts, as was the custom for those raised in the South, where revolving doors created instant friendships. The birth of our two sons gave our home an even more inviting atmosphere. Settled into the floral-print cushions of our overstuffed couch, friends shared their near-death experiences—with Avery and Sam sitting enthralled on their laps.

Several points spring from these remembrances. Sam and Avery were introduced to death in a respectful way. My wife and I always encouraged our sons to express their feelings and thoughts about what they heard. Not only did they grow up in a home where survival of bodily death was discussed, but also it was during a time when near-death experiences were being prominently covered by the media.

Both of our sons recently experienced the deaths of three grandparents. Unashamed and unrestricted, they shed tears as they reminisced. Witnessing their gentle expression of grief was heartwarming for me, and proof that my old unhealthy familial pattern for coping with loss was broken.

Introduction Leaves Impression

Based on reports, case studies, and valid and reliable research, it is certain that your introduction to the concept of death exerts an ongoing influence on your attitudes toward death, loss, and grief. Thus far, we have considered four influences on the ability to cope: prebirth, birth, attachment, and introductory experiences. Can early feelings surrounding mortality contribute as well?

Personal Existence

Some psychologists believe that from birth every human being carries an innate fear of no longer existing. Accordingly, when exposed to death, children are catapulted into an existential crisis; that is, they become overwhelmed by the notion that they will someday die.

Funerals often give children a platform from which to examine the end of their existence. Studies with the bereaved population suggest that during funeral services attendees are too emotionally raw to absorb much, if anything, said by the clergy. After four months, however, children in the study recalled statements that focused on existential matters. After twenty-five months, the children remembered details of many salient facts. Furthermore, years after the funeral, the children still clung to critical existential statements. Concerns about mortality linger into adulthood, and our attitudes toward animals furnish a portion of the evidence.

Symbols for Existence

Animals are symbolic of life and death. Our basic feelings and beliefs toward mortality surface with the death of an animal. More relevant than the death of animals in general is the death of an animal companion. Each pet's death, unconsciously, is mirrored as our own.

"I just feel like I am dying too"—Dianne's Story

While her husband was being admitted to the hospice inpatient unit, Betty and I talked in the family meeting room. She had recently sold her gift shop, one of the most thriving businesses in town, to spend more time with her four grandchildren and with her husband, who was dying from cancer. "I'm sixty-four, Dianne. Don't most people my age retire anyway?" she asked. "My life has been typical, so this is just the next step." Then, nodding toward her husband's room, she asked, "Will you tell him that I've gone to the cafeteria to grab us a snack? I'll be right back."

Because she seemed emotionally sturdy, I was surprised when I relayed Betty's message to her husband and he said, "I'm concerned about her going off the deep end. I just don't know what she'll do when I die. I mean if she so much as glances at a dead animal she comes unglued. If she sees a deer lying beside the road or a dead bird in the yard, she gets sick to her stomach. On two occasions, she was so traumatized by the deaths of our pets that she fainted and stayed in bed for days, but she has yet to talk to anyone about it. When I think about how distraught she was over them, well, you know . . ." He paused, leaning forward to cough. "We've been together for more than forty years," he went on, "and I'm just afraid for her. I think maybe it would help if you'd talk to her after we get back home. Can you do that?"

"Yes," I agreed, "I will."

As I neared their home the following week, the rain fell so heavily that even with my windshield wipers on high speed, I could barely see the ambulance pulling out of their driveway. Betty's husband's fever and pain were beyond their control; therefore, he was being transported back to the hospice inpatient unit. Distraught by the reality of his approaching death, Betty asked, "Can you come in for a minute?" As we talked, her grief history seemed normal—that is, until I asked, "What about your dogs?"

"I can't talk about them," she said, clutching her hands against her chest. "It's just too painful. I can't stand the thought of even thinking about it." Our long silence embraced her reminiscences. Finally, the stillness gave way to her recalling the accidental poisoning of one of her dogs, but soon her cheeks turned pale. "I feel faint," she said.

"Can I ask you something?" I asked, leaning closer to her. "What's your last thought before you feel this way?"

"Why, I . . . I don't know," she stammered. "I just feel like I'm going to die. Why?"

Betty began exploring her thoughts and feelings and discovered that at the moment of each animal's death, she sensed her own. "For as long as I can remember," she whispered, biting the corner of her lower lip, "I've had this fear about not being here. Actually, I never think about it until one of my dogs dies. Then I lie in bed and try to imagine what that room will be like when I'm dead and gone. Sometimes, I'll get up and walk around the house, trying to comprehend the incomprehensible. There is no way that I can imagine myself not *being* anymore, or that this house can continue to exist without me in it."

Betty realized that her style for coping was not in her best interest and sought resolution by reading about life after bodily death. In addition, she developed a support network where she could talk with others about her concerns. As a result, she stayed by her husband's side until after he died and then faced her own death with dignity and peace years later.

"She cared more for that dog than she did for her own mother"

A wiry-thin, energetic woman, Estelle was the pillar of strength for her family. Imaginative and fast on her feet, she effortlessly exhausted her young nephews with boisterous games. Like a sturdy mountain, Estelle seemed unshakable. Her family was sure, however, that she would collapse after her mother's death because the two women were unusually close. "But she remained our support after her mom died, and even after her favorite uncle died too," remarked a family member.

Several months later, one of Estelle's canine companions unexpectedly became ill and died. For the first time, she moaned and sobbed with great gusts of grief. Distraught, she fell into a deep depression. "How could she remain so intact for her mother's and uncle's funerals, yet be so grief-stricken over that animal?" her family questioned in disgust. When the poor woman became crippled by sorrow, they snapped in anger, "She cared more for that dog than she did for her own mother."

When listening to Estelle's story, there are three points to consider. First, her reaction was not "abnormal" or even very unusual. The death of her pet threw her into an existential crisis—she was left to consider her own mortality.

Second, her pet's death opened the gates of backlogged grief. Similar to fluid trapped in a clogged drain, unexpressed tears back up and continue to palpitate within until a crisis causes the backup to burst forth.

The third point is that Estelle's style for coping with loss was as distinct as the way she walked and talked. Her family expected her to grieve exactly as they did, and as a result she did not receive the love, comfort, or support she needed.

Keep in mind that Betty and Estelle were *adults* working through an existential crisis. How do children manage?

The Child Still Responds

Our childhood experiences with grief can either help us or add to the burden of our current losses. Perhaps something grief-related happened while you were in the womb, and then birth left sensations. Your introduction to the concept of death and early separations created an internal, interwoven pattern for adjusting to loss. Furthermore, like most human beings, you still hold early feelings about your mortality.

Remnants from childhood experiences are observable. Have you ever noticed the childlike qualities of adults expressing deep grief—

bottom lip protruding, awkward hand and foot gestures, or preschool utterances? Current loss can reignite our childhood responses to grief.

Updating the Little Child

This chapter ends with good news: childhood issues surrounding separation, loss, and grief can be released. The first step is to bring early experiences into conscious awareness. Identify what still serves you, and what does not. The next step is to develop beneficial methods for dealing with grief (which we will cover in chapter 7). Meanwhile, remember that coping is learned—and anything learned can also be unlearned. We were taught to avoid the bridge of grief, but the mountain on the other side still awaits.

TWO

The Stress of Grief

> The secret of health and happiness lies in successful adjustment to the ever-changing conditions on this globe; the penalties for failure in this great process of adaptation are disease and unhappiness.
>
> —HANS SELYE

From the beginning of recorded time, civilizations have reported illness and death among their bereaved. It is only within the past forty years, however, that we have been able to identify the link: grief causes stress, and prolonged stress can cause disease and death.

A Personal Experience with Grief-Related Stress—Dianne's Story

No matter how busy or rushed our lives were, supper was the time for my family to gather around the table and leisurely discuss our day. Even when I was very young, my dilemmas were an intricate part of the dialogue. "Well, when I was a little girl like you," my dad often responded, unable to hold back his grin, "I had the same problem."

"What did you do, Daddy?" I would ask with an anticipatory giggle.

His chuckle let us know that he was about to create an outrageous tale. If, however, he pushed his plate to the side, we knew that he would draw upon reality. Either way, his responses were always funny, nurturing, and thought-provoking. Dad often ended our family discussions with his philosophy, "Honey, everything changes. Nothing lasts forever." I always walked away from the table feeling confident that I, like every human being, could resolve my own problems, in my own way and time.

My mother used to declare that my "easygoing" personality was the result not of nurture but of nature. "You were born with such a struggle-free spirit," she explained, "that nothing ever upset you. You have always been calm, no matter what the circumstances." During college, psychological examinations indicated that I easily adapted to change and was not prone to stress, anxiety, or emotional disorders. Nevertheless, when I was thirty-eight years old, my adaptability was put to the test as never before.

Nineteen eighty-four had been typical in all ways except one: my gynecological problems required that I have a hysterectomy. While unwrapping new bed slippers for my stay in the hospital, I surprised even myself by suddenly announcing, "I'm going to drive my car to the medical center tomorrow."

"That's ridiculous!" a friend scolded as she tried to reason with me.

"I don't know why," I persisted, "but I have this strange feeling that an emergency will come up. I'm going to need my car handy so I can leave quickly." Although I did not understand my premonition, I remained steadfast and drove the twenty-five miles to Houston alone.

My surgery was scheduled for 7:30 A.M., and at 6:45 a nurse and two aides entered my room, pushing a gurney. "Here," snapped the nurse, holding out a cup.

"What is that?" I asked.

"Valium," she answered. "It will prepare you for the trip to the operating room."

"No, thank you," I said.

"Oh, you have to take it," she said. "Just going into the surgical area is scary, so all patients must take a sedative."

"No, I'm fine," I said, adding, "and I have to remain in full control of my senses."

We argued back and forth until one aide good-naturedly interrupted, "Come on! Come on! Let's get going! Can't keep the good doctor waiting any longer." Just then, the telephone rang.

Although reluctant to transfer the receiver to my hand, the grim-eyed nurse finally said, "It's St. Joseph's Hospital, in Hot Springs, Arkansas. Your father is in their coronary care unit and a surgeon wants to speak with you." Not surprised that a crisis was developing elsewhere, I took the phone.

A male voice spoke as if dictating a memo, "Mr. Davidson's condition is critical. He survived a stroke early this morning. It appears that he is going into cardiac arrest. He is being prepped for surgery now. It is doubtful that he will leave the hospital. If he does, he will never be the same."

Tossing the receiver to the nurse, I leaped from the gurney, threw on my clothes, and dashed to my car. The doctor was correct when he said Dad would never be the same, but, then, my life would never be the same again either.

By the time I arrived at the hospital in Hot Springs, doctors had performed the surgery. When I saw Dad, I was numb. The incision on his chest looked as if an animal had ripped him open. More horrifying was to see him laboring for every breath. Because he had always been an optimist, his words, "I'm going to die," frightened me.

"Why do you say that?" I asked, wanting to prevent his terrible prophecy.

"It's my time, honey," he said tearfully, trying not to sob.

Oh, God, please help us, my heart begged, as I watched him drift back to sleep. I found a telephone and left a detailed message for my husband, Joe, in Houston. Anxiety and dread accompanied my exhausted body to the waiting-room chair. Staring straight ahead, I nevertheless saw nothing. Minutes passed before I became aware that the pay phone next to me was ringing.

Joe had consulted with a distinguished heart surgeon at the Texas Medical Center, and a crisis team was preparing for our arrival. While I checked Dad out of St. Joseph's Hospital, two physical therapists set up an oxygen tank and a makeshift bed in the back of my car. Within an hour we were on Interstate 20, bound for Houston. All during the eight-hour drive, my eyes vaulted back and forth between his face in my rearview mirror and the road before us. Smothered by an incalculable alarm, I feared that my dad would die before we could reach the hospital.

Finally, at 2:00 A.M., I saw EMERGENCY illuminated in red just ahead. Like lifeguards preparing to dive into the water, members of the medical team surrounded our car as we approached the designated canopy. "Joe Davidson?" they asked, opening every door as they paced beside us. The team shifted Dad to a gurney and wheeled him into an evaluation room and then straight to an emergency quadruple bypass operation. The surgery was successful and his prognosis was for a full recovery. Recovery, however, was not meant to be.

The third of June, some six weeks later, brought a double celebration. It was Dad's birthday and we were cutting the cake when his doctors stepped through the door. "We're just in time to give you our gift," they announced. "You can go home in the next day or so."

We enjoyed a grand celebration and then wondered why Dad could not go home that day. His doctors had left, so I asked a nurse. "Mr. Davidson has one problem," she replied. "Before he can be discharged, he must sleep through the night. Right now, his days and nights are mixed up. He gets up in the middle of the night and wants to talk, or write, or *do* something."

"My dad is a Baptist minister," I tried to reason with her, "and that's his lifestyle. He always sleeps a few hours in the evening and then gets up to write his sermons after midnight. He's simply on *his* schedule."

"He isn't leaving until he sleeps through the night," she said and walked away. I anxiously pleaded with other nurses and the doctors on call, but when every effort failed, I left messages for Dad's internist.

"I'll be back first thing in the morning to get you out of here," I assured my dad later that night, "and they can't stop me."

The next morning I was met outside his room by the director of nurses, hospital administrators, dad's surgeons, and an anesthesiologist. "There was an accident last night," an administrator began. "A nurse gave your dad a full dose of Valium at 9:30, at 10:30, and again at midnight." The anesthesiologist chimed in, frowning and shaking his head in disgust, "Your dad was given enough Valium to kill a young healthy man in his twenties. I don't understand how he can still be alive."[1]

The horror did not sink in until I was escorted into Dad's room. His face was frozen in agony—he must have known what was happening at the time but been unable to prevent it. Eighty torturous days later, on the twenty-second of August, at 3:30 A.M., my dad's fight came to an end. I received the call I had been dreading: "I'm sorry, but your dad just died."

A long-stemmed red rose from Dad's casket was just browning around the edges when, once again, at 3:30 in the morning, I was startled by the ringing of our telephone. The news was devastating: my sister-in-law, Peggy, had just ended her own life.

Until this point in my life, the word *stress* had held no real significance, but now I heard it reverberating all around me. "You've had far too much stress," "You'll get cancer from this much stress," "No one can survive this much stress." My mother, friends, doctors, and co-workers reinforced their warnings with horrific stories.

After my weight had gone down to eighty-three pounds, one of my college professors lightly remarked from across the room, "Hey, Dianne, a new class is being offered this semester—Stress 101. Go sign up!"

"Who, me?" I asked.

"I'm serious," he said, holding up the spring schedule for me to see. "You must take this class." Although I did not feel the need, I respected his insight enough to comply.

For a college course, the first class began in an unusual way. "I want each of you to say your name," the professor said, "and then in one sentence answer this question: What is the most stressful thing in my life right now?" Words from overburdened hearts began to flow.

"I'm Faye," one young mother said, choking back her tears, "and my five-year-old son is in the hospital dying of leukemia."

The lady beside her took the question. "I'm Julia. My husband died six weeks ago from cancer."

"My name is Greg," the school's star athlete spoke up, "and my friend was killed in a motorcycle accident."

"My brother was accidentally electrocuted . . ." began a twenty-year-old, too tearful to continue.

By the final introduction, it was evident that every student in the room was grieving over the death, or impending death, of someone close.

As softly as a whisper, the professor eased her small frame onto the corner of her desk. Her silk skirt draped over the edge like an expensive tablecloth. "I don't usually begin the first class this way," she said, pausing to look around the room. Leaning forward, she continued, "But since all of you are dealing with loss, well, this is important for you to understand. The moment you hear catastrophic news, your brain releases powerful chemicals. They circulate through every cell of your body, and within minutes you've been affected all the way down to the molecular level. It takes approximately six weeks for your body to eliminate those toxins. If, however, you have another crisis within that six-week period, your brain releases another hit. The brain's initial reaction is only the beginning."

As she diagrammed and described the dynamics of stress throughout the semester, I finally understood. Although I was given months to prepare for my dad's death, the moment I heard "I'm sorry, but your dad just died," chemicals spontaneously and instantly released within my brain. From there, they continued to circulate throughout my body. Then I received another "hit" the moment I heard that my sister-in-law had died by suicide. Before those chemicals were completely flushed through my system, another circumstance caused another stress reaction. Although I knew that I was struggling mentally and spiritually with many changes, unbeknownst to me my body was in a perpetual state of stress. My heart and thyroid gland were being seriously affected.

That class was fundamentally life-changing because until then I had ignored the term *stress*. Furthermore, I was accustomed to the turmoil inside my body; therefore, like most people, I ignored that too. But once I understood, I began to transform every stressful circumstance into a positive driving force. If this book had been available, my health challenges could have been avoided.

Defining Stress

Stress is an automatic, inborn, biological function. It is the body and mind adapting to, or resisting, any change. Much as turning the key in the ignition of your car starts its engine, any change in your environment is the key that ignites stress within your body.

Purpose and Levels of Stress

The purpose of stress is to send an internal alarm: *A change is taking place; begin adjusting now.* Each change and adjustment carries its own level of intensity, which can be compared on a universal level or scale.[2]

Lowest on the scale are environmental changes that require unconscious survival-related adjustments: change in light causes adjustment in eye dilation, fluctuation in temperature affects respiration, and so on. Challenges such as unsolicited phone calls, uninvited guests, or traffic jams place higher on the scale. Ranking more intense are canceled appointments, unmet deadlines, late arrivals for meetings, and so on. Holidays and serious legal problems produce even greater levels of stress. Still higher on the scale are personal or family illnesses, job changes, retirement, changes in residence, and such. Divorce, separation, and serious illness are intense and rank second highest. The death of a loved one usually holds a place of its own, at the top of the scale.

LEVELS OF STRESS SCALE

- Death of a loved one
- Divorce, separation, serious illness
- Illness, change in career or residence
- The holidays, serious legal problem
- Traffic jam, unsolicited phone call
- Survival-related changes

Although the stress scale is considered universal, we each carry a personal pocket model. For example, the same traffic jam can place low on one person's scale but higher on someone else's. An unmet deadline is mildly stressful for one employee yet can be incredibly stressful for a co-worker. During legal problems, someone with an experienced and competent lawyer feels less stress than someone without good legal counsel. Response to the death of a loved one varies as well. No two people, not even identical twins, respond to the death of a loved one with the same level of intensity.

There is more to the personal scale. The same individual responds to each death differently because every loss is novel. For example, Dianne's dad's expected death, described earlier in this chapter, was not as overwhelming as the later sudden death of her mother.

Universally, however, the death of a close loved one produces the highest level of stress for several reasons. Loss is shocking—physically, emotionally, spiritually, mentally, and socially. Survivors face profound changes and challenges. Furthermore, stress has not evolved over time. Infants depend on their caregivers for survival; therefore, any separation is experienced as life-threatening. Although we develop into mature, independent entities, as we have learned, our instinctual response to loss remains. In adulthood, as in infancy, we are distressed upon being severed from our loved ones, and that distress initiates the first phase of stress.

Three Phases of Stress

Stress progresses in three stages or phases.[3] The first phase, alarm, begins the instant the brain perceives a problem. Within seconds, the entire body prepares to run or to fight. Heart rate, breathing, perspiration, and blood circulation elevate, and muscles tense. Explosive energy results.

Initial Cognitive Symptoms of Grief-Related Stress

– Depression, Decreased concentration, Distorted concerns,
– Exaggerated worry, Headaches, Increased distractibility,

– Increased irritability, Mental fatigue, Memory loss, Mood swings,
– Obsessive thoughts, Sleep disorders, Cerebrum aching[4]

The first recognizable symptom of stress is often the inability to function mentally as one usually does. When early symptoms are not understood, stress is often exacerbated. "I'm in such a fog," "I'm so disorganized," "I can't think straight," "I just can't get going," survivors cry out. Overwhelmed by confusing thoughts and intense feelings, many question their sanity: "I must be losing my mind." Let us assure you that these confusing states of mind and emotions, although seemingly strange or abnormal, are actually normal during the alarm phase. Remember, two strong forces are at work within: the mind is trying to comprehend somehow the reality of the death, and, at the same time, the brain (an organ within the body) is responding biologically.

Biologically speaking, the human system usually returns to normal within six to eight weeks. Mourners, however, are especially vulnerable to other crises. Survivors often experience conflicts surrounding the funeral or burial. In the Scott and White Grief Study (1994–97), 43 percent of survivors reported "adverse" occurrences surrounding the funeral or burial.[5] Moreover, other changes that cause stress may fall within the six-week period (holiday, wedding, birth, illness, or another death).

If stress is prolonged or reignited, the alarm phase advances to the second phase—resistance. Parts of any machine will either adjust to change or resist and break down. Mechanisms of the body are no different. By the first anniversary of a death, more than 90 percent of the bereaved population report having seen a doctor for such things as allergies, asthma attacks, backaches, coronary heart disease, headaches, hypertension, hyperthyroidism, hypothyroidism, immune disorders, irritable bowl syndrome, migraines, and skin disorders. Healthcare professionals warn that 75 to 90 percent of their patients' visits are attributable to stress-related illnesses.[6]

If stress is further prolonged, then the second phase advances to the third—exhaustion. Quality machines wear out when overtaxed for an extended period. The body is no exception.

Symptoms of the Exhaustion Phase of Stress[7]

Physical: Accidents, allergies, appetite disturbance, backaches, blood pressure elevation, breathing difficulties, chest tightness, dehydration, digestive problems, dizziness, dry mouth, eye disturbances, fainting spells, fatigue, headaches, heart palpitations, heart rate increase, illnesses (colds and infections because of low resistance), insomnia, menstrual abnormalities, muscle aches, nervous laugh, nervousness, nightmares, noise hypersensitivity, numb or tingling extremities, worsening of previous medical conditions, rashes, restlessness, dulled senses, shortness of breath, skin problems, sleep deprivation, speech problems, sweating, substance abuse, teeth grinding, tension, urinary infections, voice change, vomiting, weight change.

Behavioral: Frowning, grimacing, grinding teeth, head bowed, moaning, negative attitude, nervousness (foot tapping, finger drumming, nail biting, etc.), posture changes, rocking, sighing, sulking, speed of walking and talking changes.

Emotional: Agitated, angry outbursts, anxious, crying spells, depressed, discouraged, dread, fearful, frustrated, helpless, hopeless, hypersensitive, irritated, joyless, moody, nightmares, obsessive/compulsive, panic-stricken, short-tempered, tearful, void or lack of emotions, worrying.

Intellectual: Bored, compulsive thoughts, concentration difficult, confused, decision-making difficulties, dissociating, errors increase, forgetful, indecisive, irrational thoughts, irritable, poor judgment, lack of focus, errors in language, lethargic, memory loss, negative thoughts, obsessive thoughts, preoccupied, low productivity, low self-esteem.

Social: Blame others, critical, distrusting, hiding, intolerant, isolating, jealous, lack intimate connection, lash out, lonely, manipulate others, nag, relationship disturbances, avoid any reminder, resentful, self-centered, sexual dysfunction, withdrawal.

Spiritual: Apathy, cynicism, distrust, doubt, egocentric, emptiness, judgmental, loss of direction, loss of meaning, martyrdom, unforgiving.

Stress-Related Death

Short-term stress can become long-term stress. Survivors may not be aware of the tax being placed on their bodies, or the seriousness of it, until exhaustion has already taken its toll. In the following, three families share their accounts of stress left unattended.

"Hell, it's normal"

Normally a jovial, outgoing, hardworking man, Ernie reduced his work hours and shunned all social ties after his wife died. Although his large family was supportive, he remained inconsolable. Mediums (who he insisted were in contact with his deceased wife) were Ernie's only source of comfort.

"Dad, you must go to the doctor," his children insisted when they noticed his decreasing weight, increasing irritability, and lost interest in work.

"Every person loses weight over something like this," he grumbled. "Hell, it's normal."

"But you're so stressed out," they said, trying to reason with him.

"Now you're making me steamed," he said. "I'm doing okay for a man who lost his wife of thirty-three years."

Within six months, Ernie's mental and physical health deteriorated to the point that he stopped working completely. His family and friends again emphatically voiced their concern, but he insisted, "Stop worrying about me. I'm still grieving and need time to myself. Why can't you understand that feeling this way is normal?" Indeed, it seemed normal to Ernie because, like many bereaved individuals, he was used to his symptoms.

While sitting on his front porch one evening, he suddenly remembered the day's mail waiting inside his mailbox. As Ernie stepped onto the grass, he fell to his knees. He struggled to right himself but collapsed. A neighbor rushed him to the hospital's emergency room, where doctors found his blood pressure and heart rate to be dangerously high. Although his disintegrating health was obvious to others, the widower refused to believe that his condition was serious. Ernie was treated and released from the hospital, and one month later, on the first anniversary of his wife's death, he suffered a cardiac arrest. He joined his beloved just after midnight.

Whereas stress can be apparent to family and friends, as in Ernie's case, it can be concealed, as the general's family attests in the following story.

"Oh, Dad is doing so good"—Raymond's Story

Jim, a retired air force general, was easily recognized from a distance because of his confident gait and vibrant health. Running in marathons was so deeply ingrained in his body and psyche that he routinely carried himself as if pushing through the finish-line tape. After the death of his wife, his appearance remained the same. "Oh, Raymond, Dad is doing so good," his children exclaimed to me.

The general, however, was suffering digestive problems and made an appointment with me for a physical. Sauntering into my office the next week, he tried to disguise his grief by wearing his full military uniform. He attempted to conceal it on his second appointment as well. On the day of his third appointment, however, he wore plainclothes and his demeanor was reduced to obvious devastation. All pretenses were discarded. He was already in the exhaustion phase of stress, his immune system broken. A short time later, he died from illnesses that were triggered by the stress of grief.

"She moped around all the time"

Betty's death occurred suddenly, on the second day of hospitalization. Her family searched for a cause. "She lost her zest for life after Dad died," her son said. "She was still eating with that voracious appetite of hers, and she seemed physically healthy, but we couldn't get her interested in anything. She just moped around all the time. That was so unlike her because she was always so full of life."

"I went with Mother to her internist for a thorough examination," her daughter explained. "The tests were negative. The doctor said she was just depressed and gave her a prescription for an antidepressant, but she was afraid to take it."

"He told her to find a hobby or something she'd enjoy doing," her son said. "We were talking about that on the morning before she died. None of us, not even the doctors, had any clue that death was near."

Now staring at their mother's handprint, still etched on her large crystal punch bowl, her family struggled to contain their sorrow. They wondered if Betty had literally died of a broken heart. They retrieved her medical records from the hospital, which indicated that her thyroid count had been zero. "Could unattended stress cause someone's thyroid gland to shut down?" they asked. "Could grief be the reason that Mother died?"

Bereaved individuals are at greater risk for death.[8] Each of us carries a predisposition for certain illnesses. A family medical history can pinpoint which body organ is the most likely to be vulnerable, and for which specific disease. An illness, however, may not develop until a weak organ is affected from intense, prolonged stress. Therefore, grief itself does not cause death, but chronic stress kills through heart attack, stroke, suicide, violence, and perhaps even cancer. People wear down to the final, fatal breakdown.[9]

The long-held belief that grief shouldn't last beyond one year is outdated. Considering the rate at which mourners fall victim to illness, however, the statement holds merit if changed to: the *stress* of grief should not last more than one year.

Fortunately, there are many solutions to stress. Because grief-related stress creates the most explosive energy, it can be the most transforming.

Transformative Power of Stress

Today we know that stress links grief to death. We further understand that stress is not the important issue—the way in which we handle it is. Alarm clocks and deadlines can be motivating. Aging and illness can lead to improved health care. Loss can be a catalyst for self-understanding and growth. Nothing generates more transformation than grief.

THREE

Grief Carries Strong Emotions

> Love knows not its depth until the hour of separation.
>
> —Kahlil Gibran

> To experience and embrace the pain of loss is just as much a part of life as to experience the joy of love.
>
> —Alan Wolfelt

Ours is a death-denying society, and no wonder—grief can be so strong, complex, and confusing that our equilibrium is thrown totally off kilter. However, like a lighthouse beacon illuminating the midnight sea, knowledge shines its light on the valley of loss. In this chapter, we will focus on the emotional side of bereavement, beginning with definitions.

Defining Grief, Mourning, and Bereavement

Grief is an instinctive response to loss; it is a process with a host of feelings. New grief is continuous; that is, it consumes the body, mind, and soul around the clock, for many days or weeks.

Mourning is learned. Mourning moves us through grief. It is the outward expression of grief—any *action* that helps us adapt to our loss. Mourning is influenced primarily by the culture in which we grew up, and secondarily by the culture in which we live as adults.

Bereavement is the state of being deprived after a loved one's death.

Emotions Hold a Positive Purpose

Just as each human being is structured differently and has a unique purpose in life, each emotion has its own structure and purpose. The function of an emotion is to signal a like or dislike. *Notice!* it cries out. Every feeling generates internal electrical charges. The life span of an emotional charge is less than one minute *when it is naturally acknowledged and expressed.* Let's consider an example.

"Si real mad now"—Dianna's Story

"Mores?" he asked, holding up his hands covered with finger paint. Silas was almost two years old and beginning to form sentences.

"We are all out of paint," I said, standing to put his art set away.

"Back, back, Mimi!" he exclaimed, motioning for me to sit down again.

"Let's do something else now," I said, putting his paints in the drawer.

He jumped to his feet, folded his little arms across his chest, turned his back to me, and said, "Si mad."

"Oh, you are mad," I acknowledged, kneeling in front of him.

He turned to the side, looking at me out of the corner of his eyes. "Si *real* mad now," he grumbled and then pouted his lips.

"Yes, I see you're real mad now," I reflected.

Raising his arms and shoulders like a Frankenstein-type character, he looked directly at me, "Si monster mad!" he said with a growl and furrowed brows.

"Oh, yes, you are monster-ously mad."

With that, he dropped his arms, cocked his head, and in a melodious voice asked, "Have a puppet show now?"

* * *

Feelings quickly and effortlessly dissolve when children are allowed to feel and express their emotions.

As children, most of us were told (and are still being told in some cases), "Don't be mad," "You don't feel that way," "That's not nice," and so on. We were taught to repress our emotions, which takes more energy than expressing them. Furthermore, bottled feelings become deep-seated and distorted. Anger can grow into rage, grief into bitterness, and jealousy into hate. By understanding our emotions, we can deal with them before they reach that point.

Abandonment

Feeling abandonment is to sense separation as desertion. It sends an internal signal, *Someone you needed deserted you.* Watching Mother's car pull out of the school parking lot or a friend leave for home often causes feelings of abandonment during early childhood.

Adults, as well as children, can sense death as an abandonment. "I'm so mad at him for dying and leaving me alone," widows frequently say. "But how can I be angry at him when I know it wasn't his fault? He didn't want to go." Feeling abandoned may not be rational, but once the feeling takes root, it resurfaces with every loss. Until the origin is unveiled, sufferers are left bewildered by these emotions.

Anger

We feel anger when someone or something we hold dear seems violated. Anger's purpose is to send the internal warning *Stop! This cannot continue.* The experience related next could have happened to anyone.

"The hell you did!"—Dianne's Story

I dropped my clothes off at the dry cleaners, an establishment that I had frequented for more than ten years and had highly recommended to others. As always, Dave, one of the two owners, greeted me by saying, "I'll have these out this afternoon."

"I'm leaving town," I said, "and won't be back until next week, so take your time."

"Well, maybe you'll be back this way later today," he insisted, "so I'll get these ready just in case."

"No," I persisted as I waved good-bye, "I won't be back for at least a week; no need to rush."

One week later I stopped to pick up my clothes. Dave was busy with another customer, so, for the first time, the other owner came out from behind the glass partition.

"You need to pick something up?" he snarled, stomping toward me with his fists on his hips.

When he brought my clothes to the front, he slapped the plastic bag and yelled, "Where the hell were you last Tuesday?"

"What do you mean?" I asked.

He ripped the ticket off the bag and threw it on the counter between us. "You see this red tag?" he shouted, punching it with his fist. "It means we rushed like hell to get these out and you didn't even have the decency to pick them up for a week! I just want to know where the hell you were instead of here like you were supposed to be."

Again, I calmly tried to explain, motioning to Dave. "I told him that I would not be back for a week. He took it upon himself to get them out anyway." Dave, glancing toward us, did not intervene.

"The hell you did! This red tag wouldn't be on these clothes if you hadn't insisted." I felt anger's energy circulating through me. The man's remarks violated my self-image, that of being decent and considerate. Furthermore, his behavior violated the way I deserved to be treated, especially since I had clearly told Dave that I would not be back for a week.

This has to stop! my anger signaled. *You cannot allow him to treat you with such disrespect.*

I understood why I felt angry and wanted to think over my options before responding. I could have tried, again, to explain the circumstances, suggested we wait to speak with Dave, or talked to Dave alone. Other alternatives crossed my mind as well; however, on that day, I chose to vote with my feet. I paid the man as if he were a vending machine, offering no eye contact, words, or gestures that could give him an opportunity to offend me further. As I walked out, I said, "Good-bye." It was clear that I would not return, and that resolved my anger. I knew the man could never offend me again.

This simple story illustrates that anger is a natural signal for feeling violated in some way. If we understand its purpose, we are more likely to resolve it by one of many rational choices.

Grief-Related Anger

Grief-related anger is more complex, however, and for a number of reasons. Thinking is difficult and emotions are raw and easily stimulated. As a result, mourners bypass intellectual reasoning and react to their feelings alone.

Anger is often culturally taboo, which further complicates matters. Many children are told, "That's not nice," when they exhibit angry feelings. Therefore, as adults, they believe that any display of anger will cross a moral line or denote a loss of control. Holding it in causes needless suffering because there are a number of ways to express healthy feelings. Although we may place lower on the "nice scale," we will certainly measure high for honesty and integrity.

Further complications arise when the source of the anger is not an acceptable target. For instance, feeling angry at the deceased or at God can bring guilt. Few cry out their deepest fury, "Where were you, God? Why didn't you answer my prayers?"

Anger is confusing when the source is unidentifiable. Survivors usually discover the cause through talking it out. "Cancer is horrid," they hear themselves say, identifying the cause. "I'm mad at those doctors" detects another source. We ourselves can be the target of our anger: "I'm so mad at myself for leaving." Mortality is often unveiled as the root of "Death isn't fair."

Regardless of the cause, it is imperative to release anger; otherwise, it manifests as rage, bitterness, resentment, and hatred. Mrs. A's case illustrates our point.

When Anger Escalates

Initially, Mrs. A felt anger toward her daughter for ending her own life but refused to face her emotions. The anger flashing from her eyes began to frighten her young grandchildren. Then her increasing temperamental outbursts and sour withdrawals caused her marriage to disintegrate. Other family members were horrified to find themselves on the receiving end of her wrath, and those relationships ended as well. When no longer able to deny her anger, Mrs. A violently blamed her daughter's psychiatrist and friends for the death. Teachers, the public school system, and the community at large were the next targets of her venom. An employer finally demanded that she see a grief specialist. The therapist consulted with one of us after Mrs. A suddenly flew into a rage and stomped out of his office, but the woman never returned to therapy or to work. Clearly, her anger had become dysfunctional.

Today, the hate and bitterness she conveys alienate everyone who comes into contact with her. Mrs. A still moves from job to job, state to state, without one moment of peace in her heart. Traumatic loss makes us better or bitter—it is up to each person to choose.

ANXIETY AND PANIC

Anxiety and moments of panic are common after loss. If left untreated, though, they can develop into panic attacks or panic disorders. Let's compare anxiety, panic, panic attacks, and panic disorders.

Anxiety

Anxiety is a state of feeling nervously concerned. It signals, *This could affect my future.* Most people feel anxious from time to time—while waiting for an important meeting or phone call, for instance. Anxiety also arises under extraordinary circumstances such as pregnancy, childbirth, serious illness, and bereavement.

Mourners know that their emotional state is linked to their loss. Widowers, for example, are aware that their anxiety is caused by the dread of another lonely night.

Panic

Anxiety can be accompanied by sudden, brief, and intense pangs of panic. Sufferers of panic, like sufferers of anxiety, know the cause of their distress. Whereas widowers are anxious about their lonely nights, widows experience moments of panic upon sensing that their safety and security in life are compromised.

Panic Attacks

Grief-related panic attacks are more complex than panic alone because they occur without warning or apparent reason, and death or insanity can seem imminent. Although panic attacks continue to be researched, three things are clear: they are caused by biology, not personality; the stress of grief is a factor; and episodes are more likely to occur when the sufferer has not expressed his or her feelings.

An Unnerving Experience—Raymond's Story

I have never exposed my feelings of sorrow. My family taught me to hold it in, so even as I grew into adulthood, I continued to repress it. Consequently, after my newborn son died, I tried to carry on as usual.

Two months after his death, I was enjoying a pleasant dinner with friends when I suddenly began to feel a smothering sensation. My body and mind seemed to be caving in from stress. I was having a panic attack. Although I tried to understand, the attack seemed without cause.

Later, however, I realized that my entire being was fighting to keep my sorrow repressed. When I recognized that my son's death was at the root of my attack, I longed to prevent another frightening occurrence. Even though I knew about the importance of externalizing feelings, I intellectualized about my loss, struggling with my grief the only way I knew how. If I had mourned at the time of his death, that episode would never have occurred, but I refrained, just as I was taught in childhood.

In Raymond's case, two months elapsed between his loss and the panic attack. In other cases, many years separate the two events, as in John Paul's account.

"At least I could have chosen the time and place"

John Paul, a regal gentleman in his sixties, had served as a tail gunner in the Army Air Corps during World War II. When the war ended, he returned home to resume his life. In the side corridor of his bank, forty years later, a bank teller found John Paul collapsed on the marble floor, gasping and clutching his chest. When the woman began to call out for help, John Paul wheezed, "No, no," so she sat with him until he regained his composure.

"I don't know what happened," he finally said. "All of a sudden the building seemed to be collapsing around me. I couldn't breathe. I thought I was having a heart attack. I am shaken and weak. I just need to sit and regain my strength."

Fearful of another occurrence, John Paul entered therapy, where he discovered that stifled grief had caused his attack. "I never told anybody about the deaths I witnessed during the war in Europe," he sighed, shaking his head in sorrow.

Sufferers who finally express their feelings remain free from further panic attacks, as was true for John Paul. "I had no control. My grief attacked me—which was tragedy upon tragedy," he said. "I could have grieved back then and chosen the time and place."

Few aspects of grief are certain. However, there is one certainty: repressed sorrow will surface at some point, in some way.

Symptoms of Panic Attack

The American Psychiatric Association (APA) lists the symptoms for a panic attack as chest discomfort, choking or smothering sensations, faintness, fear (of losing control, dying, or insanity), feelings of unreality, heart palpitations, hot (or cold) flashes, nausea or abdominal distress, shortness of breath, sweating, tingling sensations, trembling, and unsteadiness.[1]

If four or more symptoms occur at the same time, and the person feels certain that he or she is having a heart attack or going crazy, the episode is considered a classic attack. Chronic panic attacks left untreated advance to panic disorder.

Panic Disorder

A panic disorder has developed when more than one attack occurs within thirty days. According to the APA, if a panic disorder is treated early, nine out of ten people completely recover; on the other hand, if the problem is untreated, other psychological disorders develop. The following story chronicles one example.

"I just want my mama and daddy back"

Whenever Sarah heard a train's whistle and the clatter of the rails, she rushed to watch. She loved the trains and living on the farm, but the serenity of her life was shattered when her parents were killed in an automobile accident. She was adopted by relatives who lived in a large city, and although she seemed well cared for, she was never allowed to talk about her mother and father, her rural home, or the trains.

During the first week of elementary school, Sarah experienced a panic attack. "It's just the change, moving to a big city and all," her family said. "It won't happen again if we ignore it." The attacks continued, growing more intense and occurring more frequently. By the time she was in high school, Sarah was homebound, and her condition had progressed to include physical as well as emotional problems. Psychiatrists were consulted, one of whom suggested that he could best treat her disorder in the state's psychiatric facility. When the family opposed that idea, he suggested in-home treatment by a team of healthcare professionals.

During her first session with a bereavement counselor, Sarah said, "I just want my mama and daddy back." The core of grief is the desire to have the loved one back, and once Sarah struck that deep chord, her disorder began to dissolve. She was eventually able to treat her attacks and now enjoys a full life as a wife, mother, and nurse.

Depression

Feeling depressed is normal during bereavement. Most sufferers describe it as a wavelike sensation rolling in and out, especially when memories are evoked. Feeling depressed after loss is different from clinical depression. The key words are *intensity* and *duration.* "Feeling depressed" does not hold the intensity of clinical depression, nor does it last as long.

Sufferers from both types of depression appear much the same. Their voices are monotonal, lower in volume, and slower in rhythm. They are less attentive during conversations, and the content of their speech is less optimistic. They sit less erect, move listlessly, and often keep the head bowed. Almost everything about them seems downcast.

Whereas many people feel a sinking sensation the moment they hear that a loved one has died, it can come on days or weeks later. People from across the globe report that when they grew weary of fighting waves of sorrow, they found a safe place to let the sorrow go.

"When there is illness in the conch shell . . ."

While teaching in the United States, Dr. P was deeply saddened by news of his father's death. Just getting out of bed to go to work was a major effort. Within months, he moved back to India to be near his mother and siblings, but he could not shake his depression. After several years, he decided to travel to Dharamsala, where he could receive a blessing from the Dalai Lama. Dr. P described what happened.

"His Holiness said, 'Sometimes when there is illness in the conch shell, the only way to get rid of it is to blow it out.' So I went to my father's bed, curled into a ball, and cried. After twenty-four hours, I sat up." He paused to chuckle. "I was bored. So I got up, got dressed, went back to work, and sadness for my father never came back to me like that again."

"It's just a case of the blues"

Mark seemed to be adjusting to his mother's death, but after two months, he felt tearful without any apparent provocation. *You just have a case of the blues*, he rationalized.

"When my sadness didn't go away," he explained, "I went to a counselor, who explained that, as children, we British are taught to keep a stiff upper lip. He suggested that I try letting go of my tears . . . so I wasn't going back. The next day, though, I felt depressed and tried his suggestion. I felt relief, so I still see him."

Dr. P and Mark illustrate three important distinctions between feeling depressed and suffering from clinical depression. Those who feel depressed after loss are more likely to seek help, remain more open to it, and find it beneficial.

DISAPPOINTMENT

Almost every loss carries elements of disappointment. Feeling disappointed signals, *It's over. Nothing more can be done.* Mourners often say, "I'm disappointed that I didn't get to see her before she died," "I'm disappointed that things turned out this way," "I'm disappointed that her son wasn't at the funeral." Regardless of the cause, survivors usually reach a transition in their grief when they acknowledge their disappointment.

FEAR

Fearing something is apprehending it as dangerous or unpleasant. The purpose of fear is to signal, *Warning! Danger approaching.* A vast range of fears usually surface during bereavement. Survivors fear forgetting certain specifics about their deceased loved one—face, voice, mannerisms. They fear forgetting the private jokes, the shared secrets, or other unique features of their relationship. Many clutch their grief tightly, fearing that if they release it, their memories will go as well.

The opposite is true for mourners who witnessed unpleasant deaths or long illnesses. They fear that their worst and last memories will prevail.

Control issues surface as well. Some mourners fear that if they allow one tear to flow, they will lose control and sob unbearably. Men, especially, struggle to contain their emotions. They fear that crying will make them appear weak.

Beyond our personal little world seeming out of control, the entire world seems askew. Grief awakens many realities—one being that life on earth is limited.

FRUSTRATION

Being unable to accomplish a task over an extended time leads to frustration. It signals, *You're stuck. Resolve this.* When the situation or problem is settled, frustration ends.

Feeling frustrated after the death of someone close is common. The casket, clothes, music, and so on must be chosen for the funeral. Failure to contact family members, missed flights, and miscommunications cause additional frustration. Whereas most trying situations are remedied, others can linger or become monumental, as in the following example.

"What difference does it make?"

They were a matriarchal family, mostly widows. The ninety-eight-year-old mother was the elder of her native village in Arizona; therefore, her family and the villagers assumed she would be buried there. Unbeknownst to them, her only son, who lived more than four hundred miles away, arranged for her funeral and burial services to be held close to him.

When the woman died and the son informed the others about his arrangements, they complained, "That doesn't make sense. We can't all travel that far in the August heat."

"What difference does it make?" he grumbled over the telephone. "She won't know."

Not wanting to add more stress to the situation, a small caravan of family members begrudgingly made the long trip, and their frustration ended when they arrived back home. Frustration grew, however, for the mourners who had been unable to make the two-day journey. They moaned and complained until a chaplain finally suggested that they hold their own memorial service. On the woman's favorite spot alongside the village stream, family and friends honored her life, mourned, comforted one another, and at last were able to end their frustration.

GRIEF

Every human being carries grief, if only for the little everyday losses. Grief is not an emotion but a process with a host of emotions. At the core of grief is deep sorrow and a longing to have the loved one back.

Crying is a basic expression of grief, but some people equate crying with weakness. Like many men, Raymond thought he would appear less masculine if he cried; therefore, he could not allow himself to shed a tear when his son died in 1970. Even though he now tells everybody, "Cry; it's good for you," he still finds it difficult to cry himself.

GUILT

Guilt carries remorse, humility, sadness, and anger directed at oneself. Its purpose is to teach self-forgiveness: *You made a mistake; now learn from it so you won't repeat it.*

If survivors sense death as a failure, they search for something they could have done differently. The list of if-onlys can be endless. "*If only* I had stayed," "*If only* I had called earlier," "*If only* I had known." Let's turn to Sue's example.

"If only I had called for an ambulance"

As soon as Sue's husband complained of chest pains, she called for an ambulance. The driver arrived and transported them to a small hospital within minutes of their home. Although her husband survived, Sue was angry. "The driver was stupid," she said. "He took us to that poorly equipped, ill-managed little hospital."

Years later, when her husband suffered a second cardiac arrest, Sue drove him to a medical center more than forty-five minutes away. When he died the following morning, she felt riddled with guilt, crying out, "If only I had driven him to the hospital close by. If only I'd called for an ambulance. If only I hadn't . . ."

When Sue perceived the ambulance driver as making the mistake, the target for her anger was outward. But when she perceived herself as being in the wrong, she focused inwardly. Although her relatives and friends begged, "Sue, you did your best. There's no reason to feel guilty," she nevertheless did.

The death of a loved one often brings guilt about failures in the relationship—arguments, lies, adultery, betrayals, and so on. The one left behind reflects on and feels guilty about the slights.

Ultimately, many survivors feel guilty just for surviving.

Shame

Whereas feeling guilty is self-imposed, feeling ashamed comes from others. Shame carries a social and cultural stigma. It cries out, *They're imposing their values on you.* Individuals can feel guilt, shame, or both. Just remember the difference: guilt is internally generated; shame is external.

Sue (in the case above) brought guilt upon herself by thinking, *I should have called an ambulance.* If someone had echoed her statements, "You should have called an ambulance," then she could have felt shame as well.

Shame-producing messages include "Be thankful she didn't suffer," "He wouldn't want you to cry like this," "Be happy you had him that long," "You aren't the only widow," and so on. Such statements minimize the loss and imply that survivors are wrong for mourning. Even if verbal communication is absent, those whose loved ones die by such things as suicide, murder, and AIDS often feel shame. And, actually, there is shame in just feeling ashamed.

Isolation

Being deprived of a loved one and everything the relationship granted causes a sense of isolation. As a normal aspect of grief, it signals, *You're all alone now.* The profundity of the survivor's loss is understandable only to that person. No one else can fathom her or his feelings, thoughts, level of stress, or adaptive mechanisms.

Feeling isolated can be especially difficult for men and for introverted personality types. Most men bond with one person as friend, confidant, and partner—their spouse. Similarly, introverts often connect with only one or two people. Therefore, the death of a loved one leaves them with little support, and social support is a main ingredient for coping with loss.

To avoid confusion, let's clarify that feeling isolated is an emotion. Isolating oneself is a behavior; it is imperative that mourners take time to withdraw temporarily from the world in order to process their loss.

Envy

Envy identifies desire: *You want that too.* When a bereaved son, for example, witnesses other boys with their mothers, he naturally feels envy; he longs to be with his mother too. Envy strides along with comparing and distancing, as in the following example.

"She would be walking now too"—Dianne's Story

My mother and her best friend were pregnant at the same time. Mother's baby, Josephine, died at birth; her friend delivered a healthy, blue-eyed blonde named Marie. Every time Mother saw Marie, her thoughts compared, *This would be Josephine's first Christmas too . . . Josephine would be walking now too . . . Josephine would be starting school today too*, and so on. For years, Mother avoided her friend and Marie because they evoked memories of what could have been. As she adjusted to her loss, however, her envy subsided and she was eventually able to enjoy their company.

Most bereaved parents feel envious at some point. Whereas some turn their heads to escape their pain, others entirely avoid places where parents and children congregate. Envy usually fades with time and adjustment.

LOVE

Love includes many layers of our being: spiritual, emotional, physical, and intellectual. For most of us, love is not a balance of the four but leans toward one level. Mother Teresa shared emotional love with the dying (by allowing them to grieve), physical love (by holding them), and intellectual love (by answering their questions), but she primarily shared in a spiritual love. The levels and degrees in which we love are also the levels and degrees in which we mourn.

Altruistic Love

Altruistic love is spiritual, selfless, and unconditional. Mother Teresa and the Dalai Lama are examples. Their love is rare and difficult to understand, as is their mourning.

"Your people-pleasing is irritating"—Dianne's Story

While we were facilitating an Elisabeth Kübler-Ross workshop, one of my colleagues said, "Dianne, your people-pleasing is irritating," and he continued in that vein for some time. I said nothing in return because I was once where he was.

It was my good fortune that a number of psychologists were practicing students of the Dalai Lama, and of Geshe Yeshe Phelgye, many years before me. During my first week as a student of Buddhism, I noticed that the monks put other people before themselves. They offered food from their plates to those who were finished, they stopped what they were doing to assist others, and so on. In the field of counseling, those behaviors were considered codependent or "people-pleasing"; therefore, I pulled the therapists aside. "If I acted this way, my colleagues would thoroughly chastise me," I whispered. "Yet you champion these monks. I don't understand."

"Keep observing," they whispered in return. "They are in a higher realm than we are. It can't be explained. You'll have to get it on your own."

We think it can be explained to some extent. Most people act with kindness from selfish desire: they want to gain something. Altruistic love is a selfless gift, given from a heart of compassion, for the good of the recipient. It has nothing to do with self.

Emotional Love

Love between close family and friends revolves around emotional attachment. Detaching is painful. Perhaps artist and teacher Jack McClendon explained it best.

"This mother holding her baby represents healthy love," he said, unveiling one of his paintings. "Her arms drape loosely around him, adequate enough for his safe support, but without stifling him. In his own time he will crawl, walk, and eventually move completely away from her. She will grieve for each step he takes that further separates them, but will love him all the while. Mothers don't understand that just because they give birth and love their children doesn't mean they own them. Love does not denote ownership in any relationship. We have to learn the balance between holding on and letting go."

Emotional love creates such a strong attachment that mourners often cling to their grief as a way of remaining attached (this is covered more thoroughly in chapter 7, "Adjusting to the Loss").

Physical Love

Love based on physical attraction is usually passionate, sexual, and short-lived. "You're in lust, not love," those individuals are teased. But it is a form of love and usually results in its own form of grief.

"I'm a serial monogamist, Raymond"—Raymond's Story

His courtship list was long. "I'm a serial monogamist, Raymond," he joked. Now in his forties, he had struck up a relationship with a much younger woman from our church, claiming as usual, "She's the love of my life." Six months later, the young woman was killed in an automobile accident, and he mourned intensely. Soon, however, he was introducing his new partner, "This is the love of my life."

Intellectual Love

Certain people think their way through love and grief. Charles was one of them.

"I can't marry her when she could turn out like her mother"—Dianne's Story

My friend Charles was an intellectual. For as long as I could remember, he had carried a long list of criteria that a girl needed to meet before he showed an interest. She had to be smart, pretty, and devoted. She was required to have a good figure, proper manners, a nice family, a sense of humor, and so on. At the beginning of his senior year in college, Charles called late one night. "I met someone during registration today," he said, "and I think she'll work out just fine. We have a date Friday night. You can make it, can't you?" Charles and I were like brother and sister, so I was usually the first "family member" to meet his prospective love interests. On our way to her dorm he tapped down his list of standards, making certain she met them all, and then went over them again after we dropped her off. I agreed with him—she was stunning in every way.

He called every night to intellectualize about their conversations and relationship. Then the week before Thanksgiving, he said, "I'm thinking about taking her home to meet the rest of the family, and if it goes well, I'll propose." Exactly as he had imagined it, his family approved of her, he proposed, and she said yes.

The following week, he called his parents.

"I like her," his mother began, "but what about her mother? Do you like her? Would you want to be married to her? Do you want to be sitting across the table from her every day? You know that over time daughters become their mothers."

Charles was not fond of his fiancée's mother, so from that point on, our conversations totally revolved around his mother's comment, with him repeating, "Well, her mother isn't Miss Universe." After two days of debating, he finally determined, "I can't marry her when she could turn out like her mother," and broke off their engagement. He constantly intellectualized about the mother and how he had no choice but to end the relationship.

In the extreme, intellectual love is controlling, demanding, clinging, possessive, and insatiable. When obsessive love ends, obsessive grief begins, and that carries a potential for disaster.

"I have to win her love back"—Raymond's Story

Slim was in his early thirties when his parents became concerned. His love was so obsessive that his girlfriend broke off their relationship, at which time he began stalking her. Months later, his parents consulted with several psychiatrists, of which I was one. During our therapy sessions he remained focused on his mantra, "I have to win her love back, Dr. Moody. I have to win her love back." When he was certain that she would never return to him, he ended his own life. Professional support can make a difference, but it must be timely.

Love Evolved

A rare form of love evolves over time. It is often physically, emotionally, intellectually, and spiritually intimate. No other love creates such a strong bond.[2] Because the two individuals often sense themselves as one person, death is devastating, as Otis testifies.

"I told some folks that she was my sister, 'cause we were so close"—Raymond's Story

Their love progressed from next-door playmates to best friends. "I told some folks that she was my sister, 'cause that's how close we were," he explained. Gradually, they became high-school sweethearts and then married. Unable to have children, they devoted all their energies to each other and to their farm. One was seldom out of the other's sight.

When I met Otis, his thick black hair and taut skin gave me the impression that he was much younger than his middle sixties. His wife, in the final stages of cancer, appeared much older. Although neither of them spoke about her upcoming death, they reminisced most of the time and prepared themselves. No amount of preparation, however, could have readied Otis for the ordeal that lay ahead of him.

"I feel like one-half of me was ripped away," he said at his wife's funeral. Within months, he had lost fifty pounds and gained fifteen years. Mourning was especially difficult because Otis lacked social support. Few people can relate to love that evolves over time and is shared on all four levels.

Regret

Regret carries unfinished business. *I wish it could have been otherwise,* it signals. What is unfinished business? It is an uncomfortable stirring in the pit of the stomach. Whether that person is alive or deceased, if viewing a photograph, hearing the person's name, or being reminded of the person in some way causes an unsettling sensation within, then something is incomplete.

One or more of the following six statements lie at the heart of all unfinished business: *Thank you. I forgive you. Will you forgive me? I forgive myself. I love you. Good-bye.* Actually, unfinished business is finished. It just ended in a manner that was not to your liking. It is never too late to go back, even after loved ones have died. Glen shares his example.

"Thank you, Dad"—Dianne's Story

"Dad was my role model," Glen began. "He was always compassionate and caring, so why do I feel uneasy when I look at his pictures?" As he reminisced about their relationship, I noticed that one of the six statements was missing; thus, I asked, "What do you need to say to him?"

"Thank you. I never thanked him for a lot of things," he said, scrambling for his wallet. Turning to his father's picture, Glen began, "Thank you so much, Dad. Thank you for being there for me, for teaching me to play ball, for helping me with my homework, for telling me how proud you were of me, for making my life important and meaningful, for helping me learn how to drive, for . . . ," and he continued to declare a lifetime of appreciation.

Sudden death brings regret because relationships are incomplete. The bereaved report that writing letters to their deceased loved ones or journaling helps them vent their feelings and tie up loose ends. We remind you, however, that people also need someone to mirror their feelings in order to work them through completely.

Relief

When a terminal illness has caused prolonged suffering, death is usually a blessing for all involved. Relief for mourners, however, can be delayed, as in Dot's case. When her son died after a long bout with cancer, her friend said, "He's an angel now." Dot resented those words. It was several years before Dot felt relieved enough to agree, "Yes, he is an angel in heaven, playing and free from pain."

Resignation or Acceptance

Most survivors feel resignation instead of acceptance. Resignation passively signals, *This is the end. Nothing else can be done.* Hopelessness and helplessness can accompany resignation.

Acceptance, on the other hand, brings grace, comfort, and peace. It actively signals, *This is not* the *end, merely the ending of things as they were.* Contentment about the past and hope for the future accompany acceptance. Survivors who believe they will reconnect with their dearly departed after their own bodily death are more likely to reach acceptance, as Aunt Lu's example demonstrates.

"I'm curious to see what happens then"—Dianne's Story

Aunt Lu, young and soft, was resigned to her dad's death. "I don't like it, but death is part of life," she said to me with a sigh. "Nothing we can do about it." Some forty years later, her soft countenance remained the same, but she was now a woman of the world. "Death is nothing to fear," she said during our Christmas reunion. "I look forward to being with my parents and grandparents again, and meeting generations of relatives. I'm curious to see what happens. I guess we'll have a big party in the sky," she said with a chuckle.

Thus far, we have identified some universal attributes of people who grow from loss: they are aware of early experiences that still influence their grief responses, they understand the effects of grief-related stress, and they do not deny their emotions. Now let's turn to the more individualized facets of loss.

FOUR

The Many Faces of Loss

> All changes involve loss, just as all losses require change.
>
> —Robert A. Neimeyer

No two snowflakes falling from the winter sky will ever be alike. Similarly, no two survivors adapt to loss in exactly the same way. Identical twins do not mourn the death of their mother identically, because each is unique in thoughts, feelings, beliefs, personality, and the relationship held with the mother. Each can try to learn how the other is being affected, but neither will completely understand.

Not only does each survivor grieve differently, but the same person grieves each loss differently. This is because each circumstance is unique. In addition, the survivor is constantly changing.

The observable differences among those in mourning often lead to confusion. Let's sort through some of the variables, including age, grief history, manner of the loved one's death, family dynamics, personality, relationship with the deceased, meaning of the loss, social support, and health.

Age of the Loved One

The death of our parents and other elders gives us the sense that our history, our connection to the past, has been lost. We can no longer turn to them for answers to questions such as: Where did you get my name? Did I ever have chickenpox? Was cousin Marty adopted? Has diabetes ever been detected in our family? How old was Grandma when she was diagnosed with cancer? How did it go into remission? Why did Grandpa move from Italy?

As orphaned adults, we are left to carry the family legacy. Although we grieve, we understand that nature is flowing on its normal time line: elders die first.

The universe seems in disarray, however, with the death of a child. "Why?" mourners ask. "The young are supposed to survive."

Bereaved parents find it difficult to cope with such a devastating loss, in part because their sense of the future died too. So many of their hopes, dreams, and plans were shattered. No parent or grandparent anticipates being left to carry on the legacy of a beloved child or grandchild.

When a spouse of many years dies, widows and widowers often sense that their present, their past, and their future are all lost. For them, life stops. *Where have I been? Where am I going? What am I to do now?* they wonder.

Age of the Survivors

Until the age of twelve, most children do not understand that death is real, permanent, and can happen to them, but they grieve nonetheless. Intermittently, they play, mourn, then play some more, mourn again, and so on. *If* children are allowed to feel and express their grief, they usually adjust to loss. Resilience can be a gift of youth, *but only* if their mourning is properly supported.

Resilience is lost over time. For most people, as they gain in years and wisdom, their capacity to adjust is reduced by accumulated grief and stress. That fact alone makes learning how to cope with loss more imperative.

Grief History

Our grief history begins at birth, and each loss thereafter affects the next. Current bereavement is preparatory, as a father explains.

"My grief was different the second time"

Roger survived the deaths of his daughter in 1989 and his son in 1995, both from similar birth defects. "After my daughter passed away, I was not the same person. The death itself changed me, but I had no control over that. I vowed that I would never, ever feel that helpless again, and that I *could* control. I read every grief book I could find and went to lectures and workshops. My son's death wasn't one bit easier for me, but my grief was different the second time around. I understood more about what was going on inside me, and I handled everything better. I had grown in so many ways."

Mental, Emotional, Physical, and Spiritual Health

Our mental, emotional, physical, and spiritual health are major factors in how we cope with loss. People already in crisis (facing major surgery, serious illness, or complicated pregnancy, for example) may choose to postpone their deepest mourning until their condition has stabilized. Under certain circumstances, the bereaved may never reach a state conducive to adapting. Appearances, however, are not always accurate barometers, as Guy's story illustrates.

"We see no difference in him since his mother died"

Guy lived in a small town where he was known by all. Mentally challenged, he nevertheless worked in the lawn maintenance department of a university and volunteered as groundskeeper for his church on weekends. After his mother died, he seemed fine to most of the townspeople. Several citizens, however, voiced their concern, "We see no difference in him. He is continuing with his life as if nothing happened." A nurse at the university's psychiatric unit brought Guy in, and physicians and psychologists administered a full range of physical and psychological tests. According to standard IQ tests, his intelligence was below normal. When they talked with him, however, it was obvious that, spiritually, he was far above the norm. Individuals with less cognitive ability often compensate by developing spiritual enlightenment. Guy was pronounced healthy and is, to this day, a valuable part of his community.

Cultural Influences

Confusion and misunderstandings often occur when mourners were raised in vastly different cultures.

A Buddhist couple, bereaved while living in the United States, insisted that their infant's body be cremated as they watched. Funeral directors explained that igniting the fire with the chamber doors open was against crematorium procedures in that state—it would endanger everybody present. After days of negotiations, a remote facility was located where the director found no problem in granting the request. Crematorium operators, however, were appalled to see the parents leaning forward to watch the tiny body being placed inside the furnace.

One of the Tibetan monks who, along with the Dalai Lama, was forced into exile, explained it this way: "To not see is cheating death," he said, holding the backs of his hands up in front of his face. "Must look," he paused, lowering his hands into his lap.

People in certain regions of Africa orchestrate their grief by gathering for rituals steeped in emotional display.[1] Our colleagues have facilitated workshops in those areas and found such expressions of sorrow refreshing. Visitors, however, are normally disallowed because people from other cultures are frightened by such intense mourning.

Havoc often breaks out when two contrasting cultures are represented within a single family. Religious differences—as between Jehovah's Witnesses and Catholics, for example—are a special case of such cultural differences.

Family Dynamics

Each person within a family plays a certain role. Dad may be the authority figure, Mother the caregiver, an aunt the historian, a cousin the martyr—and someone almost always emerges as the star of every show. Familial roles are more pronounced during mourning.

The authoritarian steps in as producer-director, busying himself with funeral arrangements and other details he thinks need orchestrating. Meanwhile, the caregiver makes certain that everyone's needs are being met, the martyr complains that he has been wronged in some way, and the star positions himself where he is the most prominently seen and heard.

A great deal of grief is concealed by the roles we play. The producer is so engrossed in controlling every scene, including the way everybody "should" be grieving, that she cannot feel her own grief or allow others to feel theirs. The caregiver is so focused on caring for others that she is not aware of her own needs. The martyr is too self-absorbed to care about anybody else, and the star is too busy performing to be in touch with her sorrow or that of others. These examples may or may not be extreme, but you get the point.

Not only does bereavement accentuate these dynamics, but the death of a family member leaves a hole in the system. In most families, one person normally steps in to fill the role vacated by the deceased, which keeps the system generating. For example, one parent is usually the family authoritarian. An unspoken pecking order has naturally been established over the years, and the highest one in that order unconsciously assumes the position left by the senior's death.

In Dianne's family, Aunt Lu was the senior historian, preserving the family's English/Scottish heritage for future generations. After Aunt Lu died, Dianne and her cousin Tod stepped in. Instead of one person carrying the entire load, they alternate. Being aware of familial roles enables survivors to make choices. Let's consider Sue's family next.

"He knows I'm just a poor old widow woman"

Sue, an elderly widow and mother of three, portrayed herself as a martyr. She often complained to her daughters, "Your brother keeps asking me for money, and he knows I'm just a poor old widow woman." The two women always rushed to their mother's side, soothing, pampering, and vowing to protect her. Their brother was aware of the situation but did not want to embarrass his aged mother or create "an ugly scene" within his family. Thus, he let the occurrences pass.

Their system fell apart with Sue's death. With the martyr gone, there was no one to defend or protect. Before one of the two daughters could assume the mother's role, their brother gathered them together. They all agreed to lay their old system to rest.

Whether consciously or unconsciously, if family dynamics are to remain the same, someone must secure the role once held by the departed. Sometimes that is desirable and healthy. The system is functional as long as all those involved are happy and in agreement.

RELATIONSHIPS

Relationships never end—they are simply given different labels. A bowl containing candy is labeled a candy bowl. If we fill that same bowl with soup, it is thought of as a soup bowl. Put dog food in it, and it suddenly becomes Bowser's bowl. The same bowl can serve many functions. Relationships also assume many labels, according to the roles they play. Gail lends us her example.

"He's now my motivator"

Gail's employer's role was "boss." Within two months, his label became "friend" as well as boss. Eventually he became her "lover." After they married, he acquired new labels: husband, business partner, gardener, chauffeur, tax consultant, computer programmer, and family photographer. Gail, likewise, assumed her new roles as his wife, business partner, cook, social coordinator, housekeeper, and family caregiver. He took out the garbage twice a week, and she took their clothes to the dry cleaner.

Like most survivors, Gail did not realize the cast of characters they had each played in their relationship until her husband died. It took time to identify and adjust to all that was lost. On the first anniversary of his death, Gail said, "Our relationship didn't end; it merely changed. I didn't want to die from heart disease like he did, so I began jogging. I'm eating vegetables and fruit and taking vitamins too. I don't think of him as my business partner anymore. He is my jogging partner, my motivator, the driving force behind my getting healthy."

* * *

Most bereaved parents report that the death of a child is by far the most devastating of all losses. Mrs. Stuart is one exception, and her story highlights a number of the points already mentioned. First, no two people grieve alike. Twins, siblings, bereaved parents, widows, widowers—every person's mourning process is different. Second, each loss for the same individual is unique. And third, relationships strongly influence grief.

"Nothing in my life has been so difficult"—Dianne's Story

Life had not been easy for Mrs. Stuart, a mother of four. Her two daughters had died, one from SIDS (sudden infant death syndrome) and the other from leukemia. Years later, her mother died, and then her younger son—"my fair prince," she called him.

"How are you doing?" I asked upon seeing her again.

"Oh, we British keep a stiff upper lip, you know," she said, tears filling her eyes. "But my mum's death almost put me over. I never thought that losing her would be the worst thing that ever happened to me, but nothing in my life has been so difficult. My mum was by my side during the hard times, for most of my life. I used to call her my rock, because she was my only constant. I knew that my children would leave someday but my mum would be there. I never imagined life without her. I think of her every day and will grieve for her until the day I die."

Gender

Research findings indicate that women and men respond very differently to loss. Women immediately dive into their feelings, sobbing and mourning for their loved ones. Men's grief, on the other hand, is delayed; they throw themselves into work, hobbies, and other distractions.

Bereaved mothers cry out to their husbands, "You didn't even love our child or you'd be grieving too." Husbands respond, "You're just too emotional to think straight." After more than a year, the fathers return to deal with their loss, leaning on their wives for support. But by that time, the woman's pain is much less intense; thus, she retaliates, "You weren't there for me."

It was long believed that these gender-based differences in grieving caused a strain on marriages. Divorce rates among bereaved parents were thought to be higher than among the general population. Then, in 1997, an organization for bereaved parents called Compassionate Friends hired an independent research firm to conduct a national survey. Of the fifteen thousand bereaved parents who participated in the study, only 12 percent were divorced.[2] These latest statistics suggest that the divorce rate among bereaved couples is actually lower than the national average.

Many husbands report that their sorrow was as intense as their wives' but that they chose not to display it, in part because they did not want to add to their wives' already heavy load. Family members commonly shelter one another from their pain.

Genders biologically and culturally contrast in their mourning, but then *all* survivors differ. Categorizing or stereotyping presents problems because there will always be exceptions. In addition, mourning patterns change over time.

Manner of Death

The manner of death—whether it was anticipated, sudden, or violent—strongly influences the grieving process.

Anticipatory Loss

Death comes as no surprise to the very old and to those suffering long terminal illnesses such as cancer and Alzheimer's disease. On one hand, family and friends are given time to say their good-byes and to begin preparing for the loss. On the other hand, by the time death arrives, caregivers are often emotionally and physically exhausted. They do well just to weather the funeral.

Sudden Death

When loved ones die suddenly, family and friends have more energy to support one another and mourn. Their mourning, however, is more intense for three reasons. They were not given time to say their final good-byes. They feel strong emotions, such as sorrow and regret. Survivors have little on which to focus their energy (their loved ones are no longer there as recipients of their time, energy, thoughts, and feelings).

Violent Deaths

Every loss brings its own unique form of grief, but violent deaths create circumstances far removed from all other types of loss. When loved ones die by murder or suicide, life turns upside down in ways unimaginable to those who have not survived such a tragedy. Finding a murdered friend and colleague in the darkness of her home was the end of innocence for Dianne.

"Okay, Dianne, we have a problem here"—Dianne's Story

Originally from Japan, Judy stood less than five feet tall, but her honorable character made her seem twice that size. My husband, Joe, and I enjoyed working with her at the dry-cleaning franchise we owned, and we looked forward to her stopping by with her dog on our days off. One Sunday evening, Joe said, "That's odd. We didn't see Judy all weekend."

"I thought so too," I replied, "but I didn't call her because maybe she needed a break."

The following morning, when she did not arrive for work early, as was customary for her, I called her house. Alarmed that she did not answer, Joe and I rushed to her home. Upon arrival, we saw her car parked in the driveway. After knocking and ringing her doorbell, I turned the knob and eased the door open.

The house was dark and quiet, and an eerie feeling crept over me. "Judy . . . Judy," I called. Nothing stirred within her small home. Stepping inside, I instinctually recognized the smell of death. Glancing around, I saw her blood-soaked sandals by the sofa and her handprint, etched in blood, on the door behind me. *Run! Run! Get out of here!* my mind warned, but my heart forced me to look for her. I followed a trail of smeared handprints around the corner, down the hall, and into her bathroom. There, her crumpled body lay on the floor. Just then, Joe said in a voice I had not heard before or since, "Call the police."

My body functioned automatically. I walked to the telephone and picked up the receiver, but my brain would not produce the phone number (911 was not yet available). Joe took the phone from my hand but then said, "Oh, what is it . . . what is it? I can't remember the number either. We shouldn't be in here anyway. It's a crime scene." We ran from one house to the next, knocking on doors, but when no one answered, we were forced to call from Judy's telephone.

Within minutes, we could hear police sirens. The first officer on the scene approached us. Recognizing that we were terribly shaken, he said, "Can I get you a drink of water and a place to sit down?" The police captain stepped in, however, and quickly separated us, making certain that Joe and I were driven in different squad cars to the precinct for questioning.

I was sick to my stomach, obviously in shock, but I volunteered to describe every detail I knew about Judy and finding her that morning. My shock turned to fear, however, when, at three o'clock, the investigating officer assigned to me said, "Okay, Dianne, we have a problem here. There are some discrepancies between your story and your husband's. We'll have to begin at the very beginning again."

They resumed questioning, with several detectives intermittently storming in and out of the room. One was especially confrontational. "Your answers and Joe's don't tally up," he said, standing over me. My statements, such as "I saw her lying on the floor; then Joe said to call the police," were followed by, "You were first to see her, then? Your husband told homicide detectives that he was."

Until that day, I had escaped being at the mercy of the United States justice system, but now my mind kept recalling stories of innocent people being accused, convicted, and punished for crimes they did not commit. Numbed by the day's events, all I could do was trust that my testimony differed from Joe's only in insignificant details, which investigators confirmed before releasing us.

The aftereffects of finding Judy's body left me fearful about entering my own home alone. In fact, pulling up to our house brought chilling thoughts, *Could someone be inside waiting to strike?*

Then, one week later, a twist of fate occurred. I arrived home from work to find a real-estate agent removing her signs from our neighbor's lawn. Although overpriced and on the market for years, the house had been sold and vacated that day. "What happened?" I called out.

"The buyers needed to move in immediately," the agent yelled back, "and I'll tell you, they sure paid a hefty price to do so."

That evening the new neighbors came by and introduced themselves. "We lived on Oak Street," the wife explained, "across the street from a murderer. At first he was just a Peeping Tom type, but then he started stalking the women on our block, including Judy, the lady who was killed last week. Detectives found his glasses and cigarettes under her window, so we are sure that she must have caught him peeping in and screamed, and then he panicked and killed her. We had to move away from that neighborhood."

With some amount of closure about Judy's death behind me, I was now able to mourn for her, and for my loss of innocence. Being exposed to certain circumstances brings us to a new level of sophistication, and from that point on we can never return to our original naïveté.

Bereaved by Suicide

In 1998, there were 30,575 *recorded* suicides in the United States alone, which left over four million mourners needing social support.[3] Unfortunately, social stigma, shame, and fear separated most of them from social networks. One of us discovered this firsthand in 1985.

"Nobody wants to be sick"—Dianne's Story

After my sister-in-law took her own life, I happened upon a family friend. "I heard about Peggy but I refuse to go to the funeral," she said all in one breath and then turned and dashed for the door.

"Wait. Why won't you go?" I asked, chasing after her.

"It would mean that I approve of committing suicide," she said, turning around.

"Would you go if she had died from cancer?"

"Of course," she said with a smirk. "Nobody wants to be sick or die from some illness."

"Well, nobody wants to be sick with a biochemical illness or brain disorder either, and that is the major cause of death by suicide," I said.

"Well, I just don't believe in going to the funerals of people who committed suicide. It puts ideas in other people's heads."

"Whose heads? What people?" I asked.

"Anyone who goes might think it's okay and do the same thing," she replied.

"Can I bring you up to date?" I asked in exasperation.

In the past forty-five years, the worldwide rate of suicide has increased by 60 percent; in this year alone, approximately one million people around the globe will die by this form of death.[4] These numbers are forcing people to look at the causes and prevention of suicide, as well as the social stigma and shame associated with the aftermath.

As for causes, chemical imbalances and depression are most at fault (90 percent). A great deal of ongoing research and data focus on those who are most likely to act upon suicidal thoughts and on how to prevent suicide.[5] Education is gradually dissolving the social stigma, shame, and fear associated with this manner of death.

Educators, for instance, are replacing the outdated "committed suicide," which originated in early Rome and England, where it was believed that persons killed themselves in order to avoid paying taxes (a criminal offense). "Suicided," "completed suicide," and "died by suicide" are being used instead.

Libraries, bookstores, and the Internet offer a vast range of information. Organizations, among them the American Association of Suicidology, the National Resource Center for Suicide Prevention and Aftercare, the Australian Institute for Suicide Research and Prevention, and the World Health Organization, are storehouses of information. For readers wishing to investigate further, we refer you to the resources section at the end of this book, where we have listed associations, organizations, grief centers, books, journals, Internet sites, and other sources of information on this topic.

As suicide is better understood, the negativity and social stigma surrounding it will disappear. Meanwhile, those bereaved by suicide deaths are already finding themselves enveloped in support. The devastation of this form of loss can be unequaled, but it also carries unequaled growth potential for the bereaved.

Meaning in the Loss

"Why?" is a question that comes from the soul; yet, many health-care professionals discourage mourners from asking it. "Don't ask why because trying to find the answer will only drive you crazy. It's a waste of time. You'll never find it," they insist.[6] We disagree. Many survivors benefit just by searching for an answer; finding it is liberating.

"Why, God?"—Dianne's Story

Although mentally alert, Dad was hooked up to life support and unable to speak. He lay in his hospital bed at the Texas Medical Center for four months, totally dependent on others. His suffering made no sense to me. Dad had worked as a Baptist minister, devoted to helping people, so I agonized, "Why, God, could you allow that to happen to a devotee, someone who could have continued to do good work in your name? Why did you let him suffer his greatest fear and die his worst death. Why?"

My dad, for as long as I could remember, had repeatedly said, "I must be physically, mentally, and financially independent until the day I die." He was so uncomfortable with others doing things for him that he did not even enjoy Christmas. He always answered my question "What would you like for Christmas, Daddy?" by patting me on the head. "Oh, honey, just buy yourself a nice dress or something. That's what I'd like as my gift." His face would turn red from embarrassment when presents were handed to him anyway. He was, simply put, neurotically independent.

"Why? Why? Why did he die like that?" I cried during the many workshops I attended in the years after his death. Then, I awoke one morning with perfect clarity. In my mind were remembrances of Dad's distress while hospital staff brought his food, water, medication, and so on. The tension in his face was obvious to all—his nurses, physical therapists, roommates, friends, and family. During his final weeks, however, I saw his discomfort dissolving. In the end, on the day before he died, he watched for his caregivers and softened as they neared. Finally, Dad had learned to receive. He conquered his greatest fear. Like most survivors, I was comforted and relieved by discovering my answer to "Why?"

Searching for an answer to "Why?" is an important part of the grief process for many survivors, but not for others. Some bereaved parents report that they don't know why their children were brought to earth, or why they died the way they did, but have found meaning in their losses nevertheless. One mother wrote to us:

"I didn't ask why"

"My husband and I wanted a child so badly. We were thrilled to have a son, but when Carter died we grieved our hearts out. It was so painful. Even after our other children were born, I still had a hole in my soul. Every year at the anniversary of Carter's death, I was so depressed that I thought about suicide. My husband and our other children suffered because of my grief. Gradually, over ten years, my grief and depression were no more.

"I didn't ask why Carter was here or why he died. I just knew that he was here, and because of that my husband, children, and I are better people today. I was grateful to have had him in our lives for the time we did. Today, I still think about him but I don't feel grief. I'm just thankful."

PERSONAL HISTORY

Each subsequent death reactivates previous feelings of loss. If we were not taught to deal effectively with death, then our grief history can cause problems. The good news is: just as yesterday influences today, this day will influence tomorrow. Your reading this book is generating a healthier future for you and those you love.

Personality

An individual's response to loss depends in part on his or her personality type. Some people are grief-prone. They form strong attachments, and any separation produces deep sorrow and longing. How much is innate, and how much is learned, we do not know; regardless, adjusting to loss is difficult for that type of personality.

Introverted and extroverted types differ in the way they deal with loss. Whereas introverts usually secure one or two close friends, extroverts gather them in mass quantities. Extroverts, therefore, are able to call on a large network for support—and social support is an important element in coping with loss.

Stoic and dramatic personalities contrast as well. Stoic types make unemotional and brief statements, such as "Life goes on." Their counterparts are flamboyant in their display of emotions, often swooning, "I'll never, ever get over this." That display, however, does not necessarily reflect their genuine feelings. Paradoxically, stoic individuals often "never get over it," and sometimes "life goes on" as usual for the dramatists.

Certain personality types attach to *things.* They suffer over their Mercedes being clipped or a business deal falling apart, rather than when they lose a relationship. After the death of a close loved one, however, these individuals often switch priorities—their relationships with other people become more important than their possessions. Most of these personality types revert to their former selves over time, but, meanwhile, attempting to predict their mourning process is futile.

Materialism

Materialism and fear of death go hand in hand. The more wealth and possessions people accumulate, the more likely they are to go screaming into the good night. Because they have much to lose, they deny every aspect of loss, including bereavement. The exceptions are those whose spiritual and material assets are equal.

RELIGION

Survivors often rely on religious doctrine to bring reason into the chaos of grief. Beyond sermons and scriptures, they seek hope, compassion, and comfort from their congregation or religious community. Unfortunately, mourners sometimes meet fear and persecution instead.

Accounts of religious abuse have been reported from the beginning of recorded history. Many have suffered at the hands of their faith, just when they needed spiritual nurturing the most. Religion becomes emotional, intellectual, and spiritual abuse when it robs individuals of their free will. As Geri Colozzi Wiitala testifies, spiritual care can be found outside as well as inside organized religion.

"I became more curious than fearful"

After the tragic death of her daughter, Heather, Geri wanted to read about life after death. She knew that doing so was forbidden in her Bible-based religion; therefore, she asked church elders for permission. They insisted that reading anything mystical was not in compliance with their beliefs and ordered her to refrain or be driven from the church. "I became more curious than fearful," she said; thus, Geri chose to explore spirituality without the blessings of her church.[7] Religious beliefs can be shattered or strengthened by loss.

We are often asked, "But am I religious? I believe in God, but I don't go to church." Anyone who attends some form of organized religion, or practices a doctrine, is considered religious. This includes those who prefer, or are forced by circumstances (such as illness), to practice their faith at home.

Another question people ask is "Will attending a house of worship [church, synagogue, temple, mosque, etc.] help me?" The results from one study[8] indicate that people who attend religious services and hold strong spiritual beliefs find grief less problematic. Their opposites, those who do not attend services or hold spiritual beliefs, find bereavement difficult. In between are individuals who attend church without strong spiritual convictions, as well as those with strong spiritual beliefs who do not go to church.

SPIRITUALITY

Spirituality is our birthright—we come to earth as spirit beings. Spirituality is remembering that something greater than self exists. Those who are spiritually enlightened conduct their lives with compassion, reverence, conscientiousness, serenity, and joy. They trust that the world is evolving as it should; thus, they feel at peace with the world, others, and self. Life, death, and mourning, for them, take place at a different level, as in Dee's case.

"You're religious, aren't you?" Dee's physician asked. "I can tell by the way you've handled your son's death. Religious people cope with loss better."

"No, I don't go to church," she replied. Dee's spiritual countenance owed to her believing in something much greater than herself, living from a kind heart, and practicing good deeds.

Spirituality can become buried or forgotten over time, as with Babe.

"What will God do with an old sinner like me?" —Dianne's Story

Not because she was cowardly, but because she was confused, Babe requested that a hospice chaplain visit with her in her home. Dying of lung cancer, Babe asked, "Dianne, what will God do with an old sinner like me?" Propped up on pillows, she struggled to continue. "I've never been to church. After my husband walked out, I worked two jobs on the docks just to buy food and clothes for my kids and put a roof over their heads. I had no time for myself or anything except my family. I started smoking before I knew better—and ran wild for a spell too. What will happen to me when I die?" Before collapsing into her pillows, Babe held on to ask, "God knows, I never meant no harm to nobody, but what does He do with folks like me?"

As she lay staring at me, I kept thinking, *You did the best that you could.* Finally, she raised one hand only a bit and, pointing her finger my way, forced out the words, "You know, I did the best I could."

Over the next few weeks, we talked a great deal. Babe's sense of humor and inner strength were much larger than her five-foot body, which was weakening rapidly. "I must live until next month because my son will be home from Holland," she wheezed. But her survival until then did not seem possible, and, in fact, I was called to her side the next day. Babe was actively dying, and no one expected her to make it through the evening.

Early the next morning, I was once again summoned to her home. "Dianne! Hurry! Come here!" a hearty voice exclaimed as I entered the room. I could hardly believe my ears and eyes—it was Babe. Speaking with ease, she began, "In the middle of the night I felt my lungs collapse. I tried so hard to catch my breath, but I couldn't. I knew that was *it*, but I hadn't seen my son yet, so I started yelling for help, not out loud, you know. I was begging, 'Please, please, oh please, I can't die yet.' Then I saw something right here," she gestured to her left side. "A giant hand appeared, went under my back, and lifted me up, underneath my lungs. A big whiff of air went in, like this." She gasped in demonstration. "The hand kept pushing my back up and then letting it go back down again until I started breathing on my own. It was the hand of God. He saved me. He granted my dying wish," she said, pausing to smile. "God knows that I lived the best life that I could, and now I know that He will welcome me home."

Babe's son arrived from Amsterdam several weeks later, and, with all her family gathered around, she died peacefully.

Beyond forgotten, spirituality can become blocked by strong emotions. Have you ever tried to enter solemn prayer while feeling outraged? Forgiving, like praying, is an act of spirituality.

"I couldn't hold him responsible anymore"

Tammy could not forgive her husband. He and their daughter had quarreled that evening, the night that ended with the teenager intentionally driving her convertible over a cement seawall into the ocean below. Tammy repressed her anger for years, allowing it to grow into resentment and bitterness. Finally, she attended a week-long workshop, where she screamed and cursed. "That was a turning point in my life," she said afterward. "I couldn't hold him responsible anymore. He had a role in her death, but she drove the car. That was very hard for me to face."

Families disagree. Parents and children, like husbands and wives, normally quarrel over their differences, but the ending of a life is not the normal result. Forgiveness may come down to forgiving someone for not being who we needed them to be. Then we can accept what is and move on.

Like capping anger, sitting on buckets of tears blocks spiritual growth, as Ellen's experience illustrates.

"I'm just existing, not living"—Dianne's Story

"All the meaning in my life died with my husband," Ellen said. "I'm just existing, sweetheart, not living. I've not cried since he crossed over; it simply isn't done in this family." I handed her a pillow and asked, "What would you like him to know?" She buried her face and sobbed, "I want you back. I want you back." Months later I received a card, "Thank you for the pillow talk." With her spiritual crisis behind, Ellen was living again.

SOCIAL SUPPORT

Transcending loss depends on social support. Survivors need to reminisce, often telling the same stories over and over. Raymond's grandmother was typical.

"Raymond, your grandpa Waddleton died"—Raymond's Story

In Porterdale, Georgia, neighbors were more like family. "Raymond, your grandpa Waddleton died," Mother said, waking me up early one morning. I was an eleven-year-old boy, yet I remember still. Mrs. Crowel and Mrs. Day took over Grandma's household chores so that she was free to reminisce. Everybody in the community visited, bringing food, listening hearts, and their own stories to share.

Because towns like that have fallen into extinction, today's survivors turn to peer groups and professionals for support. Our field hosts many qualified specialists, and most bereaved individuals can benefit from their help in some way.

PROFESSIONAL SUPPORT

Facilitate is derived from the French word *facile*, "easy." Grief facilitators ease grief's journey by educating and by helping survivors sort through their thoughts and feelings. We suggest choosing a therapist who works from a perspective that is the opposite of yours. If you are a feeling type person, for example, then a cognitive therapist can interject rational thinking. If you are an intellectual, a therapist who focuses on feelings will foster your emotional development. Challenge promotes growth. Some survivors need confrontation. Confrontation, however, is best left to professionals. And this brings us to an important feature of bereavement—communication. So let's turn to the next topic, giving and receiving sympathy.

FIVE

Giving and Receiving Sympathy

> Blessed are they that mourn: for they shall be comforted.
>
> —MATTHEW 5:4

As Jill sat on a beach in Crete, watching the waves wash between her toes, she noticed a young girl dancing in and out of the surf. Warmed by the child's carefree frolicking, Jill greeted her as she neared.

"Oh, hello," the little girl answered. "What are you doing here?"

"Just watching the ocean. And you?" Jill asked.

"I'm on vacation," she said, swinging her arms from side to side.

"How old are you?" Jill asked.

"Four," she answered, holding up four fingers.

"And when will you be five?"

"Hmmm." She paused to think. Then, putting her hands on her hips, she answered, "When I'm finished being four."

"Ah, of course," Jill said, smiling. *Of course, of course,* she thought.

Colin Caffell used to relay this story about his friend Jill during Elisabeth Kübler-Ross's "Life, Death, and Transition" workshops. He made the point that in a perfect world everyone would understand life's timeliness—that grieving, like aging, follows a natural rhythm. Most cultures, however, stifle mourning. Survivors are asked, "When will you stop grieving?" "When will you start going out?" "When will you start dating again?" "When will you have another child?"

"When I'm finished mourning for what I've lost, of course."

In this chapter, we will look at the way people communicate after a loss, beginning with sympathizers. They are almost always well-intentioned; nevertheless, they can say things that are offensive or hurtful. It may be a matter of poor timing, or their statements may be inappropriate. Or they may be projecting their own feelings onto the mourner.

TIMING

Appropriate timing is imperative: timing in relation to the circumstance, and timing in relation to the survivor's psychological process.

Considering the Circumstance

When grief is acute, emotions are raw. Mourners are often trying just to make it through the day on their feet. "If you encounter other bereaved individuals," we advise at support groups, "do not walk up and ask about their loss. If you see someone in a restaurant, that person may just want to eat lunch and not be reminded of her grief. Greet any bereaved individual as you normally would, 'Hello . . . How are you?' and let that person determine the direction of the conversation." The following experience illustrates how not to approach a survivor.

"I didn't feel like talking"—Dianne's Story

Darlene's entrance into my office was as stormy as the afternoon weather. "I had to come tell you," she said, slamming the door with her heel. "I was talking with someone at church when Sue walked up." (Darlene and Sue had once been members of a hospice grief-support group.) Darlene continued, "Peering at me with those penetrating eyes of hers, she blurted, 'How did everything turn out? Did they catch the guy who murdered your son?' I hated her for bringing that up. I didn't feel like talking about it right then, but I didn't know what to say. So I stood there and told her everything she wanted to know."

Etiquette calls for sensitive communication, and not only for the newly bereaved. Poor timing is always an invasion of privacy, as in the following example.

"Hey! Dianne!"—Dianne's Story

After attending to terminally ill patients and their families all day, my body and soul were in dire need of nourishment. I was carrying a tray of food to a remote corner of the hospital cafeteria when I heard a former support-group member call out from across the room, "Hey! Dianne!" Delighted to hear her voice, I turned to walk to her. But then she motioned to the group of women at her table, shouting, "I told them about your dad's death and how you made meaning of it. Come sit over here and tell them about it."

"Oh, no, not right now," I said, and hastened to the quiet corner.

"I don't want anybody asking me about my loss"

"I'd like for you to write my story in your book," a number of friends and family members told us, "but I don't want anybody asking me about my loss. Just change my name, sex, occupation, location, or whatever you need in order to guarantee my anonymity." In every case, if excluding certain details compromised the integrity of their stories, or if their stories seemed too personal for us to disclose, we did not include them. Each person deserves a right to privacy.

Consider Their Process

We advise those in mourning to be careful with whom they associate for several weeks after their loss, because most people do not understand the grief process. For instance, few sympathizers realize that, immediately after a loss, a survivor usually needs physical and emotional care. The most appreciated sympathizers are those who give practical support such as chauffeuring relatives to and from the airport, mowing the lawn, caring for pets, or just sitting with the mourner. Even experienced sympathizers can be out of sync with the mourner's process, however, as the following story illustrates.

"No more good-byes"—Dianne's Story

"It was the last death she will ever experience," my mother's minister said to me shortly after she died. "You'll never have to say good-bye to her again. No more good-byes, Dianne, because there is no more separation. She is now with you always." His words were frustrating because I wanted many more good-byes. Seeing Mother's little head peek out from her kitchen window as I backed out of her driveway meant the world to me. I wanted her with me on this physical plane. Several years later, however, I remembered and appreciated his sentiments. His declaration had been correct, but premature. His words would have been well received if spoken at a time when I was further along in my grief.

In sum, communication problems are less likely to occur when sympathy is offered at the appropriate place and time, and when the statements coordinate with the survivor's process. Sensitivity is the key for interacting with the bereaved.

Inappropriate Statements

Inappropriate statements, although irksome, are usually made by those who are simply doing the best they can. Knowing that their words are not spoken with malice can lessen the sting. The newly bereaved are often thrust among those inexperienced with loss, as in the following example.

"It's a beautiful day"

The sunshine, country breeze, and meadow of bluebonnets comforted Robert. He picked a single flower and brought it to his grandmother. "It's a beautiful day, Grandma," he said, lifting his eyes to the hills surrounding them.

"Nothing beautiful about it," she grunted and kept walking, head down, not seeing the hurt come over her young grandson's face. Her husband was being laid to rest, so, in her eyes, there was no beauty in this day. Although she was too emotionally raw to see Robert's intentions, everyone else knew that he was only trying to comfort her; after all, the burial scene was not the drizzly, cold, or dismal sight so often pictured in movies.

The newly bereaved sense when they are becoming overwhelmed. As a result, they find some way to postpone their mourning. Some throw themselves into busywork, painting rooms, cleaning out closets, or finishing projects. Others turn to nature by planting trees or tending to their gardens. Dianne initially coped by blending the two.

"What a Shame"—Dianne's Story

In Texas, January is the time to plant rosebushes. Mother and I had just purchased six for her flower garden the day before she died. After her funeral, while aimlessly wandering around her house, I suddenly remembered the roses. I sensed that feeling the dirt in my hands and finishing our project would somehow be comforting, so I gathered tools from her garage and commenced planting. (Survivors instinctually know what they need.) For the first time since her death, I felt serene and totally at peace.

I had just placed the last rosebush in its hole and reached for the shovel when a neighbor approached. The young woman, known to everybody as abrasive and crude, struck her stance. Towering over me, with her hands on her hips and feet wide apart, she smirked, "What a shame you didn't do that while your mother was alive to enjoy it." The neighbor was lucky that I did not bury her in the garden and report her missing.

In every situation, for one's own good and the good of all involved, it is best to consider the source before reacting. In this case, I knew the woman was insensitive, and I had no intention of forming any type of relationship with her. I only wanted to preserve my serenity; therefore, I stood up and walked into the house.

PROJECTION

Projection simply means judging others by one's own perceptions. Projectors assume that other people think and feel as they do. Sympathizers who are experienced with loss are oftentimes the most guilty. "I understand" and "I know how you feel," they say. Impossible. No one knows the internal life of another. No one understands the suffering and hardship one loss might bring to another. Sympathizers divide themselves from those they want to support when they say "I know" or "I understand."

"I understand"

Jenny's mother succumbed at age fifty after a brief illness. Months later, Jenny attended the funeral of her friend's elderly mother. "I'm sorry," she said. "Losing your mother is almost more than a daughter can bear. I understand. I know exactly how you feel."

"No, you don't," her friend said. "Mother suffered all those years, in and out of hospitals. She was miserable, and I'm grateful to see her finally out of her misery. There's no reason to be sorry."

Judging others by ourselves can lead to disappointment, even for sympathizers.

A Projection Was Stopped Short—Raymond's Story

While dressing for the funeral, I glanced out our bedroom window and saw that a blanket of snow had fallen overnight. "Oh, no!" I called out to my wife. "The first snowstorm of the season is here. Poor Bill—snow on the day he has to bury his daughter. This will make it even more unbearable for him and his wife. They will be so overwhelmed." On our long drive to the cemetery, my wife kept talking about their little girl and the tragic automobile accident that had taken her life, with me reiterating, "And now, how awful—all this snow."

As we stood at the graveside, snow blowing in our faces, I tried to gather the words to express my condolences and sympathize about the unfortunate weather. Before I could, Bill's wife exclaimed, "Oh! What a perfect day! It's snowing just for Emily. She was wishing for snow the other morning, and here it is, just what she wanted." Something that seems unfortunate to one person may bring comfort to others. Giving sympathy requires getting out of our world and into theirs.

Entering Their World

Toward the end of the twentieth century, the grief-awareness movement introduced new etiquette surrounding loss. Sympathizers were advised that the only appropriate phrase to say to mourners was "I'm sorry." As a result, much like "Good morning," it often reflects good manners rather than genuine sympathy. Further still, it does not always meet the circumstance.

"Oh, no, don't be sorry"—Dianne's Story

When I first met Linda, she was returning to graduate school in order to cope with her husband's death. "We were so in love," she cried. "After sixteen years of married bliss, I feel so alone now. He died three years ago, and I know that I'll never get over losing him to cancer. He was such a wonderful man."

Linda bought grief books, which she carried and referred to throughout the next four semesters. She was growing into such an independent woman that we were stunned one morning to hear her announce, "I've met the most wonderful man and we're getting married in two weeks. I'm here to drop my classes and say good-bye."

The summer and fall passed before Linda appeared again. She stood in the doorway of the lab looking around and then moved slowly toward me with her head bowed. "Oh, Dianne, the most terrible thing happened Sunday," she whispered, leaning across the table. "My husband's heart exploded while we were making love. I called 911, but it was no use. He died almost instantly."

Knowing that Linda had been distraught after her first husband's death, and that the ability to adjust decreases with age, I surmised that she must be devastated. My heart ached for her. "Oh, I'm so sorry," I said.

Leaning back with a smile, she exclaimed, "Oh, no, Dianne, don't be sorry! He died doing what he loved. Besides, I've been thinking about that old saying 'Men die before women because women deserve a few good years.' Well, I'll tell you, I've been married most of my life and I'm tired of entanglements. I want to be my own person from now on."

"What was 'the most terrible thing,' then?" I asked.

"At first, it was just the shock of his dying like that," she answered, biting her bottom lip. "Then it was having to face the paramedics. And now, people keep asking how he died. It's so embarrassing. I mean, can you imagine? People asking—that's the terribleness of it." Once again the little smile appeared on her lips. "This time it was a good death."

That exchange highlights a number of points that we have covered thus far: the manner of death influences grief; each loss carries its own unique set of circumstances; a survivor grieves and grows after each loss but in a different way each time; both survivor and sympathizers can be caught off guard by grief's unpredictability; and "I'm sorry" does not always suit the situation. Linda's story brings us to the next point—I was willing to enter her world and empathize, but she wanted sympathy. What is the difference?

Sympathy or Empathy?

Sympathizers give care and compassion. "Oh, you poor thing. You closed the door on your finger," they say. Empathizers feel the pain as if it had happened to them. "Ouch! That hurts!" they exclaim, holding their finger.

Applied to bereavement, those who empathize step into the loss and carry half of the survivor's load. In doing so, they experience change and growth. Not everyone is able or willing to do that, and not every survivor wants or needs it. Choosing between empathy and sympathy depends on both individuals.

TERMINOLOGY

Bereavement research and education has led to a better understanding of grief. As in most growing fields, however, new concepts elicit new problems. In a later chapter we will look at some misunderstandings about and misinterpretations of grief theories, but let's stay with communication for now. Whereas "I'm sorry" became the phrase for sympathizers, *closure* became the catchword for healthcare professionals.

Closure

A deep, open wound is terribly painful and vulnerable to infection. Doctors gather the material they need to repair and close the affected area as soon as possible. As a result, they protect the healthy cells and initiate the timely process of healing. Grief counselors adopted the term *closure* from the medical profession, and initially it was an effective metaphor. When the deep wound of loss occurs, the psyche needs protection from further injury, the gathering of loose ends, and precious time for rebuilding.

The bereaved often experience numerous closures with each loss.

Mourning Judy—Dianne's Story (Continued)

The moment our new neighbors described the circumstances surrounding the murder of my friend Judy and identified her killer (see chapter 4), I sensed my open wound beginning to close. I no longer felt fearful and vulnerable. With that part of my anguish resolved, for the first time since her death, I was able to mourn for what I had lost. Several years later, I felt another sense of closure when Judy's murderer was captured.

Closure was never intended to describe grief's finale—the closing of a door. Nevertheless, some people have used it in that sense or misused it in other ways, and now many bereaved men and women recoil when they hear the word. In one case, a physician turned to the mother of an infant moments after the baby's death and said, "It's time for closure on this one."

Genuine sympathy requires entering the other person's world without assessing, judging, and advising, but closure statements incorporate all three. Most clinicians now use the term only among themselves.

Sympathy via Letters and E-mail

Much is to be said for handwritten, hand-delivered, and handheld personal mail. Many bereaved people report that letters containing special memories of family and friends are among their treasured keepsakes.

Given the immediacy and convenience of e-mail, many sympathizers have begun beaming their condolences instead of sending conventional cards and letters. If sympathizers receive the news about an illness or death *from the mourner* via e-mail, then electronic sympathy is appropriate. When two people have often kept in touch by e-mail, this form of communication can become a major source of support in times of loss.

We suggest sending a card or letter to express sympathy and then staying in touch by e-mail or phone.

Internet Support

For many years, those in mourning reported that tapping on their typewriters gave them tremendous release. The advent of the personal computer took this one step further. In the privacy of their homes, survivors can now pound on their keyboards and find social support at the same time. Over the past six years, the World Wide Web has experienced a groundswell of domains designed by and for the bereaved. Tom Golden, for instance, constructed a site called Crisis, Grief, and Healing (www.webhealing.com) in honor of his father. It currently receives about 500,000 hits each month from people around the globe.

Survivors can create online memorials for their loved ones at sites such as Link for Lights (www.1000deaths.com). Angel Babies, A Place to Remember, and GriefNet also provide free online memorials, chat rooms, e-mail support, directories, and other services.

The field of bereavement, however, is like any other: among these dedicated and remarkable people are some who are less than honorable. Beware of expensive online services. Listed in our resources section are some of the free or minimally priced (at the time of this writing) Internet domains that provide the same quality service as those that charge exorbitant fees.

Keep It Simple

Simplicity is the key to good taste, and that certainly applies to giving sympathy. Simplicity and a quiet presence can bring tremendous comfort. Survivors long remember friends who sat beside them, allowing them to mourn.

Their Slight Presence—Raymond's Story

After the death of our infant son, my wife and I were visited by the couple who lived next door. Instead of having the florist deliver their flowers, they carried a beautiful bouquet in their arms and handed it to us. We were so comforted by their gesture, along with their silent presence, that I wondered if they too had survived the death of a child. Silence is difficult for those who have not needed it for themselves.

"She was sleeping"

"After my husband's funeral," Ellen said, "a member of my church called to ask how I was doing. When I began to cry, she said, 'I'll be right over.' She sat beside my recliner until I finally sobbed myself to sleep. When I awoke the next morning, she was sleeping on the couch. That was one of the kindest things anybody has ever done for me, and now I do that for other widows."

"Dianne, you just did"—Dianne's Story

For more than twenty years Doc served as a minister for a large metropolitan church, and now, as a patient in our hospice, he enlightened me on a regular basis. On the day of this visit, Doc was in a great deal of pain from an infection in his leg. As I prepared to leave, we held hands. "I'm grateful for our time together today," I finally said. "I'll be thinking of you."

"And I of you," he replied.

"Would you like for me to say a prayer before I go?" I asked.

"Dianne, you just did," he answered. Clearly, our thoughts and feelings in sympathy and prayers do not need to be elaborately expressed to be effective.

Practical Support

Condolences can also be expressed by attending to practicalities. After Dianne's mother's funeral, the family arrived home to find the lawn mowed, and they still wonder who was responsible for the good deed. Tending to young children, answering the telephone, preparing the house for guests, and chauffeuring relatives to and from the airport are all expressions of sympathy.

Although social support is a necessary aspect of mourning, sympathizers can overstep their boundaries. Let's now consider how mourners can respond to inappropriate sympathy.

Responding to Uncomfortable Statements

Insensitive statements can be so offensive that mourners retaliate in anger. If sympathizers try to explain or defend themselves, matters usually escalate. As a result, relationships are often damaged or shattered beyond repair.

"Relationships cannot be replaced"

Jerry was handsome and charming and could entertain like Elton John, but rather than leaving his good looks and talent as his legacy, he left his character. The true character of a person is displayed by the way he treats his uninvited guests, and no matter how sick Jerry felt, he always showered uninvited guests and phone callers with his undivided attention.

Before he died from an AIDS-related illness, Jerry shared his wisdom with his mother, who was upset after breaking a piece of her glass menagerie collection. "It's okay," he said. "Just remember, Mother, life is about relationships, not things. If you crack an object, you can mend it or buy a new one, but if a relationship is cracked, although it might be mended, it will never be the same. And a broken relationship cannot be replaced."

Relationships depend on communication. Unfortunately, sympathizers can make such offensive statements that, in that moment, a survivor only wants to drive them away. Because many relationships end on that note, it's important to consider the *intentions* of both sympathizers and the mourner.

Sympathizers' Intentions

Every human being on earth carries grief. Nevertheless, many remain naive or unsophisticated about loss; in other words, they are grief-challenged.

Sympathizers who make inappropriate statements are unconsciously pleading, *Don't grieve; I can't bear it.* Their intention is to avoid their own discomfort, which is stirred by fear (of their own grief surfacing), imagination (for losses that could occur in their future), concern (about their mortality), and innocence (they have no experience from which to interact).

"You're young and can marry again," "But you have other children," and "Well, just go get another dog" sound as if loved ones are dispensable. Clichés such as "She isn't suffering anymore," "Be happy you had him that long," "Be happy she is with God now," "You'll heal in time," and "Oh, don't cry; he wouldn't want you to be sad" demean the loss. They can also produce shame. *You're wrong to grieve*, they signal. Just remember, the stronger their statement, the more they need to avoid their own pain. For the most part, sympathizers say what they need to hear.

"You need to take it easy," "You need to stop working so hard," "You must exercise" are projections, wherein the speakers express their own needs. We never know what another person needs; therefore, truer words would be, "I need for you to take it easy," "I wish you would stop working so hard," or "I think you should exercise more."

When sympathizers say, "You need to get on with your life," "You need to get out more," or "You need to stop grieving," they are really expressing their own needs. They need for the survivor to get on with life, to get out more, or to stop grieving, because at the heart lies their own unconscious need—which is (or was) to get on with their lives, get out more, or stop grieving.

The Mourner's Intention

As a survivor, your response to offensive statements depends on your intention. Do you want a relationship with the sympathizer? If the answer is yes, then what kind of relationship? Is it worth your effort? The following puzzling incident illustrates that an absence of communication can result in no relationship whatsoever.

"You'll have to excuse her"—Dianne's Story

At a civic meeting, a respected volunteer approached me. "Hi, Dianne. I'm Tanya. I'm sorry to introduce myself like this, but I need someone to help me with a Christmas project for the elementary school. They gave it to me at the last minute. Is there any way you could volunteer at my place tomorrow?"

"Sure. I'll be happy to help," I said. "I can be there from about noon until three."

I felt especially invited the next day by her flower garden, wind chimes, and a doorbell that played "The Eyes of Texas Are Upon You." It was even more inviting when Tanya opened her door smiling and squealing, "This is so good of you! Come in! Come in!" Motioning to the foldup chairs and portable table in the living room, she said, "Sit down and I'll get us something to drink and our things."

Her drapes overlapped, preventing any light from entering the room, but a small lamp provided enough illumination for me to see where photographs had once hung. The dreariness inside was so strikingly opposed to the appearance of the exterior that an eerie sensation crept over me.

Tanya returned with a box of felt pieces and began instructing in an authoritarian voice, "This will be easy, but time-consuming. All we have to do is glue all these . . ." Without lifting her gaze from the material, she continued methodologically describing how she wanted the project done. As we began our work, I attempted to make conversation, but, seeing that she was not interested, I harnessed my extroverted mouth and tended to the job. The next hour was uneventful, until Tanya suddenly looked up and blurted out, "My son was killed." After she described his death and the convoluted aftermath, I said, "How tragic. I don't understand why bad things happen to good people." With that, she stood up and left the room.

When she did not return after some time, I began to speculate, *She must be looking for something we need for the project, or maybe she's trying to find a photograph of her son to show me.* Then three o'clock came, time for me to leave. I was concerned about her long absence and wondered if my comment had annoyed her. I gathered my things and was about to call out her name when I heard the back door opening.

"Hi, Dianne," her husband said. "I see you're here. Where's Tanya?"

"I don't know," I answered, walking toward the entrance. "I need to go but wanted to tell her good-bye."

"Wait just a second and let me go see what's holding her up," he said. Within two minutes he rounded the corner, whispering, "You'll have to excuse her."

"I'm afraid I offended her," I said, walking outside.

"Oh, she gets this way," he said, as he escorted me to my car.

"Please tell her that I'll be glad to help her finish."

"Yes, I will, and thank you," he said, waving good-bye.

Tanya was foremost in my mind for weeks. *Perhaps she felt tearful and needed the privacy of her bedroom,* I thought, *or maybe she found photographs and became overwhelmed.* I also thought about her husband's blasé attitude. One question, however, dominated: was she insulted by what I said? At twenty-one years of age, I was a survivor of numerous losses but had not yet been involved with anything of this magnitude. I knew that I was still naive and uninformed, and if

I was at fault I wanted a chance to make amends. I was willing to learn, grow, and be her friend, but I never saw her again.

I happened upon her husband at various meetings and he always stopped to converse. "How's Tanya?" I sometimes asked. He always answered by shrugging his shoulders, saying, "Oh, you know." But I didn't know. I was only a passerby in her life.

Many relationships are ended by communication blunders; therefore, your first consideration before responding to a sympathizer is to know if you want a relationship with that person, and, if so, what kind.

Three Basic Types of Relationships

There are three basic types of relationships. Passersby are people with whom you have brief encounters. Acquaintances exchange thoughts and ideas. Interpersonal relationships hold more depth. If such a relationship is to be emotionally, spiritually, physically, and intellectually gratifying, both people must communicate openly and honestly.

Respond Accordingly

While we are in mourning, some sympathizers briefly cross our paths (hospital staff, postal workers, florists, probate lawyers, and so on). They do not know us; therefore, they can only offer vague, and oftentimes inappropriate, condolences. If we intend to hold them as passersby, then we can remember their gestures of kindness and allow them to continue on their way.

Other sympathizers are acquaintances (co-workers, teachers, employers or employees, fellow students, friends of the deceased, clergy, and so on). They are on closer terms with us than passersby, but they can nevertheless make inappropriate statements. "It was her time to go," "Don't be sad," or "He's an angel now," they often say. If we intend to preserve these relationships, we can absorb their well-meaning gestures and acknowledge them for trying to be supportive. "Thank you for caring," we might say.

Interpersonal relationships are much more involved—and each to a different degree. They include our relationships with parents, spouse, children, grandchildren, close friends, anyone with whom we share close emotional ties. Although these people know us well, they can speak words that strike deeply, words such as "Don't be sad," "You can have another child," "She wouldn't want you to cry."

Loss causes growth. If we want our close relationships to flourish, our family and friends must grow along with us. "But I am sad and I need to grieve," "Maybe I can have another child, but it won't be this one," "This is devastating for me and I deserve to grieve for what I've lost" are replies that give them the opportunity to learn about our loss, how we are being affected by it, and what they can do to support us. Interpersonal relationships require reciprocal self-disclosure.

"Your attitude stinks"

Gloria received a call from a hospital in another state. She was told that her son had been involved in a serious skiing accident and was in critical condition. He would probably not survive, but if he did, he could never be normal again. To Gloria, everything seemed chaotic; therefore, she rushed to her friend Nancy, a bereaved mother many years previously. Gloria was tearfully describing the situation when Nancy suddenly yelled, "Stop! Your attitude stinks! You have to think positively."

"But I'm grieving over what we lost. Even if he lives, he'll never be the same, and he was such a good—"

"Stop it!" Nancy interrupted again. "Modern medicine can do miracles these days. You've got to shake this lousy attitude of yours. Get a grip."

"Nancy stunned me at first," Gloria recounted later. "But then, the more I tried to talk, the louder and more anxious she became. Finally, it was obvious to me. Nancy was still in too much pain over her child to be able to sit with me and hear about mine. On my drive home, I kept thinking about that old saying, 'We cannot take someone farther than we have been ourselves.' I realized that I didn't know one person who had moved to the other side of grief. Who was I to turn to?"

"What is your intention toward your relationship with Nancy?" her therapist asked.

"I still intend to be friends," she said. "But it won't ever be a close friendship, because she won't let me share my grief with her."

Open communication is key for preserving relationships. In some cases, however, preservation is not in the best interests of all involved.

Recognize When It Is Time to Let a Relationship Go

Meaningful relationships are reciprocal and supportive. Grief brings change, and change can be difficult. If you, as a survivor, become clear that a relationship will impede your development, then it may be time to let it go, at least for now.

As a sympathizer or support person, the same holds true. At some point, you may realize that you have done your best but that your best will never satisfy the survivor. Remember, it is his or her process. Mourners sometimes need to work through a great deal of rage, hate, or bitterness, and they unconsciously orchestrate other people to keep them refueled. If you become enmeshed, then their process is yours as well. You may need to step back for a while, or perhaps indefinitely. Healthy mourning promotes growth for all involved—which brings us to our next topic: healthy versus unhealthy grief.

SIX

Functional Versus Dysfunctional Grief

> To weep is to make less the depth of grief.
>
> —SHAKESPEARE,
> *KING HENRY THE SIXTH,*
> *PART III*

Grief covers such a broad and individual spectrum that specialists have long struggled with terminology. These twenty-six words are only a partial list of terms we have heard applied to grief when it hindered development: abnormal, afflicted, atypical, burdensome, chronic, complex, complicated, conflicted, conflicting, continued, disestablished, disordered, disorganized, dysfunctional, extended, impaired, maladaptive, morbid, neurotic, pathological, problematic, prolonged, stored, unfinished, unhealthy, and unresolved.

We will use *dysfunctional* or *unhealthy*, because healthy grief has a function. It allows survivors to identify, acknowledge, feel, and integrate what they love but are now without. Unhealthy grief prolongs suffering, interrupts normal activities, or prevents life from being lived to the fullest. Let's turn to some of the signals or symptoms of dysfunction.

Fixated Grief

Healthy grief has a flow, a natural continuing process, although that flow can include stopping to rest, reenergize, or take stock. Fixated grief, however, causes survivors to remain stuck at one point.

Immediately after loss, for instance, mourners take time off from work or daily activities to accomplish a number of tasks: arrange the funeral and burial services, attend to legal and financial concerns, organize probate procedures, and so on. Whereas most survivors return to a daily schedule within one week, others need more time. This becomes problematic only if the bereaved slide into an unhealthy, prolonged withdrawal.

The bereaved can also become fixated in telling their story. Mourning needs a voice. People often do not know how they feel until they hear themselves say it; therefore, the more survivors give expression to their feelings, the faster their emotions normalize. Unfortunately, though, some bereaved men and women tell their story without expressing how they feel. Moving through loss depends on emotionally venting.

"Why didn't you tell more?"—Dianne's Story

After reading the manuscript of this book, several friends asked, "Dianne, why didn't you tell more about your dad's horrible death—the open bedsores, the fever, his knowing their mistake would kill him while he could do nothing but lie there? Why didn't you reveal that the doctors informed you about the overdose only because his roommate, a physician, was waiting to tell you himself? Why didn't you tell about . . ."

"Sixteen years ago," I replied, "I needed to hear myself sort through my emotional ordeal. I no longer have that need, and it wouldn't help readers. Thank goodness you allowed me to express my feelings, because several people who were bereaved at the same time are still telling their stories. Instead of their grief moving along, *they* move along—from relative to relative, friend to friend, acquaintance to acquaintance."

* * *

Never underestimate the healing ability of hearing yourself say the words that identify your feelings: "And I'm angry at them for that," "I'm just so sad without her," or "Now I feel disappointed that they did that." Those who remain fixated in their stories do not express the feelings that accompany them.

Denial

People cope with trauma in numerous ways, denial being the most common. The function of denial is to protect the psyche from a crisis initially too intense to absorb. When the impact of a loved one's death is overwhelming, denial filters out the full brunt of the blow. Within weeks, though, reality begins to intervene. Eventually, the loss is fully absorbed, and the mind and body regain equilibrium. Although denial is healthy during early mourning, it can become dysfunctional if prolonged.

Denial defends against pain or discomfort in one of two forms, conscious or unconscious. Let's survey the conscious form first.

Conscious Denial

When denial is conscious, we intentionally distort the truth. A young child avoids its mother's disapproving glare by claiming, "I didn't eat the cookies!" A criminal acutely aware of his or her guilt screams out in defense, "I didn't do it!"

Mourners defend against the truth as well, and therein lies a potential for problems. The literal, unconscious mind absorbs every thought and statement, unable to distinguish between reality and fiction. Conscious deceptions invite unconscious denial, which can develop into maladaptive delusions, as in the following two cases.

"He was murdered"

After her husband suicided, Ruth began to answer inquiries by saying, "He was murdered." As she continued to tell people that he had been killed, her conscious denial slowly shifted to the unconscious form (disbelieving the reality of a situation). Maintaining that his demise was murder, she invented a scenario and then stormed the police station, insisting that investigators open his file. A chaplain in the department was called in and gently directed the widow to an SOS (survivors of suicide) group. There she received the help and support she needed and eventually came to terms with her loss.

"Oh no, Dr. Moody, she's in Ohio visiting relatives" —Raymond's Story

A nonrespondent nursing-home resident, Douglas was diagnosed with Alzheimer's disease. Psychiatrists there shifted the elderly man to a geriatric clinic where I was working. Our team of physicians ran more psychological and medical tests, all of which indicated that Douglas was healthy and lacked any sign of illness. Nevertheless, attending clinicians diagnosed Alzheimer's again, "based on the patient's inability to recall past events and his social withdrawal." Upon hearing his case reviewed, I looked over his chart, which revealed that the widower insisted his wife was in Ohio, whereas in reality she had died six months earlier. I noted his room number and went to investigate.

Easing the door open, I saw a regal-looking gentleman standing in front of the open window. Instead of the flatness of expression that usually accompanies Alzheimer's, I saw eyes that sparkled, and he smiled when he looked at me. "Doug B?" I cautiously inquired, wanting to make sure I was in the right room.

"Yes," he said, motioning to the chair facing his. "Won't you sit down?"

As I approached, I carefully checked for any sign of Alzheimer's. His newspaper on the table beside him gave me the perfect lead-in to test his short-term memory. With almost total recall, he discussed current events. Since nothing out of the ordinary appeared, I switched the topic to world history. I was amazed at how articulate he was and that his recollections were at times better than mine. Finally, I asked, "How do you like living here?" He said that he liked it, especially the physical therapy, nursing care, and meals.

"What about your family?" I asked.

"They come to see me more than they used to," he said with a grin.

I nudged further, "I understand your wife passed away."

His eyebrows raised and his head cocked to one side—he was obviously as curious about my question as I was about his upcoming answer. "Oh no, Dr. Moody, she's in Ohio visiting relatives," he said. Upon investigating further, I was certain that Douglas was socially withdrawing in order to avoid being questioned about his wife. Refusing to acknowledge her death, a maladaptive delusion, was his only deviance from reality.

His case ended on a positive note. We changed his diagnosis to "complicated grief" and placed him in group therapy. There, the reality of his wife's death eventually pierced his armor of denial. The last time I saw Douglas, he was surrounded by friends, and that image is the one I will always hold most dear.

Dr. B is different from both Ruth and Douglas. Dr. B's case shows that when circumstances are too painful or personal to disclose, it is best to refuse to discuss them rather than distort the truth.

"Some things I never talk about"—Raymond and Dianne's Story

For a number of years, we taught "Facilitator's Training for Healthcare Professionals." Although the three days were scheduled around didactic material, personal disclosures were an integral part of the course. Each training began with introductions, at which time we asked attendees three questions, "What is your name? Where do you live? And what brings you here?" Trainees normally answered the last question by recounting how their losses had catapulted them into the field.

It was early evening and the next training group was arriving. We were glancing over the list of attendees when we noticed a prominent psychologist and bereaved father's name. "Dr. B will bring depth to our time together this weekend," we agreed. We joined the trainees in a room where rain pattering on the roof played accompaniment to our introductions. Dr. B was the last to speak. "My name is Don. I'm from Canada," he said. Then, as if reaching into his innermost sacred place, he paused before continuing, "And there are some things that I never talk about." Then he answered our last question without stepping beyond his comfort level.

Within every group, a unique essence or theme is created. That evening, Dr. B established this group's tone—strength, honesty, and self-respect. He brought depth to the weekend, not by sharing his loss, but by sharing his courage. Indeed, some things are too sacred to divulge, or the time and place are not appropriate. Honoring one's individual privacy is healthy.

Unconscious Denial

Unconscious denial involves forgetting, escaping, or disbelieving in reality. Everybody disremembers something for seconds, minutes, or hours. We forget about a cut finger until we pick up a fork to eat, and then exclaim, "Ouch! I forgot!" Bandages cover and protect open wounds.

Denial serves much like a bandage. If the full impact of a loved one's death is too intense for the psyche to absorb, the newly bereaved often cry out in a fog of disbelief, "No, he can't be dead." Many are so numbed that all emotions escape them; thus, they ask, "Why am I not feeling anything? Why am I empty inside?" Survivors create a healthy and timely defense system, which they shed in bits and pieces. Let's observe the following illustrations.

"Oh no! You can't leave Dad!"

Giuseppe's military funeral and graveside service ended with the United States flag being removed from the coffin and presented to his firstborn, Joseph. Joseph reminisced with his mother for several days and then left the small New Mexico village in which she lived and returned to his home in Texas, where he experienced the usual grief responses for his age, gender, grief history, personality, and relationship with his dad.

During a harried morning at his office several months later, he answered his constantly ringing telephone, "Go ahead."

"Joseph, I'm moving back to Texas . . . ," his mother's voice on the other end began.

Although she continued to explain, the horror of his thoughts, *Oh no! You can't leave Dad!* drowned her out. For a second or two, denial severed Joseph from reality. Taken aback by momentarily forgetting that his father had died, he shuddered. "That was eerie."

"What are you doing?"

After shopping and visiting with friends in Dublin, Terri took the long train ride home. While food cooked on her stove, she, as usual, placed two plates, cups, and forks on the kitchen table. As she poured tea into her husband's waiting cup, in her mind she heard him say, *What are you doing, my dear girl?* Collapsing into her chair, Terri sobbed for the first time since his death four months earlier. That night she slept comfortably. "A burden has been lifted from my shoulders," she told her friend, a grief therapist, the next day.

Episodes of denial can cause mourners embarrassment, but bystanders are often confused, as in Orah's case.

"Are you feeling okay?"

Orah stood behind a long line of customers at the checkout counter. She had been widowed only three months earlier, and her weekly trip to the grocery store was ending as it had for thirty years—with her picking up cigarettes for her husband. Looking down, she saw the word CIGARETTES on the top of the carton cradled in her arms. *So this is what it feels like to go crazy*, she thought.

As she stood dwelling on a lifetime of memories, a voice startled her. "Hey! Honey! You okay?" the clerk, a friend of her deceased husband, was calling out. Orah looked up to find the other customers gone and him staring at the carton. "Ah . . . ah . . . you have . . . cigarettes," he stammered. Her pale cheeks flushed.

Denying the Depth of the Loss

Survivors often deny, or are denied, the depth of their pain by making comparisons. Those bereaved by miscarriage are especially vulnerable. Parents bond with a child the moment they think about having a baby. Their hopes and dreams are lost with miscarriages; nevertheless, some of them ask, "How can I mourn when I didn't give birth?" They commonly compare themselves to other bereaved parents: "Who am I to feel sorry for myself when their child was killed?" or "They are all alone now, without other children." Likewise, sympathizers diminish the magnitude of the loss when they say, "You can have another" or "It would be worse if you had known this child" or "You have other children at home."

The bereaved often compare their losses: "At least my brother didn't die in a horrible accident," "Her husband suffered a long, painful death," "Unlike my uncle who was married for thirty-five years, I was with my wife for only three years," "But he was closer to his dad." Then sympathizers follow suit: "You aren't the only one to lose a wife," "You're not the only widow in town," "My mother died when I was two years old; at least you had yours all this time." No one's pain should ever be discounted. People grow from acknowledging and feeling the depth of their pain.

"You should be happy"

Her son lay dying in a hospice. "How is he?" asked her friend (a bereaved father). They talked for a few minutes, and then the mother began to cry. "You still have your son," the man said. "You should be happy he's still with you." Their relationship ended on that note.

Another indication that grief has become dysfunctional is when death is considered reversible.

Reversibility of the Loss

"He'll wake up," young children often say. To them, death, like sleep, is temporary. Most adults endure moments in which they expect their loved ones to return.

"Oh! He'll be back any minute"

While watching the five o'clock news, the widow suddenly thought, *Oh! He'll be back any minute.* Springing from her chair, she hurriedly prepared dinner and sat down to await his arrival. The evening seemed like any other until she realized, *He isn't coming back. He died last month.* Most bereaved individuals awaken to the irreversibility of the death; otherwise, the grieving process heads down a dysfunctional course.

MEMENTOS

The manner in which we deal with our loved one's belongings reflects our values, grief, and the relationship we held with the deceased. Let's look at four categories of objects: transitional, keepsake, lifeline, and rejected.

Transitional Objects

Transitional objects are kept for a while. Sleeping in dad's old shirt, driving mom's car, and wearing a son's ring are normal because those objects carry memories and feelings of attachment. Retaining the familiar and avoiding major changes are important. Living in the same residence, for example, helps widows, widowers, and bereaved parents process what they have lost.

Beyond articles that belonged to the loved one, other items are kept as well. Many hospices place a single red rose on the bed after a patient dies. Family members rarely return to the room, but when they do, they usually ask to keep the flower. Funeral attendees customarily save a flower from the service.

A Carnation—Dianne's Story

My dad's nurse placed a carnation in a crystal vase on his bed table. Inscribed on the front of the vase was her handwritten blessing for him. Three weeks later, on the day he died, the flower still radiated its fragrance and full color. I kept it for years as a meaningful symbol.

As part of the holding-on, letting-go process, transitional objects benefit the bereaved. Whereas they are kept only temporarily, other things become keepsakes.

Keepsake Objects

Keepsakes are objects that survivors preserve permanently. Photographs, documents, jewelry, and household items often provide mourners with a physical connection to their past. Many people find pleasure in adorning their homes with their forebears' portraits and eating with the family silverware, and they look forward to passing down their heirlooms. Such keepsakes are meaningful for everybody involved.

Keepsakes can be meaningful for pet owners as well. Small mementos are usually tucked away at some point, but paintings, headstones, and reliquaries often remain as visual connections between human beings and their beloved animal companions.

Lifeline Objects

When the bereaved become too invested in their mementos or keepsakes, those articles become lifeline objects and do not serve the mourners in a healthy way. Objects are considered lifelines under three conditions: they are kept for deceased loved ones to use upon their return; they *are* the deceased (in the minds of the bereaved); or the emotional investment in them is so great that if they were lost, stolen, or destroyed, the survivor's grief would equal the grief that accompanied the original loss. Georgia and Jan provide two illustrations for our discussion of lifelines.

"It keeps James alive"

Normally demonstratively tender and affectionate, Georgia appeared stoic during her husband's funeral. Several days later, her family noticed that she had gathered all the framed photographs of her husband and hung them in her living room. For a new widow, that was not too unusual. The next week, however, they noticed that she had removed every picture of him from the family albums and stacked them on a table. By the following week, she had plastered each of those photographs on the walls of the room. On their next visit, they saw that Georgia's photo gallery now included newspaper clippings, passport photos, and drawings of her deceased husband. Soon, her living room was an enormous collage.

When her family asked about the images, Georgia folded her arms across her chest and murmured with a scowl, "I have to have them like this. It keeps James alive."

"Jan wants to mummify the house"

Before Jan's birth, her father was transferred overseas. As her mother's only companion, Jan was breast-fed until she was four years old. After her dad's return, the couple had four other children, but Jan and her mother remained inseparable.

Jan lived with her mother even after she married and gave birth to three children. Her sons grew into teenagers, but the house did not expand with them. For the first time, Jan was forced to buy her own home; however, she purchased one just down the street from her mother. From sunrise to sunset, the two women remained constant companions.

Jan's mother, in her mid-seventies, was hospitalized with a terminal illness. From her deathbed, she told her son (Jan's brother) to take a small painting from her back porch. It was his own, painted while in art school. After his mother's death, he thought nothing about recovering it, but Jan was irate. "Taking that painting changed the house," she shouted, clenching her fists at him. "You bring that back."

Immediately after the funeral, Jan purchased her mother's house from her siblings, making certain that everything inside and out remained exactly as her mother had left it. Then she feverishly searched for a duplicate painting to replace the one her brother had taken, but when she could not find one, she again insisted, "You stole that painting. Put it back on the porch where it belongs."

"Jan wants to mummify the house," he told his siblings.

To this day Jan has not become a fully functional, independent human being. The lifeline objects allowed her to step fully into the role of the deceased, wearing her mother's clothes and even assuming her personality. Instead of handing down a wonderful family heritage, she handed down dysfunction—Jan and her own daughter are now inseparable, both guarding the house and its contents. They tried to pass the pattern down to Jan's granddaughter; however, that young lady found their lifestyle constraining and refused to carry it further.

We are often asked, "How can I tell if I'm too invested in my keepsakes?" We invite those with this concern to ask themselves the following questions: What is my purpose in keeping the object? How do I feel when I look at it? What does the item represent to me? How much of myself is invested in it? If the object were lost, stolen, or destroyed, would the loss be devastating?

At some point, most survivors realize that love is the link that forever binds. It is the one thing that can never be lost, stolen, or destroyed.

Rejected Objects

If the relationship was stormy or the death disturbing, survivors often discard all objects that could serve as reminders. Later, however, they wish for certain belongings. When people ask us about throwing away mementos, we invite them to consider the following questions: What is my purpose for rejecting the articles? How will I feel if I keep them? How will I feel after they are gone? What if I want them later? Storing belongings leaves survivors with options for the future.

Assuming the Characteristics of the Deceased

Absorbing certain characteristics of the deceased is another way in which mourners normally remain connected to their loved ones. Incorporating positive traits of departed loved ones into our own personality is called *integration*—unifying the separate into one. Let's turn to the following three illustrations.

"No more good-byes"—Dianne's Story (Continued)

"No more good-byes, Dianne. No more separation, for now she is with you always." These were the words of the minister at Mother's burial. His words were frustrating because I wanted her with me, on the physical plane. I did not want to be left to grieve for the many things that I would miss and never have again.

My mother could have produced blueprints for an entire apartment building on her sewing machine, yet I could not sew a straight line. Three years after Mother's death I needed to hem a new skirt, so I sat down at her machine, fully expecting to be there for hours, encountering all sorts of problems. Much to my surprise, however, as soon as I pushed the pedal down, I was stitching perfectly straight. "It's true! It's true!" I shouted, clapping my hands in delight. "There is no more separation. She is with me always." For the first time, I felt the advantage of no more good-byes.[1]

"I can't wait to show you this"—Raymond's Story

Ben, a stout man, often wore shorts—making the butterfly-shaped birthmarks on his left leg easily noticed. His grandson Bill and I were raised together and have remained close friends. I can attest that neither Bill nor anyone else in his family sported such markings. After Ben died, Bill, then fifty years old, stopped by my house one evening. "I couldn't wait to show you this, Raymond," he said, pulling up the left leg of his trousers. There, suddenly and unaccountably, the same butterfly-shaped marks had appeared on his calf.

Fred's Mustache

Fred, a university professor, loathed any kind of facial hair, claiming that it was unclean—even his father's small mustache. Two weeks after his dad died, Fred was washing his hands in the men's room. Glancing into the mirror, he was shocked to see that he wore a mustache identical to his dad's. He had unintentionally assumed a characteristic of his father's, one that he had previously found distasteful. He said, laughing, "Facial hair doesn't represent a lack of cleanliness for me these days."

These three cases demonstrate healthy integration. Absorbing characteristics of the deceased can be life-enhancing rather than dysfunctional. The following case, in contrast, illustrates unhealthy integration.

Reproduced Medical Symptoms

Medical abnormalities can be reproduced by survivors. In most cases, they are brief and nonrecurring. If symptoms continue, however, they can cause problems.

Tom suffered severe chest pains and shortness of breath after his brother died of a heart attack. Repeated medical tests uncovered no reason for his discomfort, but the pain persisted and grew more intense. As a last resort, Tom turned to psychotherapy, which revealed that he had never mourned for his brother. His physical symptoms disappeared completely as he learned to express his deep sorrow.

Searching for the Deceased

An unconscious searching is a normal feature of bereavement. The newly bereaved look for their loved ones as if expecting to see them at any moment—in the mall, grocery store, church, airport, and other places.

"Who are you looking for?"

As they walked through the mall, a group of widows noticed one of their number keeping vigil for someone. "Who are you looking for?" they inquired. At first, they were concerned when she admitted that she could not stop watching for her husband, but then they recalled that they too had searched for their spouses in much the same manner.

"This isn't a good sign"

After her husband died, Margie visited the art department of a local community college. She spoke with Mr. McClendon, the department director (who also worked as a psychotherapist). Margie wanted to know if as an older student she would be an outcast. He assured her that, like the other adults who returned to college after raising a family, she would be welcomed.

Margie signed up for a sculpture class, and, on her first day, she began to stack large scoops of clay in front of her. "What are you doing?" Mr. McClendon inquired.

"I've always thought it would be nice to have a life-sized sculpture," Margie replied, peeking from behind her mound.

"Have you worked with clay before?" asked Mr. McClendon.

He was astonished to hear that she knew nothing about art, yet she wanted to create a realistic bust of her deceased husband. "Why don't you start with a simple project, like a small bowl?" he suggested.

"But this is the only thing I want to make," she replied, as she continued piling heaps of clay on the table.

"Well, I'll always remember you as the student who began by attempting the most difficult project," he said with a sigh.

By availing herself freely of Mr. McClendon's time and patience, Margie succeeded in completing her project by the end of the semester. She enrolled for subsequent semesters and produced other lifelike replicas of her deceased husband. Toward the end of her third year, she invited the teachers and students to her house for a Thanksgiving party. To their surprise, they saw the sculptures of her deceased husband near the windows in her home. "This isn't a good sign," groaned Mr. McClendon. "She's fixated in the searching phase of grief." Pulling Margie aside, he questioned her.

"I was lonesome for my husband," she admitted. "I thought a sculpture of him in our house would kind of bring him back into my life. It didn't, but I liked the sculpture there at the living room window. From the outside, it looked like he was watching television. So I made another one and put that one on the other side of the house, in our bedroom. It seemed like good protection, because people passing my house would think it was a man sitting inside. So I went back to class and made another one for the back porch. This party is for you. It's my way of saying thank you and good-bye, because I don't need them for protection anymore. The one I'm working on now is for you to keep."

"I'd love to have it," Mr. McClendon said in relief. "I'll keep it in my office, and every time I see it, I'll think of you."

Margie's example illustrates a number of points. First, functional grief follows a natural course. Like most bereaved people, over the years she moved beyond searching for her deceased loved one. Second, social support is important. The art teacher, unknowingly, was a major source of comfort for his student. And, finally, no one should judge the appearance of another's grief. To Mr. McClendon, the sculptures seemed unhealthy, like symptoms of dysfunctional grief, but instead they were healthy milestones for Margie as she rebuilt her life after loss.

Mistaking Others

Bereaved persons commonly mistake others for their departed loved ones. They see them in strangers waiting at the airport, driving down a street, or sitting on the other side of a room. If the loss was especially traumatic, loved ones commonly appear in sequence—as a clerk in the grocery store one day, as a flight attendant the next day, as a voice over an intercom system the following day. Each episode occurs for only a second or two, but the wave of sorrow that follows lasts much longer.

In numerous cases, bereaved individuals have reported that their glimpses were not incidents of mistaken identity but mystical experiences. They were certain that their loved one momentarily manifested over someone else's body; that is, the loved one's spirit used another human energy field in order to materialize. Skeptics retort, "That is magical thinking, like reincarnation. Those people are in such longing to have their family back that they create scenarios to make it appear that they are."

Emotions in Disguise

Sometimes people unknowingly use the death of a loved one to disguise their true feelings, as in the following example.

"What's wrong with you?"

In a coma after a long fight with cancer, Dot was dying at the home of her younger daughter, Pam. For most of Pam's life, she had served as Dot's principal caregiver, always acting in her mother's best interest. When physicians asked about possible resuscitation, Pam turned to her mother's closest friends and pastor for advice. They all agreed that the elderly woman had suffered enough and that attempting to sustain her life would only bring more suffering. Pam, therefore, signed all the necessary forms, refusing any heroic measures.

As death approached, those closest to Dot gathered around her bed. Amid their outpouring of love, Dot's other daughter barged into the room, screaming at the stunned group, "What are you doing to my mother? How dare you! I won't let you do this to her! I demand that she get full medical attention! You're so callous, Pam. What's wrong with you? Have you no conscience?" This daughter lived across the continent, had visited her mother only twice in the past fifteen years, and had never assumed any responsibility for Dot's care. Now she tried to disguise her guilt about ignoring her family by acting grief-stricken. All in attendance, however, saw through her charade.

Anniversary Reactions

The anniversary of certain events (birthday, date of death, holidays, and other memorable occasions) can bring reactions such as mild feelings of sadness or depression. In some cases, it can cause overwhelming body sensations or unexplained phenomena, as in the following examples.

"Is there anything significant about this day?"
—Raymond's Story

Unmarried and in their sixties, the four siblings still lived together on their family farm. When the youngest, a brother, developed breathing problems and chest pains, they all rushed him to the emergency room. Our team of internal specialists thoroughly examined the man but found no physical abnormalities; therefore, they speculated that a psychiatric issue was causing his symptoms and I was called in.

I scrawlled "December 12, 1965" on the top line of my assessment form and then began our interview. When I was unable to find any psychopathology in this kind and gentle man, I desperately thumbed through his medical charts. "December 12" jumped out at me—the admittance date of his last emergency-room visit, at which time he had experienced the same symptoms and had been released without diagnosis or treatment.

Gathering the entire family at his bedside, I asked, "Is there anything significant about December 12?"

"Mama died on that day," they chimed in unison.

Whereas survivors, as in their case, can be oblivious to an anniversary reaction, outsiders often recognize the connection.

"Everything changed as the anniversary of her death approached"—Dianne's Story

Greg and Pat were so close that they were separated only by their jobs. Arriving at his office one morning, Greg was called to the phone. The news was devastating. His dearly beloved Pat had been killed in a fiery automobile accident on her way to work.

Greg tried to cope by overseeing every aspect of her funeral, including digging her grave. "It took him all day," friends and coworkers wrote me in a letter, "using his own pick, shovel, and two hands, digging in the hard, rocky, clay soil. But he said it was something he had to do, and all by himself. His initial shock turned into a deep depression. It seemed that Greg spent most of his time in that dark hole with his wife. But as the months faded, so did his sadness. At work he seemed like his old self, except when lawyers called about a $1 million insurance settlement he would get. Then he'd rant about the accident, but his anger passed quickly.

"Everything changed as the first anniversary of her death approached. He lost interest in everything, including a pending settlement. Then, on the anniversary, Greg was killed in a freak fiery car wreck on his way to work. We all argue to this day whether it was an accident or suicide."

I was Greg's professional support person, and it was difficult for me to believe that this veteran would end his life in that manner. I therefore investigated his death by reading police reports and talking with his relatives. By all indications, Greg had attempted to avoid the collision, but we will never know for sure whether it was really an accident, suicide, or perhaps a twist of fate.

This brings us to the unexplainable, which, by the way, can be studied historically. Thomas Jefferson and John Adams both died on the Fourth of July, 1826, the fiftieth anniversary of their signing the Declaration of Independence. Each man reportedly spoke about the other on the day of his death.

Beyond finding mysterious events in public records, you may encounter interesting things in your own family's history. While working up a genealogical chart for her daughter, Dianne discovered that several members of her family had died during their birth months: a grandmother was born and died in December, another grandparent's birth/death month was June, and so on. This discovery brings little comfort to members of her household as their birthdays approach!

Family members often share with us accounts of relatives who died on the same date, in the same manner, although years apart. One widow, for example, reported that her husband and son were killed one year apart, to the day, in exactly the same type of accident, on the same spot. Similarly, a grandson told about his grandmother, a widow, who succumbed to a heart attack at the precise time, on the same beach, at which her husband had died from cardiac arrest years earlier.

"Exactly twenty-four years after my son's death" —Raymond's Story

On June 3, 1970, my first son was born; however, he was too small to live past thirty-six hours. Mother saw him during his short life, and she was there when he died. Deeply affected, she mourned for her first grandchild, the baby with whom she had built such a strong attachment for nine months. Then, on June 4, 1994, exactly twenty-four years after my son's death, Mother died.

There is more to this story. Studies with siblings indicate that the firstborn child identifies with the father, the second with the mother, the third with the couple, and the fourth with the family. The sequence then restarts with the fifth child. My brother Randy was the third born and identified with our parents, the couple.

"Mama and Daddy this . . . Mama and Daddy that . . ." was his anthem. His entire life always centered around them.

Although Randy was a tough, twenty-year veteran of the police force, he never once challenged our father. Actually, he never really separated from either parent. He married once, divorced, and returned home.

On the day Mother died, Randy's face revealed desperation and despair. The following year, on that same day, he suffered a major heart attack. After quintuple bypass surgery and three months of hospitalization, he returned home again. There, he died just twenty minutes short of the third anniversary of our father's death. "Why that twenty-minute lag?" my family and I wondered. "Why didn't Randy wait until the same moment our father died?" Then it became obvious to everyone in the Moody family. He always deferred to his dad. If he had died at the same time, then he would have asserted equality.

Preparation

Anniversary dates can present problems, but these are problems with many solutions. The keys are awareness and preparation. Many survivors sense that the first anniversary will be troublesome and plan events to help soften their grief, such as traveling to cultures vastly different from their own.

"I decided to fly to Las Vegas"

"I decided to fly to Las Vegas, Nevada, for Christmas," said a widow from a small rural community. "I wanted to experience something totally different from my lifestyle. I was also thinking about suicide all the time, so I thought Vegas would give me bright lights and activities around the clock. It turned out to be perfect because when I cried nobody noticed, and that crazy town lifted my spirits. I came home in the opposite frame of mind."

Others who are bereaved have traveled to foreign countries. "My wife and I spent our summers on the road," one widower explained. "I'd always wanted to volunteer for an archaeological dig, but the wife wasn't keen on that idea. Every summer after she died, I got myself into a terrible state, just sat, feeling sorry for myself. Then last June, I joined a project in Mexico and it made all the difference."

After her mother's death, Dianne found it meaningful to explore the lands of her ancestors—England, Scotland, and Wales. Stopping along back roads and talking with people, she discovered a great deal about her heritage.

Volunteer work can be especially meaningful as well. Facing his first Thanksgiving without his wife, an elderly widower donated his time to a homeless shelter. For three days, he helped prepare and serve more than five hundred turkey dinners. Because of his loneliness as well as his good listening skills, many people shared their life stories with him. His ebullience for the program flowed over to his family, and now Thanksgivings and Christmases at the shelter are projects not just for the widower but for most of his clan as well.

Survivors can find many types of resources to help them carry their loads. Talking or writing often brings issues into conscious awareness and helps survivors sort through their feelings. Memorials can be meaningful as well. Most hospices and bereavement-support groups host candlelight ceremonies or other services during the Christmas season. In most cases, awareness and preparation help survivors during special times.

Replicated Loss

A former loss is revisited when it is replicated later. The death of a grandparent triggers memories of other deceased grandparents. Mourning a sibling brings a resurgence of feelings from another sibling loss. People who have loved and lost many animal companions can be overwhelmed by the death of another, because the current loss will trigger memories of all those who have gone before.

Replicated loss is especially troublesome if the original loss was not mourned. John Kennedy, Jr.'s, death brought an emotional flood across America. Why? Many citizens revisited the death of his father, a loss that we were not allowed to mourn. That loss—and others—will be taken up in the next chapter.

SEVEN

Adjusting to the Loss

> But there was no need to be ashamed of tears
> for tears bore witness that a man
> had the greatest of courage,
> the courage to suffer.
>
> —Victor E. Frankl

Will my life ever seem normal again? When will I stop feeling this way? What can I do to speed my recovery? How can I feel whole again? What will be the quality of my life?

The answers to all these questions depend on *adjustment.*

For some of the bereaved, adjustment means learning to live with grief. Others, however, eventually leave their sorrow behind. Let's explore both, beginning with the famous losses of the Kennedys and Princess Diana. Then we will turn to funerals, grief theories, balance, stress, and rituals.

Influence of the Kennedy Assassination

On November 22, 1963, people watching television saw a motorcade passing through the streets of Dallas. Then they saw legions of citizens gathering on the lawn of Parkland Hospital, and finally they heard the tragic news: President John Fitzgerald Kennedy had died, the victim of an assassin's bullet. Open and defenseless, our nation's leader had been shot down in his prime.

Thousands of people lined the streets. Many more gathered around black-and-white television sets to watch the slain president's flag-draped coffin roll by. The wheels of the caisson rhythmically echoed. Click, click, click, the riderless horse, Black Jack, tapped in the reality—yes, yes, yes, he really is gone.

The most photographed woman in the world, Jacqueline Kennedy, presented a new image of bereavement. The widow's black veil covered her tearless face; after all, Kennedys must never cry. "The epitome of class . . . Brave and strong in the face of death . . . To be emulated by widows and widowers . . . The perfect role model for all those who grieve," said the press releases. The media raved about her "dignity" and "grace" in the wake of losing her husband to an assassin.

Just as we had begun to understand the importance of actively mourning, especially during funerals when social support abounds, Jacqueline Kennedy's stoic face was everywhere—on television, in newspapers, magazines, and books. As a trendsetter, she became the icon, the role model for survivors, robbing us of our mourning.

Many images were crystallized in time. Perhaps the most poignant was young John Kennedy saluting his father's flag-draped coffin. He, and that image, would become a catalyst, bringing the ritual of mourning to another level.

On Saturday, July 17, 1999, John Kennedy's airplane was reported overdue and missing. Six days later, his body and those of his wife and her sister were found on the ocean floor. John's funeral and burial at sea were so private that the media, public, and even church staff were disallowed.[1]

Caskets represent a transcendence from the past and into the future. Along with the body, they give mourners a focus for their grief. In the case of John Kennedy, the public had neither; therefore, their outcries of sympathy focused only on the past. Once again, the moving image of three-year-old John saluting his father's coffin became a focal point. Feelings from so long ago resurfaced, and this time the media were left to dwell on the past.

More than thirty-five years after her husband was assassinated, Jacqueline Kennedy's struggle with his death was finally exposed. Reportedly, only the ocean was privy to her grief. Far from public scrutiny, on numerous occasions the new widow cast a private yacht out to sea and, leaning over the side, screamed and sobbed. Furthermore, she was concerned about her young son, fearing that he would also become trapped in the Kennedy persona. Jacqueline placed John in the hands of Erik Erikson, a world-renowned psychiatrist who encouraged his clients to express their feelings. Later, when John injured his knee on a ski run, he was told by his uncle, "Kennedys don't cry." "This Kennedy cries," John tearfully replied, holding his leg.[2] Accounts of his sorrowing for his deceased mother were released as well.

The aftermath of his death influenced America's mourning ritual. Princess Diana's death contributed as well, but on an even wider scale.

Diana's Influence

The many dramas that surrounded Diana's life and death touched a myriad of individuals from every class. She was an ordinary young woman with a host of problems who yet managed to accomplish the extraordinary. Diana depended on a network of people to protect and keep her safe, all of whom failed her. Because she was a carrier of hope and idealism, her death left a gulf of disappointment and sorrow.

In a culture where tears are not customarily displayed, her demise brought mourning to the British as never witnessed in public before. The royal family's stoicism set the people against them, also as never witnessed before. Hearts across the globe opened to the sorrowing of the British public. Diana, a real-life human being and fairy-tale princess, became an international icon for martyrdom.

The funerals of Diana and the Kennedys are grand-scale examples of how funerals set the tone for mourning and influence our ability to adjust.

Funerals

Funerals offer survivors an opportunity to reflect on how the deceased's life touched theirs, mourn for what they have lost, embrace what they will hold most dear, and receive support. They serve as rites of passage, and they are the cornerstone for the mourning ahead.

"It's all just a bunch of phony blubbering"—Dianne's Story

As a young girl, I longed for words of comfort during funeral services but heard few. Ministers skimmed over biblical passages, made vague comments about the deceased, shook hands with survivors, and left. That remained my experience until my daughter's friend Angela was murdered. Her wake and funeral services in a small African American community were steeped in emotion and responsiveness.

Mother and I wanted my dad's life and death honored in similar fashion. We arranged for a retired Baptist minister, a man with tremendous depth, to preside over Dad's funeral and burial. Before the announcement was made, however, my sister demanded, "No funeral and no open casket. It's all just a bunch of phony blubbering. Dianne, you know how I hate that. I won't go."

Resigned to a brief graveside service, everybody made the best of it. As we were leaving the cemetery, a family friend of more than fifty years pulled me to the side. "You white folks sure have strange funerals," he murmured, frowning and shaking his head. "When do you grieve? Who helps you?"

"I'm sorry, Johnny," I said. "This was not Mother's choice, or mine."

After Mother died the following year, the family once again arranged a simple graveside service, as my sister demanded. This time, however, I also held a ceremonial in the funeral home, with family, friends, flowers, open casket, and tears. We combined mourning with the celebration of life. I realized the profound benefits at the time, but even more so after I began working with Sonja.

"How will you remember him?"—Dianne's Story

Her essence was as heavenly as any I had witnessed. Sonja's role as a hospice chaplain seemed perfectly cast. She visited with families, listening to their reminiscences. "How will you remember him?" she sometimes inquired. "What is your favorite memory? What did you enjoy doing together?" Then, during the funeral, she addressed each mourner, sharing that person's remembrances. In doing so, she created a portrait of the life and loves of the deceased. In addition, survivors were deeply touched by having their feelings and personal memories reflected back to them. In every case, Sonja honored both the living and their departed. Funerals such as those become beacons of light for those in mourning.

Theories

Theories or models of grief have contributed to our understanding of adjustment. All those in existence are based on the original model, conceived by famed psychiatrist Elisabeth Kübler-Ross. Let's consider the model, and also some misconceptions about her work.

Kubler-Ross's Five Stages of Loss

In her groundbreaking book, *On Death and Dying*, Elisabeth[3] presented the first model of grief. Her findings suggested that individuals experience five natural grief reactions, which she termed "stages." They are denial, anger, bargaining, depression, and acceptance. Her Five Stages Theory became an international model for understanding loss. Unfortunately, some therapists began using it as a tool without reading or comprehending her book. As a result, the theory came under fire from some healthcare professionals for three reasons.[4]

The main objection resulted from some professionals' assumption that bereaved individuals literally progress through five sequential stages. As a result, they classified which "stage" the client was currently in and then attempted to guide him or her through those remaining, in linear order. They directed, for example, "You're in the denial stage, so anger is next" or "You've been in the bargaining stage long enough. It's time to move to depression, and when you complete that, acceptance will follow." In effect, each client was placed in a grief box, with an identifying label attached.

Elisabeth developed her theory from her background as a psychiatrist. When the theory is examined carefully, it becomes evident that she presented the stages as coping mechanisms (the manner in which people deal with trauma or crisis). Unfortunately, the semantics caused confusion—a difficulty that can be eliminated by replacing the term *stages* with the more flexible *states.*

Human beings experience various states of grief. Any of these states may coexist with other states, be completely skipped, occur intermittently, or repeat themselves.

Second, critics complained that the Five Stages Model dismissed the uniqueness of grief. They regarded it as a grief template. In Elisabeth's defense, she recognized that mourning is highly variable. In fact, not only is it impossible to apply one standard to all mourners, but one standard model for a single mourner is unrealistic.

The third objection to the Five Stages Theory came from bereavement specialists who alleged that its model of grief was too passive. According to them, when a loved one dies, those left behind sense a loss of control. The stage concept heightens that sense. It says, "Death happened to me, and now grief." Elisabeth explained that grief is a continuously evolving process that offers potential for growth. She did not, however, include specific suggestions for achieving that growth.

The bereavement movement is trying to move away from the misunderstood and misused model. Nevertheless, Elisabeth Kübler-Ross deserves tremendous regard. Her work continues to benefit many people. Moreover, she opened the door to the field of thanatology (the study of death and dying).

After *On Death and Dying* was published, colleges and universities began offering classes in death studies. By 1978, 938 universities in the United States alone offered death-education courses.[5] Classrooms filled to capacity, and students demanded waiting lists in order to sign up for subsequent semesters. Americans jumped forward to look behind death's door, and then recoiled, slamming it shut again. They wanted no foretaste of their inevitable demise. Now, however, four decades later, another generation of students is rushing to sign up for an evolved form of those early courses. Studies in life after death (which investigate beyond death's door) flourish. Once again, students will be introduced to the pioneer work of Elisabeth Kübler-Ross.

Active Approaches

Therapists have developed a number of active approaches for resolving grief. These goal-oriented models establish certain steps for rebuilding life after loss. William Worden's task model was among the first and is still considered basic.

Four Tasks of Mourning

Worden found a solution for the passive stance offered by Kübler-Ross's Five Stages Model.[6] Whereas Elisabeth's theory is based on emotions, Worden's assumes a more cognitive approach, requiring the accomplishment of four tasks.

In the first task, survivors accept the reality of the loss; that is, they understand that the death is permanent and irreversible. Working through emotional pain is task two. Worden reminds us that feeling the pain of loss when it occurs is much less difficult than carrying it forward.

Survivors' third task is to adjust to the environment. It takes time to realize what has been lost. A wife might serve as the couple's chauffeur and accountant, her husband as cook and gardener. Neither is aware of how dependent they have become on each other until one dies. Adjustment often requires shifting social networks, hobbies, and interests. Many widowers and widows complain that they lost not only their spouses but their circle of friends as well. Bereaved parents are separated from school functions, athletic competitions, music recitals, and other activities.

The final task involves moving ahead. Survivors acknowledge and integrate their past and then step forward to live for today and the future.

Problems with Goal-Oriented Mourning

Goal-oriented perspectives have been criticized because they include sequential steps. Certain personality types, however, need structure and direction. Those individuals never take a picture without studying photography first, or at least reading an instruction manual. As survivors they prefer organized, step-by-step procedures.

Goal-oriented approaches present problems nevertheless. One problem is that they primarily focus on the loss. Human beings act for one of two reasons: we either want to gain something or we want to lose something. We move toward or we move away from. In a goal-oriented approach, survivors who want to move away from their grief must continuously hold the loss in their minds—the very thing they want to move beyond. If, on the other hand, survivors want to move toward an ideal, then the future becomes their focus: that which they want to become.

The second problem with goal-oriented processes is that many survivors find them too limiting. Any goal requires following systematic steps or plans, all of which focus on the end result. Step one is completed, then step two, then three, and the blueprint continues.

No single path of mourning will ever be appropriate for everyone. "It's impossible to follow a map," say those who have completed their trek across the bridge of grief. Furthermore, no matter how much knowledge is acquired, each survivor will still work through grief in his or her own way. Therefore, let's consider a more flexible and creative approach.

Intention-Oriented Process

An intention-oriented process moves toward a future ideal. Survivors state their intentions, such as, "I will rebuild my life," "I will transcend this loss," "I will grow in strength and grace," "I will create meaning in my life," "I will remember to keep my life in balance." Then they flow with life as it unfolds. The trek through the valley of grief, across the bridge, and up the mountain is as significant as the end result, living on the mountaintop.

Balance

Life is in balance when our physical, emotional, intellectual, social, and spiritual needs are met. Our bodies need nourishment, rest, and exercise. Feelings need recognition and venting. Our minds and brains require intellectual stimulation. We need social connection and interaction with other people. Spiritual nurturing comes through creativity, play, relaxation, music, rituals, prayer, meditation, and so on. Loss affects all five aspects of our being; however, most survivors neglect one or more. An aspect of healthy adjustment is keeping life in balance.

Raymond has dealt with his losses by intellectualizing. He is aware that his mind outweighs his emotional essence; therefore, he advises all mourners, "Cry. It's good for you."

Dianne is the opposite of Raymond. She lives by her heart and spirit. She therefore turned to behaviorism and cognitive therapy in an attempt to keep her life balanced during bereavement. At times her brain was so overly stimulated that it ached.

Although few people keep their lives in perfect balance, aiming toward that intention aids grief resolution.

Coping with Grief-Related Stress

The stress of grief affects every aspect of our being. Relief from this type of stress requires exorcising—physical action accompanied by words or sounds. Whereas *exercising* is motivated by willpower, *exorcising* is motivated by feeling emotions so deeply that something needs to be done to move the energy forward. Each of us can learn to release grief-related stress in our own way.

"I have to find a release"—Dianne's Story

Among the first hospice patients assigned to me was an elderly gentleman who reminded me of my dad. Caring for him brought fond memories. Then, one afternoon, his wife and daughter stood in the doorway, clutching each other until they could make their way to his bedside. "Oh, honey, I miss you," the wife swooned, in the same southern drawl as my mother's. Stroking his face, forehead to chin, she continued to pamper him exactly as my mother had pampered my dad. Their daughter braced her mother's elbow in her hand, forcing back her tears. They perfectly mirrored scenes from my past—the patient was my dad; the wife was my mother; their daughter, me. The stress inside my body was overwhelming. *I have to find a release for this*, I thought and rushed to the staff dining area.

Once there, I grabbed a towel and vigorously began wiping tables. As I wiped, I gave words to the energy that was flowing from me. "I hate that you died that way, Daddy. I hate that we were alone in our suffering. If only we had known about hospice," and so on. After the tables were spotless, I attacked the mirrors with the same vigor. I kept working the energy and feelings out of my body. By the time I felt completely relieved, the staff room was immaculate.

At that point, I went back into the patient's room and was able to serve him and his family in the manner they deserved. My way of dealing with stress is to create an activity that will allow me to move my energy out. If the circumstance is not appropriate for exorcising my stress in that moment, then I do so as soon as possible.

The key word to remember for releasing grief-related stress is *intention.* Any action is only a fruitless physical activity unless it is accompanied by some form of emotionally releasing sound.

Exorcising Activities—Raymond's Story

When I was a young boy in Porterdale, Georgia, everybody's chief method of transportation was walking. By the time I was nine years old, I ran any time I felt anxious. After I learned about stress, jogging became my typical way of dealing with it. With age, I began walking again to protect my knees, and that remains my preference. Nothing stops me, not weather or even location. While on tour, I move the furniture in my hotel room out of the way, turn the volume on the television to high, and vigorously pace back and forth across the floor. Like many survivors, I am convinced that this sports-type activity helps me cope with stress and loss.

People reportedly jog in cemeteries. Their running, accompanied by crying, is ignored by groundskeepers and visitors. Others rely on sports such as golf, tennis, and racquetball. A significant element is the ball. Mourners identified the ball with the source of their stress. "I thought of the ball as my problems," several widowers explained. "I picked up the ball and said what I was feeling stressed about," one elaborated. "Then, as I smashed it with my racket, I grunted,

'Humph!' and watched it take off. I actually felt that old contaminated energy leaving many times—a victorious feeling."

A new sport may prove beneficial for bereaved individuals. BI RAK IT[7] is a racquetball-type activity played with a racquet in each hand. It promotes interaction between the left and right hemispheres of the brain. Playing BI RAK IT influences brain chemistry and the central nervous system, which means that it is more than an outlet for grief-related stress; it is also an effective method of behavior modification. Our choice of handedness is partly behavioral, and BI RAK IT tends to redirect behavioral biases, which increases learning. Because mourning is learned, BI RAK IT possibly helps the bereaved integrate some of the changes that accompany life after loss.

Exorcising activities extend beyond athletic pursuits. Many movies have depicted husbands cursing as they chopped wood and wives yelling out their anger while beating rugs. Some survivors have found that working with clay on their potter's wheel is an effective discharge for stress. Others preferred digging in their gardens, and still others played their pianos. Almost any physical motion, accompanied by sound, is releasing. Remember your intention and periodically check to ensure that your method is effectively exorcising the stress from your body.

Now let's turn to other avenues that have helped the bereaved adjust to loss and cope with their stress.

Time-Out

Children have not yet learned to push themselves. When they become sick they take to their beds, which greatly reduces the time it takes for their recovery. The young also take time out from mourning; that is, they intermittently grieve and play. We adults, to the contrary, push ourselves. Taking time away from mourning is healthy.

One way the bereaved can find respite is by socially withdrawing. Our entire being needs privacy in order to reflect, relax, and replenish. Whereas some people prefer to curl up with a book, others turn to videos, music, warm baths, or the beach. Regardless, intervals away from stress and mourning are imperative.

Nurturing the Soul

The soul, made of playfulness, humor, and creativity, needs replenishing during grievous times. Art is especially therapeutic. Grief therapist Colin Caffell gave clay to his clients, inviting, "Put what you feel on the inside, out." In this way, they externalized their emotions, and the object they created gave them a visual representation of their sorrow. Many participants from his sessions reported that, beyond being therapeutic, working with clay was delightful.

Feeling delight, however, can sound distasteful to the newly bereaved. Not only do they wonder if they will ever laugh again, but complicated dialogue is often nerve-racking. One way that Dianne nurtured her soul and brought humor back into her life was by sitting back with a large bowl of popcorn and watching Bette Midler videos.

Some survivors return to a favorite childhood entertainment—painting, playing the piano, watching cartoons—to nurture themselves. To this day Raymond retires to his room with Donald Duck and Uncle Scrooge comic books, like the ones his grandmother read to him when he was a child.

Others partake of activities they missed as children. "My parents forbade me to eat ice cream or junk food of any kind," one psychologist explained. "Asking for it only got me into trouble. So, after my father died, I drove myself to McDonald's and ordered my inner child a kid's meal with an ice cream cone for dessert. I sat there, almost forty years old, and thoroughly enjoyed treating my little one to something he had wanted all those years." Nurturing the child replenishes the soul.

Create Rituals

Rituals give us a sense of transformation. Through them, we observe and court our devotion to a greater purpose. They do not need to be elaborate or shared; instead, they can be a self-acknowledgment, honoring our rite of passage.

"Stay in the moment"

After her son, Alex, was killed in an automobile accident, Terri Huber found continuing life almost impossible. She needed a tool for living; therefore, she created a mantra that gave her direction. *Stay in the moment,* she thought during difficult times.[8] Beyond her personal ritual, the Huber family began writing, which, much to their surprise, evolved into a helpful book for bereaved parents.

Many survivors favor writing. Some write poems, stories, letters, or journals. The stress of grief travels from their bodies, through their arms, down their hands, and out onto the paper. The ink on the paper provides a visual representation for what was left behind. Other writers prefer word processors, finding that the rhythm, sound, and feel of the keys are more exorcising than writing by hand.

Rituals can be spontaneously created along the way.

"I will take a moment to think about Dad"—Dianne's Ritual

My parents built a home on their property in the foothills of the Ozarks. Through the forest behind them was a state prison. After several convicts escaped, Dad purchased a Smith and Wesson thirty-eight revolver, the first gun ever owned by a member of our family. Merely mentioning the gun could make Dad's face turn pale, but he learned to load and shoot it nevertheless.

"What are we going to do with that thing?" Mother asked after Dad's funeral. "I'm too scared to take it out of the drawer," she added, nodding toward his desk. "Me too," I replied, and neither of us mentioned it again—that is, until the fall.

"One way to cope with loss is to tackle your greatest fear," we were told during a grief workshop. My fear was that little gun—actually, any firearm. I hated them. As it happened, when I was walking out of the building that day, I noticed a bulletin posted by the police department. Their gun class for women began that evening.

Mother was stunned when I announced, "I'm going." As she stood in the corner, both of us scared silly, I opened the drawer, wrapped the gun in a thick bath towel, and drove to the police station. Once I arrived, I was too terrified to carry it inside; therefore, I decided to create a ritual.

"Every time I touch this gun," I said to myself, "I will take a moment to think about Dad and how he overcame his greatest fear. I will appreciate my effort in trying to adjust to life without him." To my amazement, this devotional became enjoyable, and I excelled in the class. "You have a natural gift for shooting," the police officers said after the six-week course. "We're hosting a competition next month and sure could use you."

Can you believe this, Dad? my thoughts sprang out as I accepted their invitation.

On the day of the competition, I felt embarrassed and out of place. Most of the other contestants drove up in vans or motor homes outfitted like small armories. They commenced to load ammunition, donning shooting gloves and glasses and speaking a lingo that sounded unlike any English I had ever heard. They experimented with their various firearms, finally choosing 357 Magnums with scopes, or something even more powerful.

My discomfort dissolved as I turned to my ritual. Standing in position, prepared to take my first shot, I reached down and picked up Dad's revolver. I held no fear. Although exhilarated and wanting to go celebrate, in honor of my teachers who surrounded me I stayed and finished the meet. Taking the second-place trophy, with my dad's little gun, was the cherry on top of my milestone cake.

Rituals help us mark a transition. Terri's ritual affirmed her choice to live; mine acknowledged my dad and me. Rituals do not need fanfare or audience; they only need meaning.

And We Fly South—Dianne's Story

The first cool front and heavy rains of fall were just moving in. I was barreling down Interstate 10, as anxious to get to my destination as the flocks of birds crossing the highway high overhead. I kept admiring the nature of their journey and the power of the bodies that enabled them to make the flight. With each hour and flock that passed, I noticed subgroups forming to the outside and behind the main formations. Those in back labored to stay in a linear path. At last, Houston's evening skyline diverted my attention—that is, until an exhausted bird passed over my windshield. I pulled to the side of the road and watched it flapping its wings, trying to keep up with its flock, until finally it landed in a field of evergreens. *Good for you,* I thought. *Your flight was not as easy or graceful, and you did not end up with the others, but you made it. You have arrived.*

And so it is with the bereaved. The journey may be graceful, or slow and laborious. Nevertheless, most of us somehow arrive. We reach either restoration or transcendence.

EIGHT

Transcending Loss

What does not destroy me, strengthens me.
—NIETZSCHE

The death of a close loved one usually causes inconceivable suffering. How we move beyond our loss is neither good nor bad, neither right nor wrong; however, the quality of our life after loss depends on moving forward. In most cases, survivors eventually reach either restoration or transcendence. To demonstrate the difference, we'll chart the journey of grief on a bell curve.

GRIEF THROWS ITS CURVE

Throughout life, personality is basically stable; that is, our concepts and opinions change, but our core values and beliefs remain the same. Before the death of a loved one, each of us moves along a personal continuum (represented by *x*).

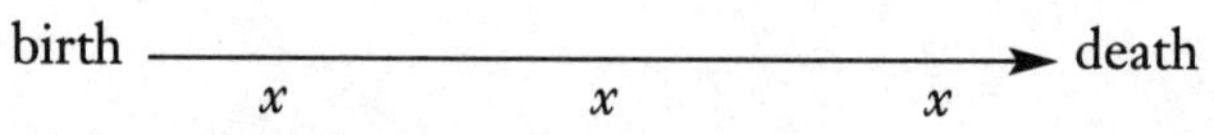

Personality normally flows on a continuum.

Loss Occurs

The death of a loved one interrupts that continuum. It generates change in the personality of survivors. We enter a period of transition that normally lasts from four to six years.

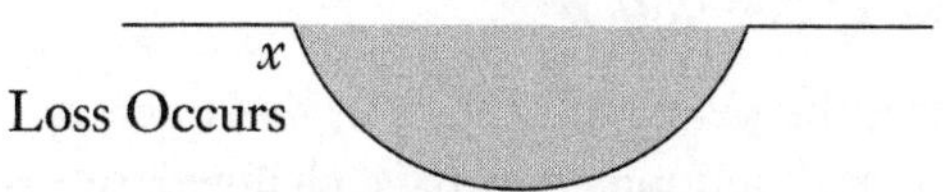

Grief's journey begins.
The continuum is interrupted.

Early Bereavement

Personalities shift during bereavement. We face our feelings of grief, or we rationalize about them, or we begin to distort them into rage, bitterness, denial, phobias, and so on.

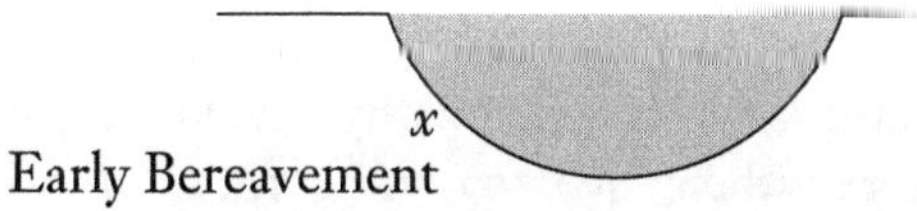

The personalities of survivors shift
during this transitional period.

Bereavement Midpoint

The more survivors release their feelings while in the valley of grief, the more they grow. At midpoint, grief's journey reaches its greatest depth.

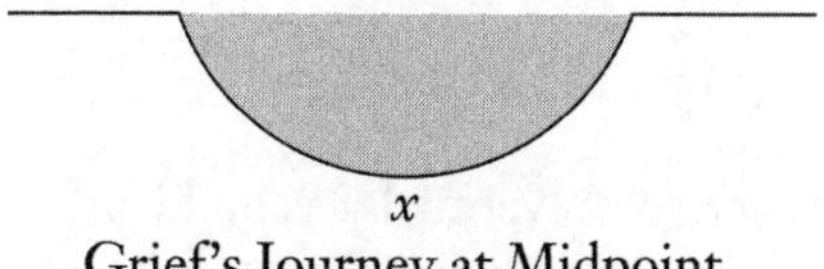

Life is being restored.

Transition Enters Completion

Beyond midpoint, the personality shift begins to enter completion. Certain concepts and opinions may have changed, often noticeably.

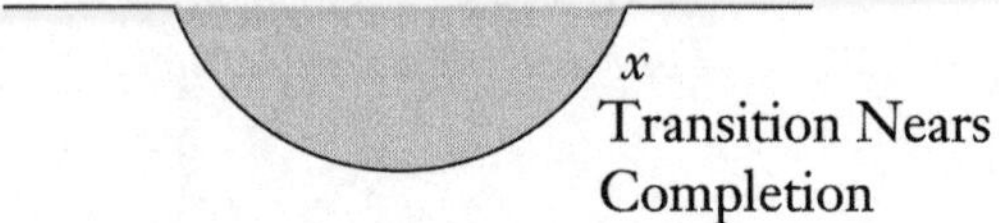

Life is rebuilt after loss.

Personality Stabilized

The average time for the transition is between four and six years; however, some survivors have reported that theirs lasted only one year, whereas for others it continued for ten years or longer. Eventually, though, the shift in personality reaches completion. Survivors have restored their lives to some form of normalcy. Because they hold their same core values, beliefs, and ideals, their personal model of the world has remained intact.

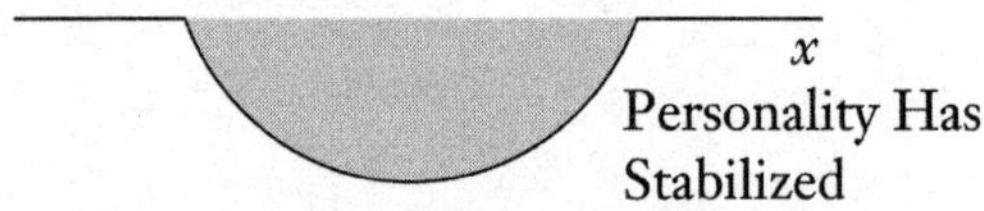

The major transition is complete.
Survivors have found some form of normalcy.
Their personalities are much as they were before the loss.
Life has been rebuilt.

TRANSCENDENCE

Whereas most survivors eventually rebuild or restore their lives, some experience transcendence. Transcendence is a spiritual rebirth. It requires stepping into the deepest valley of sorrow, which some survivors are not willing or able to do.

Transcendence at Midpoint

Although transcenders (those who are achieving transcendence) resume certain aspects of their former selves, their basic personalities are being permanently affected. Their core values, beliefs, and ideals, as well as their concepts and ideas, are becoming enlightened. Their model of the world is becoming richer. They find a new normalcy, one that has a greater quality. They are growing, and will continue to grow, beyond the person they were at the time of the death.

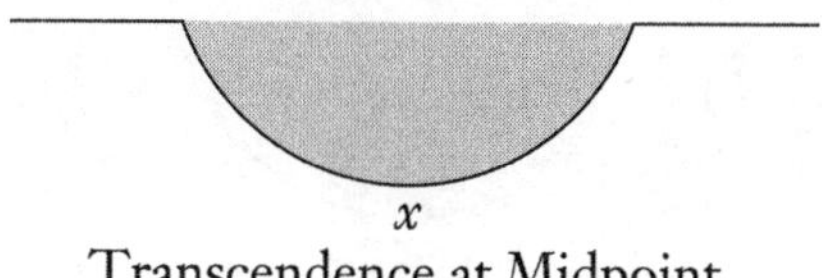

Transcendence at Midpoint

At this point survivors often feel as if they have climbed into the casket along with their deceased loved ones—a phenomenon of transcendence.

Transcended Beyond the Loss

People who transcend beyond the depth of their pain begin to feel elevated above their former selves. They become stronger, kinder to self and others, and more appreciative of life. They have gained in wisdom, compassion, understanding, and unconditional love. *Transcenders feel elevated above their former selves.*

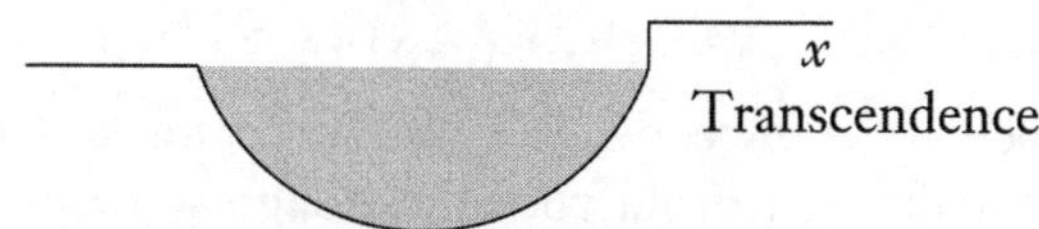

Their core values, beliefs, and ideals are more enlightened. They find a new normalcy, one that is enriched.

The Tragedy of a Hardened Heart

Whereas most survivors become better human beings, a minute proportion become bitter. Normalcy for them, unfortunately, means remaining fixated in the pit of despair, anger, bitterness, or sorrow. In most cases, these survivors lack spiritual beliefs, passionate meaning in their lives, or adjustment skills. Moreover, they may fear their own mortality, suffer from prolonged stress, or be grief-prone personality types. Others may not have been healthy individuals at the time of the loss or were perpetually traumatized by the death.

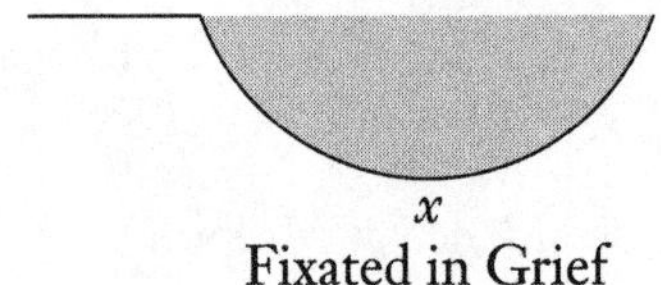

Fixated in Grief

Sufferers remain in the valley.

Personal Models

The bereaved are forever changed after the death of a close loved one. Each of us defines who we will become by creating an individual, personal model of mourning.

We, the authors, have very different personalities and perspectives. Raymond is a thinking, intellectual male; Dianne is an intuitive, feeling female. Although we have both found transcendence, we have done so very differently.

Transcendence—Raymond's Story

My model for transcendence looks different from Dianne's and may look very different from yours. Although some of my losses were expected and others completely shocking, my basic way of dealing with them was the same.

The first drawing is a model of my grief on the day my firstborn died, June 4, 1970. The circle represents my entire self, and the markings inside the circle represent my grief. Notice that my sorrow fills almost the entire circle.

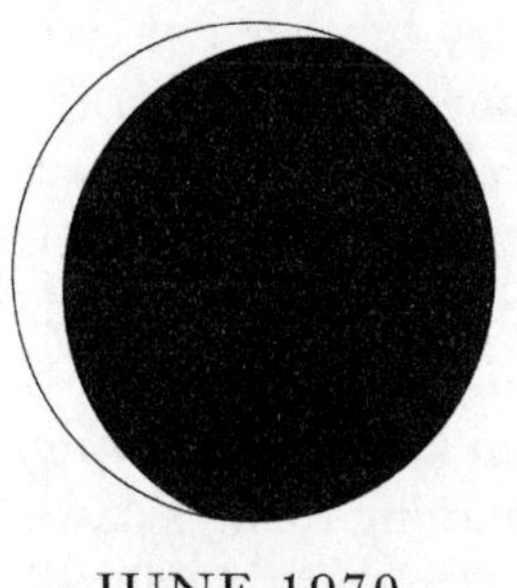

JUNE 1970

My personal model of grief on June 4, 1970
The circle, representing my entire being, was almost totally filled with grief. Only the small portion on the left remained untouched by the death of my newborn child.

By 1990, I thought of my loss in terms of inner and outer circles, as in the second diagram. The inner circle represented my grief. The outer circle, the whole of me, had expanded beyond my former self. My son's death was no longer overwhelming. It had become only one component of my makeup, along with other losses and life events.

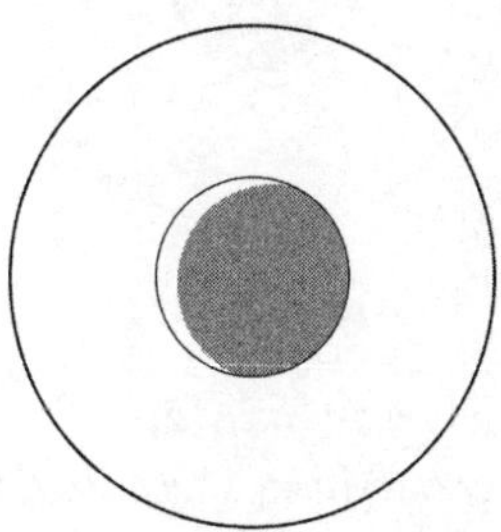

My 1990 model for personal transcendence
The inner circle, representing my grief, remained the same as on the day my firstborn died. However, it became much lighter and less defined. The outer circle, representing my whole self, grew around that loss.

As with most people, each new loss I experience brings a ripple effect. My grief intensifies because the past resurfaces. In January

1996, for example, as my brother Randy took his last breath, my mind flashed back to some fifty years earlier.

I was a little boy again, looking at a pale blue blanket. Mother opened the corner for me to catch a glimpse of my newborn baby brother, but all I could see were Randy's distinctive bald head and ears. In my mind's eye, I then revisited our hometown and imagined that my wonderful life in Porterdale, Georgia, was never-ending.

Now, along with mourning Randy's death, I longed for that wonderful cast of characters from our childhood.

Circumstances other than the death of a loved one can cause my grief to intensify. When my surviving sons graduated, I thought about their brother and what could have been. Then, while I was preparing for Avery's wedding in May 1999, the anniversary date of my firstborn's death approached. Among the many losses that ran rampant in my mind was my failed marriage to his mother. I drew the following as a representation of my grief at that time.

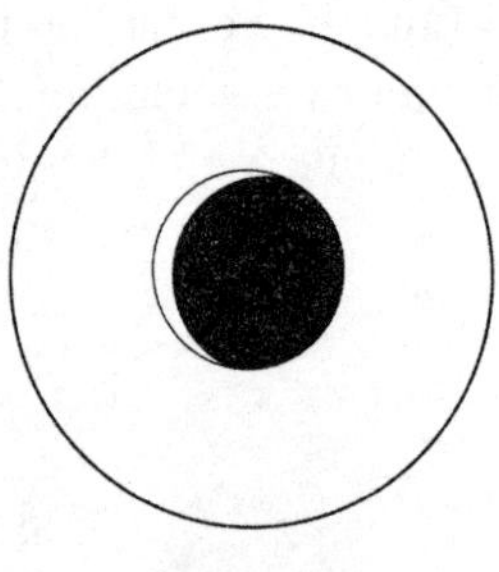

MAY 1999

My grief in May 1999
While I was preparing for Avery's wedding, the anniversary date of my first son's death was approaching. I felt more grief at this time than on the day he died. Apart from the minute area on the left, intense grief filled the inner circle.

Grief for my firstborn will always remain part of my psychological makeup. On a normal day, my sorrow (represented by the inner circle) is much less defined. My whole self (represented by the outer circle) will continue to grow and expand.

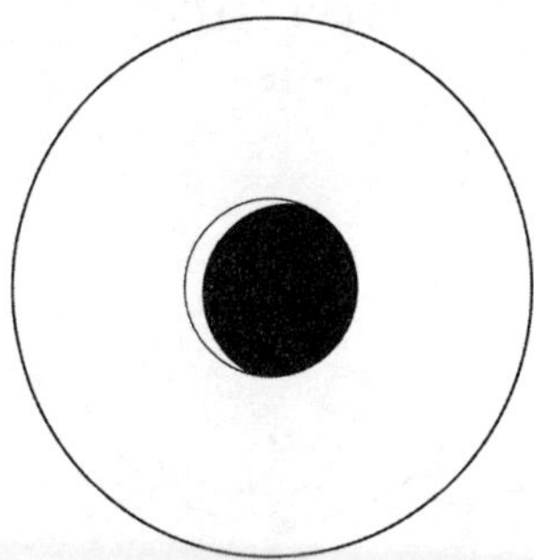

My transcendence: August 2000
The outer circle, my whole self, is larger than ever before.
I keep growing and expanding from my loss.

Although each loss was different for me, I dealt with all of them by intellectualizing, controlling my emotions, and walking.[1] This is the common method for many men, but not all. Some deal with loss as Dianne does; that is, their transcendence is based on feelings, spirituality, and leaving grief behind.

TRANSCENDENCE—DIANNE'S STORY

The beating heart of grief is fueled by the longing for reconnection. Transcendence occurs for me when that longing is resolved. My concepts of loss and transcendence are represented by one circle.

My mother and I shared a strong, healthy relationship. We were not only mother and daughter but also best friends. Unafraid of allowing each other to know our true selves, we habitually exposed our deepest thoughts, feelings, and desires. Much of my time, energy, thoughts, and feelings focused on her. Our relationship formed a circular connection, with me on one side and Mother on the other. Even when we were not together, we remained linked simply by our strong bond.

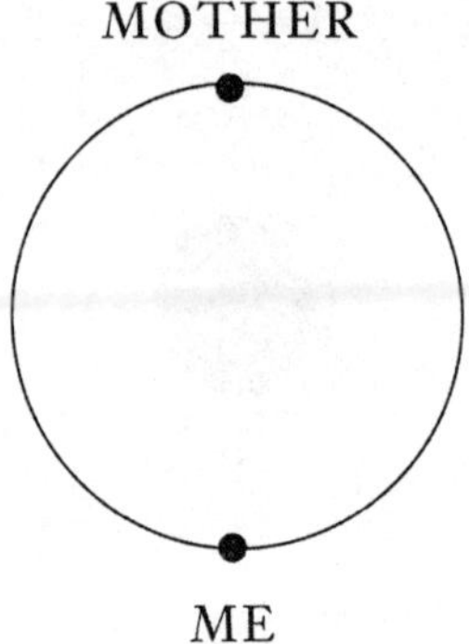

Before Mother's death, our relationship formed a continuous circular connection fueled by reciprocated energy, time, thoughts, and feelings—mine to Mother and hers to me.

Mother's death left a hole within our circle. My body, mind, and spirit still created energy, but without focus. Mother was no longer on the other side to receive and reciprocate.

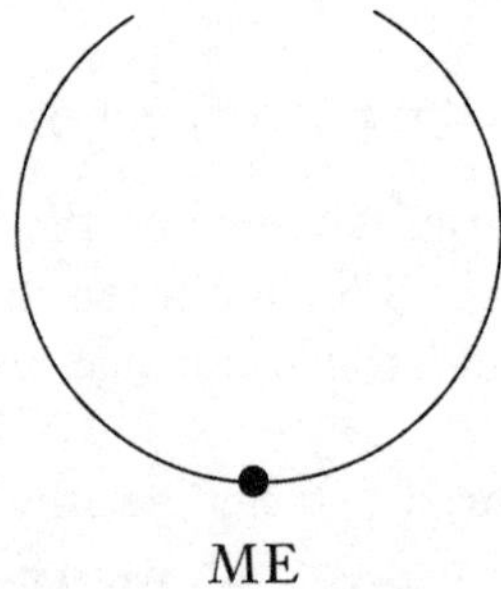

After Mother's death, our encircling connection, once sustained by sharing time, energy, thoughts, feelings, hopes, and dreams, was left with a hole.

Few things are as enduring as the bond between loved ones. The greater the bond, the stronger the connection. When a strong circle is broken, the loss can seem unbearable. Energy surging without focus lacks meaning. If we remove a light bulb from a lamp but leave the switch turned on, the generation of electrical power is pointless.

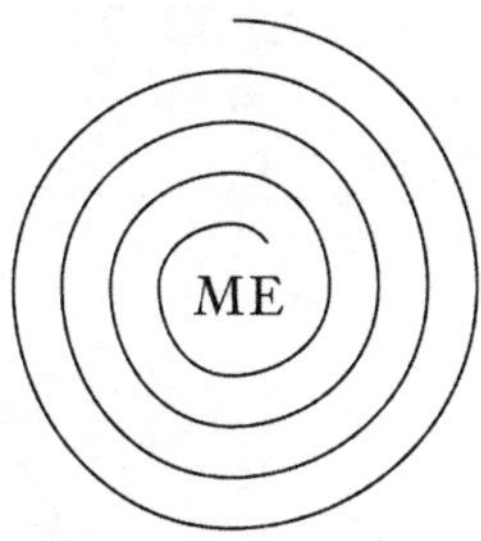

As is true for many survivors, my life seemed meaningless. Without a target for my time, love, and focus, my energy was left to swirl within and around me.

When I realized this, my transcendence took a tremendous leap forward. First, I thought about my connection with my deceased family members and friends. If life continues after bodily death, then their consciousness has places to go and things to do. My holding on to them, spiritually, prevented them from expressing their free will.

I thought about a young child carrying a puppy by its neck. If the child squeezes long and hard enough, all the life force will drain from the animal. Spirits are much the same. Holding on to our deceased loved ones drains their life force. They are not free to carry on in the other realm. The greatest gift I could bestow (for them and for me) was to let their spirits go. I can sustain my link to them through love and memories, and if I live life to the fullest, then their legacy lives vibrantly through me.

At the point that I was no longer willing to hold my loved ones back, we were all set free. I attended workshops and mourned. I used that swirling energy around me to work through as much of my grief as I could. Then I returned to sculpture, a passion I had left behind with childhood. It not only helped me work through some of my sorrow but became the recipient of my time, energy, and love.

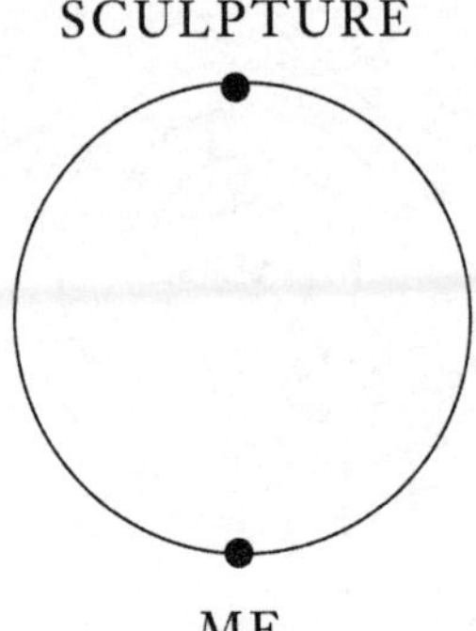

My passion for sculpture created a circle of energy, time, thoughts, and feelings.

Research and working in the field of thanatology eventually replaced sculpture. As I write this, a four-inch frame around my computer monitor holds photos, segments of police reports, notes, letters, cards, and small tokens. These mementos are visual representations of men and women who have requested these words on paper. As a reader, you are the focus of my time, energy, thoughts, and feelings.

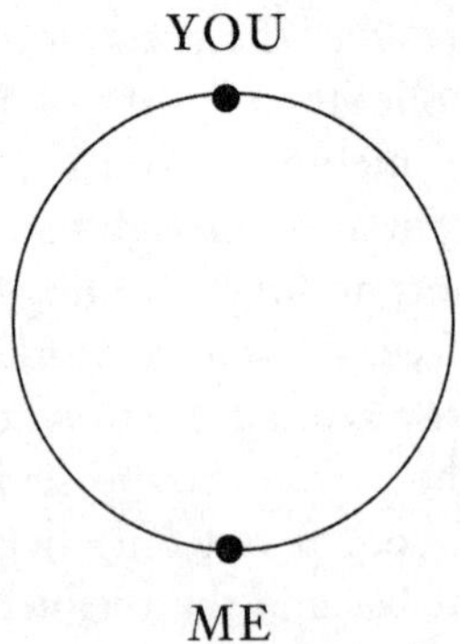

Other survivors have also found this to be their path for transcending loss, as Albert's story illustrates.

"I found passion in life and another chance"

"I was very close to my father. We were separated by more than a thousand miles, so we talked on the phone almost every day. We were always making plans to visit one place or another. All we did was talk about it, though, because I would not take time off from work to go. I thought I had plenty of time, so I kept putting our plans into the future.

"Then my father suddenly became gravely ill and was put on life support. Doctors pronounced him brain-dead, but I was never convinced of that because every time I whispered in his ear, his vital signs improved. I did this every day until nurses removed the monitors. It took months for Dad to die, and I was at his bedside almost continuously. During that time, I realized that everything at the office carried on just fine without me. I regretted that I had not taken time off to be with my father as we had planned.

"Dad's death left a big hole in my life, and I went into a deep depression. I grieved for him and for the good times that I had let pass me by. I was able to continue my life only because of the close support that my wife gave me, but, still, I was just shuffling through day by day. I had no real interest in anything. Then my grandson was born, almost three years after my dad's death, and somehow it seemed as if the hole in my life closed. I found passion in life and another chance. This time I don't just make plans—I spend as much time with the little guy as I can.

"I left so much unfinished with my dad that every once in a while I'll still feel a wave of sorrow, but they are fewer and fewer over time."

Can Survivors Leave Their Grief Behind?

An often-debated question exists in our field: Is it possible to leave grief behind? The human mind is so compartmentalized that no one can possibly expose every experience of loss residing within its deep crevices. It seems certain that we all carry some grief.

Furthermore, many survivors mourn deaths so tragic that we cannot imagine how any human being could totally resolve that kind of tragedy, at least in one lifetime. Our friend Carol Poole, whose son John died from cancer, shares the following (from *Shared Blessings*, her book in progress).

"Soldiers don't come back from war and just get over it"

"My husband worked abroad, so John, my only child, was my constant companion. John and I were exceptionally close, and I found that the death of someone with whom we have such a bond causes post-traumatic stress. Soldiers don't come back from war and just get over it. I've been in battle, I fought my private war, and although some of my battle scars still ache at times, my wounds are healing as best they can."

Some survivors extinguish the grief they once suffered over certain losses. Luanne Valkner, an artist from Michigan, shares her story.

"From tragedy came triumph"

"I was in shock and deep, numbing grief when our firstborn son, Nathan, died a day and a half after his birth. To this day, almost twenty-five years later, it is still hard to go back to that place and touch what was, at the time, unexplainable pain. It is difficult to remember the grief but not the way I got through it.

"My husband and I had good counsel from a doctor at the neonatal unit. He told us not to blame ourselves or each other for Nathan's death. He told us that a lot of marriages disintegrate over the death of a child. We decided to communicate with each other and not let this experience destroy us. If we could get through this, we could get through anything life handed us.

"We grieved together as a couple and gave ourselves the room and space to carry our grief into the corner to grieve alone. Grief is like that, sometimes needing to be shared and other times needing solitude. Time seemed to stand still. I didn't and couldn't look into the future; my pain kept me grounded in the reality of each individual day. Some days the grief became an all-consuming fire that threatened to burn my soul into ashes; on others, it was ice that anesthetized all feeling until even my extremities became unresponsive to life.

"Slowly spring gave way to summer and, with the passing of time, an awareness began to enter my conscious thoughts. It didn't come to me in the quickness of a lightning bolt's flash. Instead, it was a gentle emergence of understanding that unfolded before me, an understanding of God's love. Here I was wanting nothing more than to be a mother, yet my son was taken from me. Until this point in my life God had been a mere abstract concept. Through my son's death He was becoming a Heavenly Father who personally knew my pain. I did not willingly give up my son, but God willingly gave his. In my unspeakable pain, I saw a Heavenly Father who sacrificially gave his Son to the world. In my pain I saw God's pain, and in God's pain I saw and felt love and mercy that carried me through.

"From tragedy came triumph. What had been unbearable became tolerable as I adjusted to my loss. Grief is a process that must be ridden out like the storm it can be, but after the storm comes the stillness of a soul quieted, comforted by God if we dare to let Him in. Today I no longer carry grief for Nathan, but only think of him with love."

Leaving Grief Behind—Dianne's Story

I have known many people who no longer feel sorrow and pain over the death of certain loved ones. Years ago, I could not have imagined that I would be one of them, but today I no longer grieve for my parents, my friend who was murdered, and others whom I've loved and lost. I still feel sadness over my sister-in-law's suicide, and I grieve over deaths that have occurred in recent years.

As a result of my losses and from years of working with other bereaved men and women, I have come to believe that extinguishing grief depends on a number of things. First, the loss was not too traumatic or violent for the survivors to move beyond. Second, the transcenders found grief too burdensome to bear; therefore, they mustered all the effort, courage, and support they possibly could to work through it. And, finally, the survivors held infinite spiritual beliefs that kept them tied to their deceased, and to something far more auspicious than anything on earth.

To say we leave grief behind for a certain loved one does not mean that another piece of sorrow for that same person will not surface at some point. And it does not mean that we have worked through every loss, or that we do not mourn for more recent deaths. It means that after a long journey through the valley and over the bridge, we can now reflect on our loved one and smile.

Grief comes in one size, Extra Large. If we tuck it away in the bottom drawer where it never sees the light of day, it remains exactly the same. On the other hand, if we wear it, feel it, talk about it, and share it with others, it is likely that it will become faded, shrunk, and worn, or will simply no longer fit. When grief has served its purpose, we are able to recognize the many gifts we have gained.

NINE

The Blessings Received from Loss

> So long as we live, they too shall live and love
> for they are a part of us as we remember them.
>
> —*Gates of Prayer*

> To live in the hearts we leave behind, is not
> to die.
>
> —Thomas Campbell

> I have learned to cherish the bounty of every
> day, almost every moment.[1]
>
> —Mrs. John Connally

People who grow from loss ultimately recognize the many blessings loss has provided them. As healthier, stronger, and wiser human beings, we are empowered by our growth and the lives we have ahead. So what are some of these gifts?

All Human Beings

Grief illuminates our humanity. As part of the human species, we all come from the same source and will someday return to that source.

Meanwhile, like the moon, sun, stars, flowers, and trees, we all have a right to be here.

Celebrate Our Differences

The more the bereaved work through their losses, the more they value differences in others. As we noted, a controversy exists as to whether grief is ever extinguished, with one side claiming, "Survivors who say they are free of their grief are in denial." Those who take the opposite view retort, "The bereaved who still grieve just don't want to release it." Such simplifying and judging is unfortunate, because there are no absolutes. We wrote this book together because we exemplify opposites.

"I could never grieve your way"—Dianne's Story

"You know, I could never grieve your way," Raymond said to me during a retreat we hosted in 1995. "I wish I could allow myself to feel those feelings, but I have never been able to do that and still can't."

"Yes, Raymond, I can relate," I said reflectively. "When I met Elisabeth at one of her workshops, people all around the room were wailing. I thought, *I could never do that; it just isn't my style.* But then she orchestrated my path by pointing at me and saying, 'Your little girl needs to have her tears.' It was as if she'd hit me in the stomach. *No way I'll go back to my childhood grief,* I thought.

"Then, late that night, as I lay my eighty-two-pound body down to sleep, I suddenly realized, *I'm sick of carrying this muck inside me. It feels awful and it could even kill me. I don't want to die feeling like this.* With that, I turned flat on my back and sobbed. For five days, I continued to release buckets of tears for that little girl who moved away from her grandma, and for the orphaned adult I had become. It took me years to work through most of that.

"Leaving grief behind is not easy, pretty, or quick, but now that I know how wonderful it feels to be rid of the suffering, repressing my sorrow is no longer an option. That was my path, but one I'd never impose on someone else."

* * *

Transcenders champion every human being. Instead of assessing or judging, we celebrate the fact that no two people, or their styles of mourning, are the same.

Appreciation Is Heightened

Loss furnishes us with an acute appreciation for our departed loved ones. Until they are gone, most people take everyday events (such as saying hello or hearing their voices over the telephone) for granted. But now we appreciate what we lost.

You may recall Jerry's story, about the young man who possessed an uncanny ability to grant everybody his undivided attention, in spite of his painful illness. At his funeral, almost every attendee agreed that they were aware of his gift to them but did not appreciate it until he was gone.

Loss further teaches us to appreciate our surviving loved ones, as well as all life.

Clarification of Self

Our genuine qualities come forth after a devastating loss. We discover who honestly resides within. We search our souls, sorting through our true beliefs and values, and then set priorities accordingly.

Passion Is Enriched

Passion feeds our souls. Our lives depend on it. The death of a loved one brings passion to a deeper level. Most survivors build new priorities, allotting more quality time for those they love. Newfound passions motivate us to enrich our lives and help relieve the plight of others.

Desire to Serve Others

Many bereaved people gain a strong desire to help others. After the murder of Adam Walsh, his parents, John and Reve Walsh, fought for passage of the federal Missing Children's Act and founded the National Center for Missing and Exploited Children. In August 1987, John Walsh became the host for *America's Most Wanted*, a television program that has reunited many abducted children with their families. Since turning an international spotlight on violent criminals, AMW has brought 671 fugitives to justice (as of June 1, 2001). Among the many honors the Walshes have received is John's selection by CBS as one of the "100 Americans Who Changed History."

After her son's death, Iris Bolton founded The Link, a nonprofit counseling center funded by the United Way, and the National Resource Center for Suicide Prevention and Aftercare. Her two fine organizations have helped thousands of people (see the resources section for further information).

One of the foremost psychologists and thanatologists in the field of bereavement, Alan Wolfelt, began his career at the age of fourteen after the death of a close friend. Dr. Wolfelt has dedicated his life to helping others understand and mourn their losses. We refer many individuals, especially children, to his center (see Center for Loss and Life Transition in the resources section).

For every Walsh, Bolton, and Wolfelt, there are thousands of lesser-known survivors who are making a difference in the lives of others. Their stories and noble accomplishments could fill the pages of many books.

Gain Sensitivity

Bereaved individuals are usually more sensitive toward others because loss teaches compassion. Many of us have been accosted by inappropriate statements; therefore, we gain insight about communicating with others.

Finiteness of Life

Death reminds us that life is impermanent. Our time, and that of our surviving loved ones, is finite. Every millisecond is precious when we recognize how fleeting life can be.

Fragility of the Human Body

The death of a loved one highlights the remarkability and fragility of the human body. Our bodies are not machines, but complex, vulnerable, living organisms that can cease to function in a heartbeat.

Humility

Grief teaches humility. As human beings we do not have unlimited power. We are not divine, all-knowing, all-encompassing. Many circumstances are beyond our control, and, ultimately, death is one.

Less Materialistic

Transcenders become less materialistic and more focused on life, living, relationships, and spirituality. We turn to self, improving the quality of our inner lives, and then turn outward to enhance our relationships.

Lessons

Grief brings lessons beyond any classroom. Among them is understanding both what we have lost and what we have gained, and how to integrate the two. The ultimate lesson is knowing that only by having known, loved, and lost our loved one can we reach our highest potential.

Love Is the Link

Another gift is the knowledge that love transcends the body. Love is the link that binds two people together throughout eternity.

Mortality Faced

The death of a loved one forces us to consider our own mortality. Human beings fear what we do not understand, and although not everyone befriends death, learning about it lessens our fear. By dealing with the inevitable, we live life to the fullest.

Relationships Enhanced

Mourning creates self-authenticity, and when we are authentic we feel good about ourselves. The degree to which we love, respect, and appreciate ourselves is the degree to which we can love, respect, and appreciate others.

At one time it was believed that our senior citizens held few relationships because they had outlived their family and peers. That is not the full extent of the story, however. With each loss, survivors become more selective about the people they want in their lives. As a result, they abandon relationships they no longer desire and strengthen those they do want.

Beyond enhancing the relationship with self and others, many bereaved individuals refine their relationship with God. At the time of the death, God may be the focus of our anger. "Where were you?" we question. Feelings toward another indicate that a relationship exists; therefore, anger toward God is proof that the relationship still stands.

Spirituality Increased

Loss can catapult mourners into a quest for spirituality. Most investigate the concept of consciousness surviving bodily death, and some eventually address their questions about reincarnation. No matter what they find along the way, their ultimate discovery is: I have only one opportunity to live in this body, in this era, with these particular circumstances, challenges, and relationships. What happens during this lifetime is not always my choice, but what I gain from it is.

Wisdom Is Acquired

If you were to write your autobiography, it would contain varying events, themes, and characters. Certain characters in your story will have changed, and others will have been lost along the way. Although every person and event contributes, the most poignant will come from your losses. Wisdom is acquired through life experiences.

Bereaved parents often say they feel honored to have given their children the opportunity to come to earth. Some believe in karma and accept that their children were here to complete something unresolved from former lives. Others believe their offspring were here on a mission, possibly as teachers, and once their mission was completed, their destiny had been fulfilled. In such cases, parents feel blessed to have been hosts for those spirits' journeys.

Part of the wisdom that Dianne acquired was realizing why her dad died the way he did, and that holding on to his spirit was an injustice to everyone involved.

A Sense of Immortality

As children, we sense that death is like the moon and stars—something far away. From their perspective, we continue on and on. By adulthood, however, we know that our physical existence is limited. Transcenders merge both perspectives. Indeed, our bodies are finite, but, just like the moon and stars, we will continue on and on.

In your being, you carry a part of everyone you have ever met. They, along with every life experience, coexist within you. Some hold more influence than others, but all touch you to some degree. Likewise, some part of you resides within every person you have met. We all live through one another, and in that respect we all reach a certain immortality.

Transcendence

Although mourning is tremendously painful at the time, it is the ultimate catalyst for growth. Transcendence, rising above who we were at the time of the death, is not an end result but a never-ending process. Transcenders feel good about themselves and who they are becoming.

Beyond all these gifts, perhaps the greatest gift that loss brings is reassurance that life continues beyond bodily death, a subject that we will cover in the next chapter.

TEN

We Will See Them Again

The secret of heaven is kept from age to age.
—OLIVER WENDELL HOLMES

Most people who grow strong after the death of loved ones believe that life continues in some form. Many gather their beliefs from their faiths; others turn to science. Although science does not yet offer definite *proof*, it provides a large body of work indicating that, indeed, consciousness continues beyond the body. Let's explore some of that evidence.

NEAR-DEATH EXPERIENCES—RAYMOND'S STORY

After close calls with death, some people can recall specific details about their experiences.

In the 1960s, I read or heard two accounts of near-death experiences. The first was Plato's description of Er,[1] a warrior who was pronounced dead on the battlefield. While his body lay on the funeral pyre, Er's spirit floated above his body and through passageways. He saw his life replayed before him, and then divine beings told him to return to earth.

Several years later, I was shocked when I heard Dr. George Ritchie, a psychiatrist at the University of Virginia's Department of Psychiatry, recount his experience. His account had the same pattern as Er's.

After completing my doctorate in 1969, I was teaching philosophy at East Carolina University when a student confronted me after class one day. "Why haven't we studied the issue of life after death in this *philosophy* class?" he asked, emphasizing the word as if I had been remiss in not covering the topic.

"Why do you want to talk about *that*?" I asked, thinking that the subject was passé.

"A year ago I was involved in a serious accident," he confided, "and my doctors pronounced me dead. I experienced something during that time that totally changed my life, but I've not been able to talk about it." Delighted to oblige, I invited the young man into my office. To my amazement, he described a close call with death that contained elements identical to Ritchie's and Er's.

Having heard three similar accounts, I felt confident that there must be others; therefore, while introducing Plato the next semester, I posed the question, "Can consciousness survive bodily death?"

"Yes!" a student exclaimed and proceeded to divulge how he had been run down by a car. Between the time the front wheels and the rear wheels passed over his body, the young man vividly relived his life.

From that point on, any time I mentioned Plato I brought up the subject of life after death, and indeed one or more students from each succeeding semester described their experiences. When the university provost, a retired Marine Corps colonel, heard several accounts, he invited me to lecture at his church. My collection of stories expanded after I began speaking in public, and more so after I entered medical school the following year.

Dispelling the Myth

"Poor Dr. Moody was persecuted by his colleagues for investigating after-death experiences and dismissed as a crank," would be such a wonderful story born during this phase of my career; however, it was far from the truth. I was embraced by most of the medical community. Regardless of their belief or disbelief in life after death, physicians were interested in the phenomenon because they were hearing similar claims from their patients.

It was their encouragement that led me to write an article for the *Atlanta Constitution*, and that led to my writing *Life After Life*.

When the most prominent psychiatrist in the field, Elisabeth Kübler-Ross, stepped in to write the foreword, she confirmed that her findings were similar to mine—near-death experiences exhibited common characteristics.

Characteristics of Near-Death Experiences (NDEs)

As described in my book *Life After Life*, first published in November 1975, I considered near-death experiences under one of three circumstances: (1) persons were resuscitated after being pronounced or thought dead; (2) persons were close to death following an accident, injury, or illness; (3) persons told witnesses about their experiences before they later died.

What were the characteristics of these near-death experiences? They usually began when the experiencers heard themselves pronounced dead by a physician or other medical personnel and then felt peace as they rose above their bodies. They experienced going through or into a tunnel, seeing a brilliant light, and then meeting with an Omnipresence, heavenly beings, or apparitions of their deceased loved ones. After their life reviews, they reluctantly returned to their bodies.

The aftereffects included tremendous spiritual transformation (many became ministers or hospice volunteers); a feeling of ineffability about their NDEs; and a quest for knowledge (many returned to college). And although experiencers no longer feared death, they viewed life as a finite precious gift to savor and protect.

Updating the Past Twenty-five Years

Life After Life burst onto the national scene after it was republished by Bantam Press in the summer of 1976. Intense scientific, medical, and popular attention focused on the phenomenon of near-death experiences. Early cases from around the globe were brought to light, including the first collection ever published—the *Yearbook of the Swiss Alpine Club* (1892), written by a Zurich geology professor, Albert von St. Gallen Heim. Along with his personal account, which he experienced during a fall in the Alps, Heim included the results of his interviews with thirty other experiencers, most of whom were Alpine climbers. Other unearthed cases included one from London dating to 1911 (published in London's *Sunday Express* on May 26, 1935), one from France that took place in 1916 during World War I, and another from South Africa that occurred in 1920 during the Boer War.[2] Then, during the early to mid-1970s, at the University of Iowa, Russ Noyes and his colleagues published accounts wherein they referred to NDEs as "depersonalization in the face of life-threatening danger."[3]

Bruce Greyson: A Turning Point in Death Studies

A turning point in the evolution of death studies occurred in July 1976. Bruce Greyson was an assistant professor in the Department of Psychiatry at the University of Virginia, where I began my first year of residency. Bruce informed me that his colleague Dr. Ian Stevenson, a world-renowned investigator of paranormal experiences, held more than thirty cases of near-death experiences in his repository. With Greyson's and Stevenson's influence, scientific research began under the newly coined term *near-death experience*, and qualified investigators entered the field.

Dr. Greyson extensively researched NDEs, specializing in experiences after suicide attempts. One of his most significant findings was that, whereas attempted suicide dramatically increased the risk of later suicide, attempted suicide followed by an NDE dramatically decreased the risk of self-destructive behaviors. Those experiencers discovered that life has a purpose and that suicide prevents that purpose from unfolding. Greyson also found that the NDEs of suicide attempters followed the same pattern as the NDEs of those who came close to death from other causes.

Michael Sabom Enters the Field

Psychiatric social worker Sarah Kreutziger was intrigued by *Life After Life*. "Will you invite Dr. Moody to speak?" she asked Dr. Michael Sabom, her Bible studies classmate.

"That book is fiction," he said. As a resident cardiologist at Shands Teaching Hospital at the University of Florida, Sabom had resuscitated many patients but had never heard such claims.

"Have you ever asked one of them?" Sarah inquired. When he admitted that he had not, she responded, "Perhaps you should."

Sabom began to interview his patients, and the third patient he questioned reported salient facts about being resuscitated after cardiac arrest, including the equipment used. Other patients subsequently added their accounts, including details that occurred while they were unconscious (in the medical sense). When Sabom compared their claims to their medical records, he was fascinated and began intensive research.

Sabom has published numerous journal articles and books on the subject, and in his latest, *Light and Death: One Doctor's Fascinating Account of Near-Death Experiences*, he includes the case of a woman who was diagnosed with an inoperable aneurysm at the base of her brain. She was nevertheless transported from her hometown, Atlanta, to the Barrow Neurological Institute in Phoenix, Arizona. The institute was one of the few facilities at that time that performed a dangerous procedure called hypothermic circulatory arrest—dangerous because individuals normally cannot survive more than a few minutes without a healthy blood supply to the brain, yet the operation requires forty to sixty minutes.

The surgery normally progresses as follows: Surgeons divert the patient's blood from his or her body, through an ice-water bath, and then back into the body. When the body cools to sixty degrees Fahrenheit, its metabolism is slowed, allowing the patient to survive much longer without blood to the brain. At that point, surgeons tilt the operating table and drain all the blood from the patient's head. (If any remains, the aneurysm can burst.) Finally, surgeons remove the top of the skull and repair the aneurysm. During the forty- to sixty-minute procedure, by medical criteria the patient is clinically dead—no brain waves, no pulse, no respiration.

The patient from Atlanta suffered complications. It took surgeons longer than expected; therefore, they were forced to start warming her body faster than usual. As a result, her heart arrested twice. Without breathing, heartbeat, or electromagnetic activity in her brain for an extended period, she nevertheless survived. After awakening, she described a number of details that occurred during her operation, including the complications, songs that played on the tape deck, and the appearance of the unique saw used to cut open her skull. In addition, she reported moving through a tunnel into a beautiful light and meeting relatives who had died many years earlier.

Kenneth Ring's Scientific Exploration

I presented *Life After Life* as an overview of the phenomenon of NDE, but Kenneth Ring (a professor of psychology at the University of Connecticut at Storrs and an expert in the field of social psychology) wanted solid scientific data. He interviewed more than one hundred patients from various hospitals and published his statistical breakdown and findings in his first book, *Life at Death: A Scientific Investigation of the Near-Death Experience*. He then examined the aftereffects of NDEs and presented those findings in *Heading Toward Omega: In Search of the Meaning of the Near-Death Experience*. Ring continues to make discoveries. For instance, he tracked the impressions of blind men and women and found that the sightless regained their vision during NDEs.[4]

All this research and all these findings began to influence popular attitudes toward this phenomenon. By 1980, a national Gallup poll determined that more than eight million American adults had experienced NDEs.

Melvin Morse's Investigation of NDEs Among Children

Melvin Morse, a pediatrician in Seattle, began to interview children and found that their accounts included the same characteristics and aftereffects as the accounts of adults.[5] His repository included drawings by children in which they depicted their bodies floating up, through passageways, and so on. Dr. Morse is unique in the field because he has been able to follow children post-NDE. He reports that the children from his original interviews, now young adults, remain unusually insightful, kind, and compassionate.

In Summary

More than twenty-five years of research has verified, as well as extended, our knowledge of the NDE phenomenon. A common type of experience, indeed, normally unfolds among the dying. An early rumor that NDEs were reflective of mental illness has been dispelled—they occur evenly throughout the general population. Furthermore, those who claimed that near-death experiences were caused by oxygen deprivation or other chemical changes within the brain have found no evidence to support that theory.[6] Long-term studies reveal that NDEs result in lifelong psychological and spiritual change. If you want to investigate further, we offer a number of suggestions.

Rely on the Reliable

The international tidal wave of fascination with near-death experiences bred some inauthentic claims; therefore, our first suggestion is to rely on the reliable. George Ritchie chronicled his authentic account in *Ordered to Return.* Elisabeth Kübler-Ross, Kenneth Ring, Michael Sabom, and Melvin Morse offer an extensive body of work. An early (1982) compilation of writings by Grosso, Haraldsson, Moody, Noyes, Osis, Ring, and others can be found in Craig Lundahl's *Collection of Near-Death Research Readings: Scientific Inquiries into the Experiences of Persons Near Physical Death.*

The *Journal of Near-Death Studies,* the principal journal in the field, is another credible source. It began circulating after a group of serious investigators met at the University of Virginia and formed the Association for the Scientific Study of Experiences Near Death (now the International Association of Near-Death Studies) in 1977. Any attempt to highlight articles from that publication would be daunting, and it holds only a small portion of the literature. The journal's editor, Bruce Greyson, has alone collected more than two thousand scholarly papers.[7] In 1984, he and Chuck Flynn published an anthology of the best writings at that time in their book *The Near-Death Experience: Problems, Prospects, Perspectives.* Greyson and his colleagues at the University of Virginia are comparing pre-1975 cases with recent NDEs. Their upcoming article will describe how patterns have changed over the past few decades.

Beyond literature, do not overlook personal resources, such as relatives and friends. Just because they have not disclosed their stories does not mean they have not experienced the phenomenon. Most experiencers do not expose their accounts for a number of reasons.

One reason is that NDEs are spiritually deep and profound; therefore, no words can do them justice. Many experiencers feel, too, that their NDEs are too intimate to share. Others are concerned that listeners will be judgmental or think their stories indicate mental illness. Ultimately, most experiencers conclude that no one else could ever comprehend a near-death experience; yet many will submit themselves to inquiries or rigorous scientific investigation if they think others will be genuinely helped.

Just when NDEs are finally being understood, it is time to step into another realm. What does the future hold for death studies?

Before examining that question, let's consider a phenomenon we call death sense.

Death Sense

Death sense is the term we use for "intuiting a loss." Many people have reported waking up in the middle of the night with a sensation that a loved one has just died, only to discover the following day that, indeed, one had. Mothers have sensed the instant that their children were killed in faraway places. Relatives and friends have intuited the moment their loved ones were killed during war. Gary describes his death sense.

"Even the hairs down the back of my neck stood on end"

Trying to choose the words to describe his experience, Gary spoke slowly, "I was talking to friends when suddenly I felt an intolerable jolt. It sat me straight up in my chair like a thunderbolt. You've seen those cartoon scenes where one character gets hit with a blast of electricity, and his body extends . . . arms, hands, legs, feet . . . they all fly straight out? Well, even the hairs down the back of my neck stood on end."

Bending forward, Gary held his face in his hands for a long moment before continuing, "I don't know why, but all I could think of was my wife, Pam [who worked as an electrician at a large refinery]. When no one answered the phone at her job, I knew something had happened. I kept pacing the floor and calling again and again. Finally, I got through and one of her co-workers told me the horrible news, 'Gary . . . I'm sorry . . . Pam mistakenly grabbed a live four-thousand-volt wire. She never stood a chance.' Then I understood why I'd felt that shock. Pam was my soul mate. We were so close that I know my body reacted with hers, even though I was more than three hundred miles away."

Some people move beyond death sense or intuiting the moment of death and into death coincidents.

Death Coincidents

A phenomenon of death is being reported in growing numbers, owing in large part to two convergent social factors: baby boomers and professional practices. Baby boomers are surviving the deaths of their parents in vast numbers. Moreover, thanks to the hospice movement, family and friends are no longer ushered away from dying patients. Because of this increased involvement with the dying, more death coincidents are being reported.

A dictionary definition of a *coincident* is a "remarkable occurrence that happens in connection with something much greater." A death coincident occurs when family members or friends accompany their dying loved one into the other realm and then return to their bodies. As a shared experience,[8] it involves their momentarily stepping through death's door.

Characteristics of Death Coincidents

The characteristics of death coincidents parallel many of the standard NDE characteristics: cotravelers leave their bodies, view the scene below, sense peace, and return to their bodies. Other similar elements are a light and tunnel, life review, apparitions, and personal transformation.

The Light and Tunnel

Most death coincidents involve a light or a tunnel or both. Joan's account is typical. While sleeping beside her terminally ill husband, Joan dreamed that they were strolling down a pathway, through a meadow, and into a dark tunnel. Inside, a soft yet brilliant light surrounded them and illuminated their way. She was feeling love and peace as never before when her husband said, "Joanie, you must go back now." At first she ignored him and continued to stroll, but when he tugged at her elbow, she spun around. To her amazement, he appeared healthy, athletic, and without glasses—much as he had in his youth. "You must go back," he repeated. "It isn't your time. I'll be back for you when it is." Joan sensed that they were at a point of no return and turned to leave, but just then a noise outside their window startled her awake. Opening her eyes, she saw that her dear husband had continued his journey into death.

"For some reason I'm not grief-stricken like I thought I would be," Joan said. "Going with him like that softened the blow."

Life Review

Although not all cotravelers witness their loved ones' panoramic life reviews, those who do, describe it as heartwarming. In two cases, independently and without knowledge of the other, mothers recounted identical stories. At the moment of her adolescent son's death, each woman saw his body illuminated in a glowing light and then coexperienced the entirety of his life review. Both women reported feeling privileged and uplifted.

Apparitions

Death coincidents are becoming so common that one person in almost every group seems to have experienced the phenomenon.

"An ecstasy of peace lingers with me"—Dianne's Story

A friend invited five guests to a small dinner party. Sitting next to me was a woman, Ruth, who during our conversation inquired about my line of work. When I told her, she said, "Oh, hospice. My stepfather died three weeks ago in a hospice and they were wonderful."

"That is always good to hear," I replied.

"Yes, the entire experience, really, was quite wonderful," she said. "I was standing next to my stepfather's bed, close to him, when I began to feel a deep peace, almost as if I were in a dimension all by myself. In my mind's eye I saw a line, and there were two people waiting for him on the other side of the line. One was his son, John, who had died years before at the age of thirty. John was reaching out, jumping up and down like a little kid, yelling, 'Come on, Dad! Come on!' He looked just like he always did dressed in khaki pants and an olive green shirt. Then I saw a woman I didn't know. She had dark hair and was wearing a blue skirt and sweater. She stood there in total respect, waiting for him. I told Dad, 'When you are ready, all you have to do is reach out your hand.' He was no longer with us after that point. It was a beautiful passing.

"When I told one family member about my experience, she told me that the woman was his first wife. The main thing that stuck out to me was that although his son John was a grown man when he died, he greeted his dad like a little kid. As close as I was to my stepfather, I'm not grieving for him because an ecstasy of peace lingers with me."

Ruth was only one of many strangers who have shared their coincidents with us during dinners, on airplanes, at conferences, and in numerous other settings. Her case is typical in that she could not identify every apparition. Her account, however, is different from a classic coincident because her stepfather did not die at the time of her experience but slipped into a coma before his body succumbed hours later.

Contrasting Features

Most characteristics of death coincidents are similar to the characteristics of NDEs; however, some elements differ. Coincidents can be disorienting, be collective, occur away from the death scene, and serve a different purpose.

Disorienting

Compared to classic NDEs, death coincidents are more disorienting. Cotravelers usually realize that their loved ones have died, but it requires time to process their situation mentally, as the following accounts illustrate.

"She was standing beside me"

As a professor of internal medicine, Dr. Ash was in the awkward position of resuscitating his mother as she lay in her hospital bed. While desperately trying to bring her back, he felt himself rise above his body and then saw himself working on hers. *Oh, oh,* he thought, *I must be going into shock.* When he looked around to get his bearings, there, beside him, stood his mother. "She was different from the elderly body lying in the bed below," he explained. "She was rejuvenated, young and healthy again." Dr. Ash and his mother carried on a heart-to-heart conversation and then said their good-byes. "I watched her recede toward a tunnel, from which a brilliant, comforting light illuminated, and, as she swept toward it, I automatically returned to my body."

"Oh wow! It's me!"—Raymond's Story

Louise, a bright, wisecracking nurse, was assisting me with paperwork when her face suddenly changed. She seemed far away and, in a sense, she was—she was back in time, reliving her father's death.

Her father, dying after a long struggle with terminal cancer, was surrounded by his family. Louise, so relieved that he was dying peacefully, took his hand in hers. "Just then, I felt him go through me," she explained. "From his hand, into mine, his energy traveled up my arm and out. I was trying to gather my wits when I saw a tall, thin, blonde female step in front of me. *How rude of that woman to insert herself between me and my dad just as he died!* I thought. *Who is she?* The woman kept standing between my dad and me, staring at his body."

"Oh wow! It's me!" Louise finally gasped, unnerved that the woman's image was her own. Then she heard her father's vibrant laughter. She turned to see him standing beside her, totally rejuvenated. "Dad hugged me with a joyful, warm, and loving embrace, and at the same time endless information passed from him into me. In a flash, he told me all there was to know about life, love, and death. Then we were swept up and away by a powerful vacuum, to a passageway that seemed to lead into infinity. We both flew smoothly, almost magnetically toward a light from which human forms appeared. I could not identify every apparition, but I recognized my grandparents, aunts, and uncles. But Dad obviously knew them all because he rushed over to them. Once he was in their midst, they all closed in around him, welcoming him into their circle of love."

As her dad and the apparitions receded into the light, the tunnel closed from its perimeter in a circular motion, like the aperture of a camera, and at that point Louise jolted back into her body. "I felt like shouting with joy, but when I looked around the hospital room and saw others grieving, I knew I couldn't."

"Before my coincident," Louise said, "I didn't know what to think about near-death experiences or life after death. Now I'm convinced that there is something to it." Further still, she wonders if other family members were cotravelers. "I keep remembering," she said, "other joyful faces at my father's deathbed that day." If someone else had shared the phenomenon, then Louise would have been part of a collective coincident.

Collective Experiences

Differing further from NDEs, death coincidents can occur in groups. When more than one person escorts the departing, then the experience is considered collective. An example from one of our families follows.

A Collective Experience—Raymond's Story

During the week of Mother's Day, 1994, Dianne and I were reporting death coincidents to a group of researchers. After our meeting on Sunday, we drove to a local shopping mall, where I called my mother to wish her a happy Mother's Day. Mother informed me that she had just been to the emergency room because her body had suddenly been covered with an unexplained rash. The attending physician diagnosed her symptoms as a petechial rash, which was not a threat to her health; he suggested that she return for a complete examination the following week. Horrifically, when she did, further tests revealed that she was in the final stages of non-Hodgkin's lymphoma. She had less than two weeks to live.

My wife and I drove to Georgia, where we sat by her hospital bed. Within several days, she became unresponsive. Soon, all her family gathered around her. In her final moments, Mother's eyes opened and she looked intently into each of our faces. Then, drawing in her last breath, she warmly and audibly said, "I love you, I love you."

Within seconds, I felt a strong spiritual presence, and another family member felt the same, describing it as our father, who had died eighteen months before. Next, I sensed a tunnel spiraling open, and a light that the world does not see appeared. "Do you feel it?" whispered my brother-in-law, a minister, with tears in his eyes.

In retrospect, I think that I did not leave my body because I was focused on Mother's face. I have never had an out-of-body experience, but now I understand how easy it would be to unite with the peaceful, comforting light. I am certain that I would have left my body if I had allowed it.

Coincidents Beyond the Death Scene

Death coincidents can occur away from the deathbed as well. The following three accounts chronicle such experiences.

"I was suddenly rocked"

Amy's dad suffered from flulike symptoms and was hospitalized for tests. "I was there by his bed for two days," she said, "until finally I had to go home and rest for a few hours. I was napping when I was suddenly rocked to my feet. I tried to reorient myself, but I floated into a peaceful light and saw my father beside me. I felt disconnected from reality, but as soon as I could pull myself together, I drove back to the hospital." Upon entering her dad's hospital room, Amy discovered that he had died at the exact time of her experience.

Coincidents often occur while the experiencer is sleeping. And children as well as adults have reported them, as in the following example.

"Grandpa! Grandpa!"

Andy's mother and aunt were sitting on the front porch one afternoon when a cry rang throughout the house. They hurried to the bedroom, where they found the four-year-old in a half-sleep, reaching toward the ceiling.

"Wake up, honey, you're dreaming," his mother said, squeezing his hand.

"Grandpa! Grandpa!" he cried out, opening his eyes. "Grandpa fell down on the floor by his sink," babbled the young boy, standing to demonstrate, "like this, and a light came, and a lady he called Sarah came, with red hair, and . . ."

"Aunt Sarah," the women said in unison. Frantically, they telephoned their elderly father, and, when he did not answer, they rushed to his house nearby. Flinging the back door open, they found his lifeless body on the kitchen floor, in exactly the position his grandson had depicted. "Aunt Sarah, Papa's sister, died years before this and she came to take him home," the women later explained.

Professional caregivers can experience coincidents as well.

"But you were here"—Dianne's Story

To be placed in hospice care, patients must be diagnosed with an illness that is expected to end their lives within six months. Once they are admitted, however, their lives can extend for a year or more because the quality of living increases dramatically. Such was the case with Rodney.

Although Rodney was diagnosed with terminal cancer, he had displayed no further signs of physical or mental deterioration since being admitted as a home-care patient with our hospice. With a round face, pink cheeks, and jolly disposition, Rodney mirrored Saint Nick. He, his wife, and their large family congregated daily to watch television and share stories. They were a delight to visit, which I had been doing every week for almost two years.

Before leaving Houston, I usually informed my colleagues and the patients on my caseload that I would be gone. This one time I didn't, however, because it would only be for a long weekend and no one seemed close to death.

Manhattan pulsated below my feet, like a volcano ready to erupt. I was in love with New York, especially at Christmastime. At day's end, my energy was ablaze and I speculated that I would stay awake all night, but occasional snowflakes tapping down the windowpane of my hotel room lulled me into a peaceful slumber.

The tranquillity of my sleep was shaken by a nightmare. Rodney was in his bed, covered with perspiration and struggling to stay alive. Standing over him, I could not dismiss the unmistakable smell of death. Panic and commotion swirled about his house. Rodney, his family, and the hospice staff were not prepared for his sudden turn.

A cold wetness ended my nightmare. *What is this?* I thought and half-rose in bed to look for the cause. My own perspiration saturated the sheets. *How can this be? The room is so frigid.* Then I remembered Rodney. *It was only a dream*, I assured myself, gazing out the window to make certain that I could see New York. Still, an uneasiness permeated my soul. Lying back against the pillow, I was sure that sleep was impossible now, but I quickly nodded off and was once again at Rodney's deathbed. Almost whispering, I apologized. "I'm sorry, Rodney. I thought I would be here when the time came."

Peace soon replaced his struggle. It was over. Sobs replaced the bustle within his bedroom. Over my shoulder a familiar voice consoled, "But, Dianne, you were here." I turned to see Rodney standing behind me. "Come back for her," he said, motioning to his wife, who had gone pale.

The noise of the awakening city opened my eyes. *Rodney!* was my first thought, *I wonder if . . .* But then my mind rationalized, *Oh, that was just a weird dream.* A gnawing feeling and ruminating thoughts about Rodney caused me to drop my planned schedule and catch the first flight back to Houston. Once home, I listened to an obviously stunned colleague's message on my answering machine: "Dianne, Rodney just died. We're all in shock. Please come over as soon as you can."

My coincident brought me back to serve the family and hospice staff. Furthermore, my grief was eased by hearing them describe his death, exactly as I had coexperienced it. Rodney's wife and I continued to visit, but, regretfully, I never told her about my early-morning coincident.

Why do such experiences occur?

The Purpose of Coincidents

Kenneth Ring concluded in his book *Heading Toward Omega* that the ultimate purpose of NDEs is to make an evolutionary thrust toward higher consciousness for all humankind.[9] On a grand scale, knowledge about death coincidents offers the world population a similar transformation.

On a smaller, more personal, scale, however, the phenomenon holds three main purposes. First, separation is eased for cotravelers as well as the dying. Second, the intensity and duration of grief are lessened. And last, these experiences expand hope. Not only is the belief in life after death a key for adapting to loss, but it reduces anxiety about death in general.[10] This brings us to the question of survival.

Evidence for Survival of Bodily Death

People who have experienced NDEs and death coincidents are left with no doubt that consciousness survives beyond bodily death. Many survival researchers agree.

Critics, however, claim that NDEs are not evidence of life after death because the experiencers were alive to report their accounts. "Only the actual dead can tell us about the afterworld, and, thus far, that has not happened," they snort. But let's consider the fact that if some of the experiencers had died before modern resuscitation devices were available, they would have remained deceased. Therefore, in a sense, those individuals are the living dead. Critics will similarly say that death coincidents do not provide evidence for survival.

We, the authors, are often asked for our personal opinions and so we will state them briefly here.

Raymond: I wish that I could say mine; however, science has not proved the case one way or the other, and I have not figured it out.

Dianne: I am not certain how long consciousness survives or where it goes. I am sure, however, that it continues after the body ceases to function. My conviction comes both from my personal experiences and from years of gathering objective evidence.

Perhaps the existence of heaven is not supposed to be proved scientifically. If that is the case, then regarding the human spirit as immortal will always remain a mixture of faith and science. Regardless, believing that loved ones continue in some form, as will we, eases our passage across the bridge of grief. And we can find comfort in knowing that someday, when our lives upon this earth have reached their natural completion, we will see them again.

Supportive Resources

Articles, Pamphlets, and Magazines

American Academy of Child and Adolescent Psychiatry. *Helping Children After a Disaster.* Facts for Families No. 36. Washington, DC: American Academy of Child and Adolescent Psychiatry, 1990.

Bereavement: A Magazine of Hope and Healing. Bereavement Publishing, 5125 North Union Boulevard, Suite 4, Colorado Springs, CO 80918-2056. Telephone. 719.266.0006. www.bereavementmag.com

Cadoff, Jennifer. "How Kids Grieve." *Parents,* April 1993, p. 142.

Comer, James P. "Learning to Cope with Death." *Parents,* May 1987, p. 20.

DeFrain, John D., Deanne K. Jakub, and Betty Lou Mendoza. "The Psychological Effects of Sudden Infant Death on Grandmothers and Grandfathers." *Omega* 24 (1991–92): 165–82.

Dunne, Edward, and Menyl Maleska Wilbut. *Survivors of Suicide: Coping with the Suicide of a Loved One.* Washington, DC: American Association of Suicidology, 1993. (22-page pamphlet.)

Grollman, Earl A. *Living with Your Loss.* Batesville, IN: Batesville Management Services, 1991. (Brochure.)

Gunderson, Jean M., and Donna E. Harris. *Quetus: A Story of a Stillbirth.* Omaha: Centering Corp., 1990. (16-page booklet.)

Karnes, Barbara. *Gone from My Sight: The Dying Experience.* 1986. Available from B. Karnes, P.O. Box 335, Stilwell, KS 66085. (Booklet that educates caregivers about the dying process.)

Rosenblatt, Paul C. *Coping with Losing a Family Member in a Farm Accident.* North Central Regional Extension Pub. 484, Minnesota Extension Service Pub. FO-6205-B, 1993.

Stillwell, Elaine. *Healing After Your Child's Death.* Liguori, MO: Liguori Press, 2001.

Stillwell, Elaine. *Stepping Stones for the Bereaved.* Liguori, MO: Liguori Press, 2001.

Turnbull, Sharon. *Who Lives Happily Ever After? For Families Whose Child Has Died Violently.* Omaha: Centering Corp., 1990. (23-page booklet.)

What Is SIDS? McLean, VA: National SIDS Clearinghouse. (Fact sheet.)

Wolfelt, Alan D. "Resolution Versus Reconciliation: The Importance of Semantics." *Thanatos* 12 (1987): pp 10–13.

Books

Animal Loss

Coleman, Joan. *Forever Friends: Resolving Grief After the Loss of a Beloved Animal.* Las Vegas: J. C. Taraent Enterprises, 1993.

Montgomery, Mary, and Herb Montgomery. *Good-bye My Friend: Grieving the Loss of a Pet.* Montgomery Press, 1991. P.O. Box 24124, Minneapolis, MN 55424.

Nieburg, Herbert A., and Arlene Fischer. *Pet Loss: A Thoughtful Guide for Adults and Children.* New York: Harper & Row, 1982.

Quackenbush, Jamie, and Denise Graveline. *When Your Pet Dies: How to Cope with Your Feelings.* New York: Simon & Schuster, 1985.

Ray, William J., and others, eds. *Pet Loss and Human Bereavement.* Ames: Iowa State Univ. Press, 1984.

Ross, Cheri Barton, and Jane Baron Sorensen. *Pet Loss and Human Emotion.* Philadelphia: Taylor & Francis, 1998.

Sheldrake, Rupert. *Dogs That Know When Their Owners Are Coming Home and Other Unexplained Powers of Animals.* New York: Crown, 1999.

Sife, Wallace. *The Loss of a Pet, the Human-Animal Bond.* New York: Macmillan, 1993.

Children's Bereavement

Adams, David W., and Eleanor J. Deveau. *Beyond the Innocence of Childhood: Helping Children and Adolescents Cope with Death and Bereavement.* Amityville, NY: Baywood, 1995.

Adams, David W., and Eleanor J. Deveau. *Coping with Childhood Cancer: Where Do We Go from Here?* Ontario: Kinbridge, 1988.

Alderman, Linda. *Why Did Daddy Die*? New York: Simon & Schuster, 1989.

Arnold, Caroline. *What We Do When Someone Dies.* New York: Franklin Watts, 1987.

Aub, Kathleen A. *Children Are Survivors Too: A Guidebook for Young Homicide Survivors.* Grief Education Enterprises, 1991. 6971 N. Federal Highway #404, Boca Raton, FL 33487.

Bernstein, Joanne E., and Masha Kabakow Rudman. *Books to Help Children Cope with Separation and Loss: An Annotated Bibliography.* New York: Bowker, 1989.

Blackburn, Lynn Bennett. *The Class in Room 44.* Omaha: Centering Corp., 1991.

Bluebond-Langner, Myra. *The Private Worlds of Dying Children.* Princeton, NJ: Princeton Univ. Press, 1978.

Buckingham, Robert W. *Care of the Dying Child: A Practical Guide for Those Who Help Others.* New York: Continuum, 1989.

Buscaglia, Leo. *The Fall of Freddie the Leaf.* Thorofare, NJ: Slack, 1982.

Cassini, Karhleen Kidder, and Jacqueline L. Rogers. *Death and the Classroom: A Teacher's Guide to Assist Grieving Students.* Griefwork of Cincinnati, 1990. 1445 Colonial Drive, Suite B, Cincinnati, OH 45238.

Center for Attitudinal Healing. *There Is a Rainbow Behind Every Dark Cloud.* Millbrae, CA: Celestial Arts, 1978.

Coles, Robert. *The Spiritual Life of Children.* Boston: Houghton Mifflin, 1990.

Corr, Charles A., and Joan N. McNeil, eds. *Adolescence and Death.* New York: Springer, 1986.

Davies, Betty. "Long-Term Follow-Up of Bereaved Siblings." In *The Dying and the Bereaved Teenager*, edited by John D. Morgan, pp. 78–89. Philadelphia: Charles Press, 1990.

Dyregrov, Atle. *Grief in Children: A Handbook for Adults.* Bristol, PA: Taylor & Francis, 1991.

Fitzgerald, Helen. *The Grieving Child: A Parent's Guide.* New York: Simon & Schuster, 1992.

Furman, Erna. *A Child's Parent Dies: Studies in Childhood Bereavement.* New Haven: Yale Univ. Press, 1974.

Gaes, Jason. *My Book for Kids with Cancer.* Aberdeen, SD: Melius & Peterson, 1987.

Gaffney, Donna A. *The Seasons of Grief: Helping Children Grow Through Loss.* New York: Plume, 1988.

Gliko-Braden, Majel. *Grief Comes to Class: A Teacher's Guide.* Omaha: Centering Corp., 1992.

Goldman, Linda. *Life and Loss: A Guide to Help Grieving Children.* Muncie, IN: Accelerated Development, 1994.

Gootman, Marilyn E. *When a Friend Dies: A Book for Teens About Grieving and Healing.* Minneapolis: Free Spirit, 1994.

Gordon, Audrey K., and Dennis Klass. *They Need to Know: How to Teach Children About Death.* Englewood Cliffs, NJ: Prentice-Hall, 1979.

Gordon, Sol. *When Living Hurts.* New York: Dell, 1988.

Gottlieb, Shapiro. *A Parent's Guide to Childhood and Adolescent Depression.* New York: Bantam Doubleday, 1994.

Gravelle, Karen, and Charles Haskins. *Teenagers Face to Face with Bereavement.* Englewood Cliffs, NJ: Messner, 1989.

Grollman, Earl A. *Explaining Death to Children.* Boston: Beacon Press, 1981.

Grollman, Earl A. *Straight Talk About Death for Teenagers: How to Cope with Losing Someone You Love.* Boston: Beacon Press, 1993.

Grollman, Earl A. *Talking About Death: A Dialogue Between Parent and Child.* Boston: Beacon Press, 1990.

Grollman, Earl A., ed. *Bereaved Children and Teens: A Support Guide for Parents and Professionals.* Boston: Beacon Press, 1995.

Gullo, Stephen V., and others, eds. *Death and Children: A Guide for Educators, Parents, and Caregivers.* New York: Tappan Press, 1985.

Hartnett, Johnette. *Children and Grief: Big Issues for Little Hearts.* Good Mourning, 1993. P.O. Box 9355, South Burlington, VT 05407-9355.

Huntley, Theresa. *Helping Children Grieve: When Someone They Love Dies.* Minneapolis: Augsburg Fortress, 1991.

Jewett, Claudia L. *Helping Children Cope with Separation and Loss.* Boston: Harvard Common Press, 1982.

Kolehmainen, Janet, and Sandra Handwerk. *Teen Suicide: A Book for Friends, Family, and Classmates.* Minneapolis: Lerner, 1986.

Kolf, June Cerza. *Teenagers Talk About Grief.* Grand Rapids, MI: Baker Books, 1990.

Kübler-Ross, Elisabeth. *On Children and Death.* New York: Macmillan, 1983.

LaTour, Kathy. *For Those Who Live: Helping Children Cope with the Death of a Brother or Sister.* Omaha: Centering Corp., 1983.

Linn, Erin. *Children Are Not Paper Dolls: A Visit with Bereaved Siblings.* Incline Village, NV: Publisher's Mark, 1982.

Lombardo, Victor S., and Edith Foran Lombardo. *Kids Grieve Too!* Springfield, IL: Thomas, 1986.

Lonetto, R. *Children's Conceptions of Death.* New York: Springer, 1980.

Lord, Janice Harris. *Death at School: A Guide for Teachers, School Nurses, Counselors, and Administrators.* Dallas: MADD, 1990.

Metzgar, Margaret. *Little Ears, Big Issues: Children and Loss.* Transition and Loss Center, 1991. 11301 Fifth Avenue NE, Seattle, WA 98125.

Morgan, John D., ed. *The Dying and the Bereaved Teenager.* Philadelphia: Charles Press, 1990.

Morgan, John D., ed. *Suicide: Helping Those at Risk.* King's College, 1987. 266 Epworth Avenue, London, Ontario, Canada N6A 2M3.

Orbach, Israel. *Children Who Don't Want to Live.* San Francisco: Jossey-Bass, 1988.

Papadatu, Danai, and Costas Papadatos, eds. *Children and Death.* New York: Hemisphere, 1991.

Peck, Michael L., Norman L. Farberow, and Robert E. Litman, eds. *Youth Suicide.* New York: Springer, 1985.

Richter, Elizabeth. *Losing Someone You Love: When a Brother or Sister Dies.* New York: Putnam, 1986.

Rickgarn, Ralph L. V. *Perspectives on College Student Suicide.* Amityville, NY: Baywood, 1994.

Rofes, Eric E., ed. *The Kids' Book About Death and Dying, by and for Kids.* Boston: Little, Brown, 1985.

Romond, Janis Loomis. *Children Facing Grief.* St. Meinrad, IN: Abbey, 1989.

Schaefer, Dan, and Christine Lyons. *How Do We Tell the Children? A Step-by-Step Guide for Helping Children Two to Teen Cope When Someone Dies.* New York: Newmarket Press, 1993.

Schliefer, Jan. *Everything You Need to Know About Teen Suicide.* NY: Rosen Publications, 1988.

Schowalter, John E., and others, eds. *The Child and Death.* New York: Columbia Univ. Press, 1983.

Schowalter, John E., and others, eds. *Children and Death: Perspectives from Birth Through Adolescence.* New York: Praeger, 1987.

Schulz, Charles M. *Why, Charlie Brown, Why? A Story About What Happens When a Friend Is Very Ill.* New York: Topper Books, 1990.

Scrivani, Mark. *When Death Walks In.* Omaha: Centering Corp., 1991.

Slaby, Andrew, and Frank Garfinkel. *No-One Saw My Pain: Why Teens Kill Themselves.* New York: Norton, 1994

Smith, Judy, and Diane Ryerson. *School Suicide Prevention Guidelines.* Washington, DC: American Association of Suicidology, 1999.

Stevenson, Robert G. *What Will We Do? Preparing a School Community to Cope with Crises.* Amityville, NY: Baywood, 1994.

Stillwell, Elaine. *A Forever Angel.* Omaha: Centering Corp., 2000.

Stillwell, Elaine. *Forever Angels.* Omaha: Centering Corp., 2000.

Stillwell, Elaine. *Sweet Memories: For Children and Adults to Create Healing and Loving Memories for Holidays and Other Special Days.* Omaha: Centering Corp., 1998.

Traisman, Enid Samuel. *Fire in My Heart, Ice in My Veins.* Omaha: Centering Corp., 1992.

Vogel, Linda Jane. *Helping a Child Understand Death.* Philadelphia: Fortress Press, 1975.

Wass, Hannelore, and Charles A. Corr. *Childhood and Death.* Washington, DC: Hemisphere, 1984.

Wass, Hannelore, and Charles A. Corr. *Helping Children Cope with Death: Guidelines and Resources.* Washington, DC: Hemisphere, 1984.

Webb, Nancy Boyd. *Helping Bereaved Children: A Handbook for Practitioners.* New York: Guilford Press, 1993.

Wolfelt, Alan D. *A Child's View of Grief: A Guide for Caring Adults.* Service Corporation International, 1990. (Video also available.)

Wolfelt, Alan D. *Helping Children Cope with Grief.* Muncie, IN: Accelerated Development, 1983.

Christian/Religious

Anthony, Nancy. *Mourning Thoughts: Facing a New Day After the Death of a Spouse.* Mystic, CT: Twenty-Third Publications, 1991.

Branch, Roger G., and Larry A. Platt, eds. *Resources for Ministry in Death and Dying.* Nashville, TN: Breadman Press, 1988.

Cox, Gerry R., and Ronald J. Fundis, eds. *Spiritual, Ethical, and Pastoral Aspects of Death and Bereavement.* Amityville, NY: Baywood, 1992.

Curry, Cathleen L. *When Your Parent Dies: A Concise and Practical Source of Help and Advice for Adults Grieving the Death of a Parent.* Notre Dame, IN: Ave Maria Press, 1993.

Curry, Cathleen L. *When Your Spouse Dies: A Concise and Practical Source of Help and Advice.* Notre Dame, IN: Ave Maria Press, 1990.

Dobihal, Edward F., Jr., and Charles W. Stewart. *When a Friend Is Dying: A Guide to Caring for the Terminally Ill.* Nashville, TN: Abingdon Press, 1984.

Guntzelman, Joan. *Blessed Grieving: Reflections on Life's Losses.* Winona, MN: St. Mary's Press, 1994.

Hewitt, John H. *After Suicide.* Louisville, KY: Westminster/John Knox Press, 1980.

Johnson, Christopher Jay, and Marsha G. McGee, eds. *How Different Religions View Death and Afterlife.* Philadelphia: Charles Press, 1991.

McCurley, Foster R. *Making Sense Out of Sorrow: A Journey of Faith.* Valley Forge, PA: Trinity Press International, 1995.

Meyers, Charles. *Surviving Death: A Practical Guide to Caring for the Dying and Bereaved.* Mystic, CT: Twenty-Third Publications, 1988.

Pregent, Carol. *When a Child Dies.* Notre Dame, IN: Ave Maria Press, 1992.

Rupp, Joyce. *Praying Our Goodbyes.* Notre Dame, IN: Ave Maria Press, 1988.

Schmitt, Abraham. *Turn Again to Life: Growing Through Grief.* Scottsdale, PA: Herald Press, 1987.

Sullender, R. S. *Grief and Growth: Pastoral Resources for Emotional and Spiritual Growth.* New York: Paulist Press, 1985.

Tengbom, Mildred. *Grief for a Season.* Minneapolis: Bethany House, 1989.

Tengbom, Mildred. *Help for Bereaved Parents.* St. Louis: Concordia, 1981.

Tengbom, Mildred. *Help for the Terminally Ill.* St. Louis: Concordia, 1983.

Todd, Peter B. *AIDS, a Pilgrimage to Healing: A Guide for Health Professionals, Clergy, Educators, and Caregivers.* Newtown, Australia: Millennium Books, 1992. (Distributed by Morehouse Publishing, Harrisburg, PA.)

Wiitala, Geri Colozzi. *Don't Let Them Persecute You: Refuting the Fundamentalist Mentality.* Charleston, RI, 1998. Telephone: 401.364.7435.

Wolfelt, Alan D. *Death and Grief: A Guide for Clergy.* Levittown, PA: Accelerated Development, 1988.

Adult Bereavement

General

Aiken, Lewis R. *Dying, Death, and Bereavement.* Boston: Allyn & Bacon, 1990.

Allen, Marvin, with Jo Robinson. *Angry Men, Passive Men: Understanding the Roots of Men's Anger and How to Move Beyond It.* New York: Fawcett Columbine, 1993.

Arterburn, Stephen. *Hand Me Down Genes and Second-Hand Emotions.* New York: Simon & Schuster, 1994.

Ascher, Barbara Lazear. *Landscape Without Gravity: A Memoir of Grief.* New York: Penguin Books, 1994.

Attig, Thomas W. *How We Grieve: Relearning the Old.* New York: Oxford Univ. Press, 1996.

Baldwin, Christina. *Life's Companion: Journal Writing as a Spiritual Quest.* New York: Bantam Books, 1991.

Baures, Mary. *Undaunted Spirits: Portraits of Recovery from Severe Emotional Trauma.* Philadelphia: Charles Press, 1994.

Berkus, Rusty. *To Heal Again: Toward Serenity and the Resolution of Grief.* Los Angeles: Red Rose Press, 1984.

Biebel, David B. *If God Is So Good Why Do I Hurt So Bad?* New York: Navpress, 1989.

Bouvard, Marguerite. *The Path Through Grief: A Practical Guide.* Portland, OR: Breitenbush Books, 1988.

Bowlby, John. *Attachment and Loss, Vol. 1: Attachment.* New York: Basic Books, 1982.

Bowlby, John. *Attachment and Loss, Vol. 3: Loss Sadness and Depression.* New York: Basic Books, 1980.

Bozarth, Alla Renee. *A Journey Through Grief: Gentle Specific Help to Get You Through the Most Difficult Stages of Grief.* Minneapolis: CompCare, 1990.

Bozarth-Campbeil, Alla. *Life Is Goodbye, Life Is Hello: Grieving Well Through All Kinds of Loss.* Minneapolis: CompCare, 1982.

Brammer, Lawrence M. *How to Cope with Life Transitions: The Challenge of Personal Change.* New York: Hemisphere, 1991.

Brener, Anne. *Mourning and Mitzvah: A Guided Journal for Walking the Mourner's Path Through Grief to Healing.* Woodstock, VT: Jewish Lights Publishing, 1993.

Brooks, Anne M. *The Grieving Time: A Month by Month Account of Recovery from Loss.* Wilmington, DE: Delapeake, 1982.

Buckingham, Robert W., and Sandra K. Huggard. *Coping with Grief.* New York: Rosen Group, 1991.

Caplan, Sandi, and Gordon Lang. *Grief's Courageous Journey.* Oakland, CA: New Harbinger, 1995.

Center for Help in Times of Loss Staff and Deborah Roth. *Stepping Stones to Grief Recovery.* New York: Borgo Press, 1988.

Childs-Gowell, Elaine. *Good Grief Rituals: Tools for Healing.* Banytown, NY: Station Hill Press, 1992.

Clark, Karen Raiser. *Life Is Change, Growth Is Optional.* St. Paul, MN: Center for Executive Planning, 1993.

Cleiren, Marc. *Bereavement and Adaptation: A Comparative Study of the Aftermath of Death.* Bristol, PA: Taylor & Francis, 1993.

Cochran, Larry, and Emily Claspell. *The Meaning of Grief.* New York: Greenwood, 1987.

Corless, Inge B., Barbara B. Gennino, and Mary Pittman, eds. *A Challenge for Living: Dying, Death, and Bereavement.* Boston: Jones & Bartlett, 1995.

Cornils, Stanley P. *The Mourning After: How to Manage Grief Wisely.* Saratoga, CA: R&E, 1990.

Corr, Charles A., Clyde M. Nabe, and Donna M. Con. *Death and Dying, Life and Living.* Pacific Grove, CA: Brooks/Cole, 1994.

Counts, David R., and Dorothy A. Counts. *Coping with the Final Tragedy: Cultural Variation in Dying and Grieving.* Amityville, NY: Baywood, 1991.

Cousins, Norman. *Anatomy of an Illness as Perceived by the Patient: Reflections on Healing and Regeneration.* New York: Norton, 1979.

Davidson, Glen W. *Understanding Mourning: A Guide for Those Who Grieve.* Minneapolis: Augsburg Press, 1984.

Davies, Phyllis. *Grief: Climb Toward Understanding—Self-Help When You Are Struggling.* San Luis Obispo, CA: Sunnybank, 1988.

DeBellis, Robert, and others, eds. *Suffering the Psychological and Social Aspects in Loss, Grief, and Care.* New York: Hayworth Press, 1986.

DiGiulio, Robert C. *After Loss.* Waco, TX: WRS Group, 1993.

Doka, Kenneth J. *Disenfranchised Grief: Recognizing Hidden Sorrow.* Lexington, MA: Lexington Books, 1989.

Doka, Kenneth J., ed. *Living with Grief After Loss.* Washington, DC: Hospice Foundation of America, 1986.

Donnelly, Katherine Fair. *Recovering from the Loss of a Sibling.* New York: Dodd, 1988.

Dossey, Larry. *Reinventing Medicine: Beyond Mind-Body to a New Era of Healing.* San Francisco: HarperSanFrancisco, 1999.

Dyer, Wayne W. *Happy Holidays! Uplifting Advice About How to Avoid Holiday Blues and Recapture the True Spirit of Christmas, Hanukkah, and New Year's.* New York: Merrow, 1986.

Engram, Sara. *Mortal Matters: When a Loved One Dies.* Kansas City, MO: Andrews & McMeel, 1990.

Ericsson, Stephanie. *Companion Through the Darkness: Inner Dialogues on Grief.* New York: Harper Perennial, 1993.

Erikson, Erik H. *Identity: Youth and Crisis.* New York: Norton, 1968.

Farnsworth, Elizabeth. *Journey Through Grief.* Atlanta: Susan Hunter Publishing, 1988.

Feinstein, David, and Peg Elliott Mayo. *Mortal Acts: Eighteen Empowering Rituals for Confronting Death.* San Francisco: HarperSanFrancisco, 1993.

Feinstein, David, and Peg Elliott Mayo. *Rituals for Living and Dying: From Life's Wounds to Spiritual Awakening.* San Francisco: HarperSanFrancisco, 1990.

Felder, Leonard. *When a Loved One Is Ill: How to Take Better Care of Your Loved One, Your Family, and Yourself.* New York: New American Library, 1990.

Finn, William F., and others, eds. *Women and Loss: Psychobiological Perspectives.* New York: Praeger, 1985.

Fitzgerald, Helen. *The Mourning Handbook.* New York: Simon & Schuster, 1994.

Fulghum, Robert. *From Beginning to End: The Rituals of Our Lives.* New York: Villard, 1995.

Gibran, Kahlil. *The Prophet.* New York: Knopf, 1973.

Glick, Ira P., Robert S. Weiss, and C. Murray Parkes. *The First Year of Bereavement.* New York: Wiley, 1974.

Golden, Thomas R., and James Miller. *When a Man Faces Grief.* Fort Wayne, IN: Willowgreen, 1998.

Goleman, Daniel, ed. *Healing Emotions: Conversations with the Dalai Lama on Mindfulness, Emotions, and Health.* New York: Random House, 1999.

Goulding, Mary McClure. *A Time to Say Goodbye: Moving Beyond Loss.* Watsonville, CA: Papier-Mache Press, 1996.

Grollman, Earl A. *Living When a Loved One Has Died.* Boston: Beacon Press, 1987.

Grollman, Earl A. *Time Remembered: A Journal for Survivors.* Boston: Beacon Press, 1987.

Grollman, Earl A., ed. *What Helped Me When My Loved One Died.* Boston: Beacon Press, 1981.

Hafen, Brent Q. *Faces of Death: Grief, Dying, Euthanasia, Suicide.* Denver: Morton, 1983.

Harricharan, John. *Morning Had Been All Night Coming.* New York: Berkley, 1991.

Hartnett, Johnette. *The Funeral, an Endangered Tradition: Making Sense of the Final Farewell.* Good Mourning, 1993. P.O. Box 9355, South Burlington, VT 05407-9355.

Hartnett, Johnette. *Grief in the Workplace: Forty Hours Plus Overtime.* Good Mourning, 1993. P.O. Box 9355, South Burlington, VT 05407-9355.

Harwell, Amy. *Ready to Live, Prepared to Die: A Provocative Guide to the Rest of Your Life.* Wheaten, IL: H. Shaw, 1995.

Heegaard, Marge. *When Someone Very Special Dies.* Omaha: Centering Corp., 1988.

Heegaard, Marge Eaten. *Coping with Death and Grief.* Minneapolis: Lerner, 1990.

Irish, Donald P., Kathleen F. Lundquist, and Vivian Jenkins Nelsen, eds. *Ethnic Variations in Dying, Death, and Grief: Diversity in Universality.* Washington, DC: Taylor & Francis, 1993.

Jackson, Edgar N. *The Many Faces of Grief.* Nashville, TN: Abingdon Press, 1977.

Jacobsen, Gail B. *Write Grief: How to Transform Loss with Writing.* McCormick & Schilling, 1990. P.O. Box 722, Menomonee Falls, WI 53052.

Jaffe, Hirshel, James Rudin, and Marcia Rudin. *Why Me? Why Anyone?* New York: St. Martin's Press, 1986.

James, John W., and Frank Cherry. *The Grief Recovery Handbook: A Step-by-Step Program for Moving Beyond Loss.* New York: HarperCollins, 1988.

Jensen, Amy Hillyard. *Healing Grief.* Medic Publishing, 1995. P.O. Box 89, Redmond, WA 98073.

Johnson, Elizabeth A. *As Someone Dies: A Handbook for the Living.* Santa Monica, CA: Hay House, 1987.

Kabat-Zinn, Jon. *Full Catastrophe Living: Using the Wisdom of Your Body and Mind to Face Stress, Pain, and Illness.* New York: Delacorte Press, 1990.

Kalish, Richard A. *Death, Grief, and Caring Relationships.* Monterey, CA: Brooks/Cole, 1985.

Kalish, Richard A., ed. *Midlife Loss: Coping Strategies.* Newbury Park, CA: Sage, 1989.

Klein, Allen. *The Healing Power of Humor: Techniques for Getting Through Loss, Setbacks, Upsets, Disappointments, Difficulties, Trials, Tribulations, and All That Not-So-Funny Stuff.* Los Angeles: Tarcher, 1989.

Kolf, June Cerza. *When Will I Stop Hurting: Dealing with a Recent Death.* Grand Rapids, MI: Baker Books, 1987.

Krauss, Pesach, and Monie Goldfischer. *Why Me? Coping with Grief, Loss and Change.* New York: Bantam Books, 1988.

Kreis, Bernadine, and Alice Pattie. *Up from Grief: Patterns of Recovery.* San Francisco: Harper & Row, 1985.

Kübler-Ross, Elisabeth. *Living with Death and Dying.* New York: Macmillan, 1982.

Kübler-Ross, Elisabeth. *On Life After Death.* Berkeley, CA: Celestial Arts, 1991.

Kübler-Ross, Elisabeth. *Working It Through.* New York: Macmillan, 1982.

Kushner, Harold S. *When Bad Things Happen to Good People.* New York: Schocken Books, 1989.

Kushner, Harold S. *Who Needs God?* New York: Pocket Books, 1989.

Kutscher, Austin H., and others, eds. *For the Bereaved: The Road to Recovery.* Philadelphia: Charles Press, 1990.

LaGrand, Louis E. *Coping with Separation and Loss as a Young Adult: Theoretical and Practical Realities.* Springfield, IL: Thomas, 1986.

Leick, Nini, and Marianne Davidsen-Nielsen. *Healing Pain: Attachment, Loss, and Grief Therapy.* New York: Routledge, 1991.

Leming, Michael R., and George E. Dickinson. *Understanding Dying, Death, and Bereavement.* Fort Worth: Holt, Rinehart & Winston, 1990.

Levang, Elizabeth, and Sherokee Ilse. *Remembering with Love: Messages of Hope for the First Year.* Minneapolis: Deaconess Press, 1993.

Levin, Rhoda F. *Heartmates: A Survival Guide for the Cardiac Spouse.* New York: Prentice-Hall, 1987.

Levine, Stephen. *Healing into Life and Death.* Garden City, NY: Anchor Press/Doubleday, 1987.

Levine, Stephen. *Meetings at the Edge: Dialogues with the Grieving and the Dying, the Healing and the Healed.* Garden City, NY: Anchor Press, 1984.

Levine, Stephen. *Who Dies? An Investigation of Conscious Living and Conscious Dying.* Garden City, NY: Anchor Press/Doubleday, 1982.

Lighter, Candy, and Nancy Hathaway. *Giving Sorrow Words: How to Cope with Grief and Get On with Your Life.* New York: Warner, 1990.

Lynch, James J. *The Broken Heart: The Medical Consequences of Loneliness.* New York: Basic Books, 1977.

Manning, Doug. *Don't Take My Grief Away: What to Do When You Lose a Loved One.* San Francisco: Harper & Row, 1984.

Martin, Terry L., and Kenneth J. Doka. *Men Don't Cry . . . Women Do: Transcending Gender Stereotypes of Grief.* Philadelphia: Brunner/Mazel, 2000.

McGaa, Ed. *Mother Earth Spirituality: Native American Paths to Healing Ourselves and Our World.* San Francisco: HarperSanFrancisco, 1990.

Menten, Ted. *After Goodbye: How to Begin Again After the Death of Someone You Love.* Philadelphia: Running Press, 1994.

Menten, Ted. *Gentle Closings: How to Say Goodbye to Someone You Love.* Philadelphia: Running Press, 1992.

Miller, William A. *When Going to Pieces Holds You Together.* Minneapolis: Augsburg Press, 1976.

Morse, Don. *Searching for Eternity.* Memphis: Eagle Wing Books, 2000.

Moyers, Bill. *Healing and the Mind.* New York: Doubleday, 1993.

National Directory of Bereavement Support Groups and Services. ADM Publishing. (544 pages; $34.95; ISBN 0-9645608-8-7.)

Neeld, Elizabeth Harper. *Seven Choices: Taking the Steps to New Life After Losing Someone You Love.* New York: Clarkson N. Potter, 1990.

Neimeyer, Robert. *Lessons of Loss: A Guide to Coping.* Philadelphia: Brunner Routledge, 2001.

O'Connor, Nancy. *Letting Go with Love: The Grieving Process.* Tucson: La Mariposa Press, 1984.

Osmont, Kelly. *More Than Surviving: Caring for Yourself While You Grieve.* Portland, OR: Nobility Press, 1990.

Osmont, Kelly, and Marilyn McFarlane. *Parting Is Not Goodbye: Coping with Grief in Creative, Healthy Ways.* Portland, OR: Nobility Press, 1986.

O'Toole, Donna. *Healing and Growing Through Grief.* Burnsville, NC: Rainbow Connection, 1987.

Page, Pat. *Sad Ain't Forever.* Colorado Springs: Bereavement Publishing, 1999.

Panuthos, Claudia, and Catherine Romeo. *Ended Beginnings.* Hadley, MA: Bergin & Garvey, 1984.

Parkes, Colin Murray. *Bereavement: Studies of Grief in Adult Life.* Madison, CT: International Universities Press, 1987.

Parkes, Colin Murray, and Robert S. Weiss. *Recovery from Bereavement.* New York: Basic Books, 1983.

Peacock, Valerie S. *A Family Heritage Workbook.* Scribe Write Books, 1980. Box 9263, Missoula, MT 59807.

Platt, Larry A., and V. Richard Perseco. *Grief in Cross-Cultural Perspective: A Casebook.* New York: Garland, 1992.

Price, Eugenia. *Getting Through the Night: Finding Your Way After the Loss of a Loved One.* New York: Dial Press, 1982.

Rando, Therese A. *Clinical Dimensions of Anticipatory Mourning.* Champaign, IL: Research Press, 2000.

Rando, Therese A. *Grieving: How to Go On Living When Someone You Love Dies.* New York: Lexington Books, 1988.

Rando, Therese A., ed. *Loss and Anticipatory Grief.* Lexington, MA: Lexington Books, 1986.

Raphael, Beverly. *The Anatomy of Bereavement.* New York: Basic Books, 1983.

Revueltas, Jose. *Human Mourning.* Minneapolis: Univ. of Minnesota Press, 1990.

Rico, Gabriele L. *Pain and Possibilities: Writing Your Way Through Personal Crisis.* Los Angeles: Tarcher, 1991.

Rosenblatt, Paul C. *Bitter, Bitter Tears: Nineteenth-Century Diarists and Twentieth-Century Grief Theories.* Minneapolis: Univ. of Minnesota Press, 1983.

Rosenblatt, Paul C., Patricia R. Aralsh, and Douglas A. Jackson. *Grief and Mourning in Cross Cultural Perspective.* New Haven, CT: Human Relations Area Files Press, 1976.

Samarel, Nelda. *Caring for Life and Death.* Bristol, PA: Taylor & Francis, 1991.

Sanders, Catherine M. *Grief: The Mourning After, Dealing with Adult Bereavement.* New York: Wiley, 1989.

Sanders, Catherine M. *Surviving Grief and Learning to Live Again.* New York: Wiley, 1992.

Schiff, Harriet Sarnoff. *Living Through Mourning: Finding Comfort and Hope When a Loved One Has Died.* New York: Viking Penguin, 1987.

Schneider, John M. *Finding My Way: Healing and Transformation Through Loss and Grief.* Seasons Press, 1994. 2707 Old Mission Road, Traverse City, MI 49686.

Schneider, John M. *Stress, Loss and Grief: Understanding Their Origins and Growth Potential.* Baltimore: University Park Press, 1984.

Schuller, Robert H. *Tough Times Never Last, but Tough People Do!* New York: Bantam Books, 1983.

Selder, Florence. *Enduring Grief: Intimate Stories of Loss.* Philadelphia: Charles Press, 1994.

Selye, Hans. *Stress Without Distress.* New York: Signet Books, 1974.

Shapiro, Ester R. *Grief as a Family Process: A Developmental Approach to Clinical Practice.* New York: Guilford Press, 1994.

Siegel, Bernie S. *Love, Medicine, and Miracles.* New York: Harper & Row, 1986.

Siegel, Bernie S. *Peace, Love and Healing: Body/Mind Communication and the Path to Self-Healing.* New York: HarperCollins, 1989.

Silverman, Phyllis R. *Mutual Help Groups: Organization and Development.* Beverly Hills, CA: Sage, 1980.

Sims, Darcie. *Why Are the Casseroles Always Tuna? A Loving Look at the Lighter Side of Grief.* Carmel, IN: Bereavement Publishing, 1990.

Sittser, Gerald. *A Grace Disguised: How the Soul Grows Through Loss.* Grand Rapids, MI: Zondervan, 1996.

Slaikeu, Karl A., and Steve Lawhead. *Up from the Ashes: How to Survive and Grow Through Personal Crisis.* Grand Rapids, MI: Zondervan, 1990.

Somé, Malidoma Patrice. *Of Water and the Spirit.* New York: Putnam, 1994.

Spies, Karen. *Everything You Need to Know About Grieving.* New York: Rosen Group, 1990.

Staudacher, Carol. *Beyond Grief: A Guide for Recovering from the Death of a Loved One.* Oakland, CA: New Harbinger, 1987.

Staudacher, Carol. *Men and Grief: A Guide for Men Surviving the Death of a Loved One; a Resource for Caregivers and Mental Health Professionals.* Oakland, CA: New Harbinger, 1991.

Stearns, Ann Kaiser. *Coming Back: Rebuilding Lives After Crisis and Loss.* New York: Ballantine/Random House, 1988.

Stearns, Ann Kaiser. *Living Through Personal Crisis.* Chicago: Thomas More Press, 1984.

Stephenson, John S. *Death, Grief, and Mourning: Individual and Social Realities.* New York: Free Press, 1985.

Stillion, Judith M. *Death and the Sexes: A Differential Examination of Longevity, Attitudes, Behaviors and Coping Skills.* New York: Hemisphere, 1985.

Stroebe, Margaret, Wolfgang Stroebe, and Robert O. Hansson, eds. *Handbook of Bereavement: Theory, Research, and Intervention.* New York: Cambridge Univ. Press, 1999.

Strommen, Merton P., and A. Irene Strommen. *Five Cries of Grief.* San Francisco: HarperSanFrancisco, 1993.

Tagliaferre, Lewis, and Oary L. Harbaugh. *Recovery from Loss: A Personalized Guide to the Grieving Process.* Deerfield Beach, FL: Health Communications, 1990.

Tatelbaum, Judy. *The Courage to Grieve: Creative Living, Recovery, and Growth Through Grief.* New York: Harper & Row, 1980.

Tatelbaum, Judy. *You Don't Have to Suffer: A Handbook for Moving Beyond Life's Crises.* New York: HarperCollins, 1989.

Temes, Roberta. *The Empty Place.* New York: Irvington, 1985.

Vajentic, Annakathryn, and Nancy Newer. *Remembering: Explaining Organ and Tissue Donation—Loss, Grief, and Hope.* LIFEBANC, 1993. 20600 Chagrin Boulevard, Suite 350, Cleveland, OH 44122-5343. (Two versions: Adult and Children's.)

Viorst, Judith. *Necessary Losses.* New York: Simon & Schuster, 1986.

Walsh, Froma, and Monica McGoldrick. *Living Beyond Loss: Death in the Family.* New York: Norton, 1991.

Weenolsen, Patricia. *Transcendence of Loss over the Life Span.* New York: Hemisphere, 1988.

Weisman, Avery D. *The Coping Capacity: On the Nature of Being Mortal.* New York: Human Sciences Press, 1984.

Weiss, Brian. *Messages from the Masters: Tapping into the Power of Love.* New York: Warner Books, 2000.

Weitznan, A. G., and others, eds. *Coping with Dying, Death, and Bereavement.* New York: Foundation of Thanatology, 1992.

Welshons, John. *Awakening from Grief: Finding the Road Back to Joy.* Little Falls, NJ: Open Heart, 2000.

Westberg, Granger. *Good Grief.* Philadelphia: Fortress Press, 1971.

Wolfelt, Alan D. *Understanding Grief: Helping Yourself Heal.* Muncie, IN: Accelerated Development, 1992.

Zada, Dan, with Maria Woodard. *Forever Remembered.* Seattle: Com-Pen-Di-Um, 1999.

AIDS

Buckingham, Robert W. *Among Friends: Hospice Care for the Person with AIDS.* Buffalo, NY: Prometheus Books, 1992.

Callen, Michael. *Surviving AIDS.* New York: HarperCollins, 1990.

Donnelly, Katherine Fair. *Recovering from the Loss of a Loved One to AIDS.* New York: St. Martin's, 1994.

Fortunato, John E. *AIDS: The Spiritual Dilemma.* San Francisco: Perennial Library, 1987.

Froman, Paul Kent. *After You Say Goodbye: When Someone You Love Dies of AIDS.* San Francisco: Chronicle Books, 1992.

Kirkpatrick, Bill. *AIDS, Sharing the Pain: A Guide for Caregivers.* Pilgrim Press, 1990. 700 Prospect Avenue, Cleveland, OH 44115-1100.

Martelii, Leonard J., with Fran D. Peltz and William Messina. *When Someone You Know Has AIDS: A Practical Guide.* New York: Crown, 1987.

Moffate, Betty Clare. *When Someone You Love Has AIDS: A Book of Hope for Family and Friends.* Santa Monica, CA: IBS Press in association with Love Heals, 1986.

Pohl, Mel, Kay Deniston, and Doug Toft. *The Caregivers' Journey: When You Love Someone with AIDS.* New York: HarperCollins, 1991.

Richardson, Diane. *Women and AIDS.* New York: Routledge, 1988.

Seligson, M. Ross, and Karen E. Peterson, eds. *AIDS Prevention and Treatment: Hope, Humor, and Healing.* New York: Hemisphere, 1992.

Selwyn, Peter. *Surviving the Fall: The Personal Journey of an AIDS Doctor.* New Haven: Yale Univ. Press, 1998.

Todd, Peter B. *AIDS, a Pilgrimage to Healing: A Guide for Health Professionals, Clergy, Educators, and Caregivers.* Newtown, Australia: Millennium Books, 1992. (Distributed by Morehouse Publishing, Harrisburg, PA.)

Cancer and Other Illnesses

Anderson, Greg. *The Cancer Conqueror: An Incredible Journey to Wellness.* Kansas City, MO: Andrews & McMeel, 1988.

Blitzer, Andrew. *Communicating with Cancer Patients and Their Families.* Philadelphia: Charles Press, 1990.

Doka, Kenneth J. *Living with Life Threatening Illness: A Guide for Patients, Their Families, and Caregivers.* New York: Lexington Books, 1993.

Harwell, Amy, with Kristine Tomasik. *When Your Friend Gets Cancer: How You Can Help.* Wheaten, IL: H. Shaw, 1987.

Jevne, Ronna Jay, and Alexander Levitan. *No Time for Nonsense: Self-Help for the Seriously Ill.* San Diego: Lura Media, 1989.

Caregiving and Support

American Association of Retired Persons. *If Only I Knew What to Say or Do: Ways of Helping a Friend in Crisis.* Washington, DC: AARP, 1989.

Bright, Ruth. *Grieving: A Hand Book for Those Who Care.* St. Louis: MMB Music, 1986.

Bryant, Richard A., and Harvey Allison. *Acute Stress Disorder: A Handbook of Theory, Assessment, and Treatment.* New York: American Psychological Association, 1999.

Buckman, Robert. *I Don't Know What to Say: How to Help and Support Someone Who Is Dying.* New York: Vintage Books, 1992.

Callanan, Maggie, and Patricia Kelly. *Final Gifts: Understanding the Special Awareness, Needs, and Communications of the Dying.* New York: Poseidon Press, 1992.

Callari, Elizabeth S. *A Gentle Death: Personal Caregiving to the Terminally Ill.* Greensboro, NC: Tudor, 1986.

Carter, Rosalynn, with Susan K. Golant. *Helping Yourself Help Others: A Book for Caregivers.* New York: Times Books, 1994.

Cook, Alicia Skinner, and Daniel S. Dworkin. *Helping the Bereaved: Therapeutic Interventions for Children, Adolescents, and Adults.* New York: Basic Books, 1992.

Crenshaw, David A. *Bereavement: Counseling the Grieving Throughout the Life Cycle.* New York: Continuum, 1990.

Eneroth, Carlene Vester. *If There's Anything I Can Do: A Practical Guide for Helping Others Cope with Grief.* Spokane: Marciel, 1990.

Floyd, Maita. *Caretakers: The Forgotten People.* Phoenix: Eskauldun, 1988.

Floyd, Maita. *Platitudes: You Are Not Me.* Phoenix: Eskauldun, 1991.

Hartnett, Johnette. *Death Etiquette for the 90's: What to Do, What to Say.* Good Mourning, 1993. P.O. Box 9355, South Burlington, VT 05407-9355.

Hartnett, Johnette. *Different Losses, Different Issues: What to Expect and How to Help.* Good Mourning, 1993. P.O. Box 9355, South Burlington, VT 05407-9355.

Hayslip, Bert, Jr. *Helping Older Adults Cope with Loss.* Dallas: TLC Group, 1993. P.O. Box 28551, Dallas, TX 75228. Telephone: 214.681.5303.

Hoff, Lee Ann. *People in Crisis: Understanding and Helping.* San Francisco: Jossey-Bass, 1995.

Jackson, Edgar N. *Telling a Child About Death.* New York: Hawthorne Books, 1965.

Kircher, Pamela. *Love Is the Link: A Hospice Doctor Shares Her Experience of Near-Death and Dying.* New York: Larson, 1995.

Kolf, June Cerza. *Comfort and Care for the Critically Ill.* Grand Rapids, MI: Baker Books, 1993.

Larson, Dale G. *The Helper's Journey: Working with People Facing Grief, Loss, and Life-Threatening Illness.* Champaign, IL: Research Press, 1993.

Linn, Erin. *I Know Just How You Feel: Avoiding the Clichés of Grief.* Incline Village, NV: Publisher's Mark, 1986.

Lord, Janice Harris. *Beyond Sympathy: What to Say and Do for Someone Suffering an Injury, Illness or Loss.* Ventura, CA: Pathfinder, 1988.

Manning, Doug. *Comforting Those Who Grieve: A Guide for Helping Others.* San Francisco: Harper & Row, 1985.

Margolis, Otto S., and others, eds. *Acute Grief: Counseling the Bereaved.* New York: Columbia Univ. Press, 1981.

Margolis, Otto S., and others, eds. *Loss, Grief, and Bereavement: A Guide for Counseling.* New York: Praeger, 1985.

Milstein, Linda Breiner. *Giving Comfort: What You Can Do When Someone You Love Is Ill.* New York: Penguin Books, 1994.

Morgan, John D., ed. *Personal Care in an Impersonal World: A Multidimensional Look at Bereavement.* Amityville, NY: Baywood, 1993.

Morrissey, Paul. *Let Someone Hold You: The Journey of a Hospice Priest.* New York: Crossroads, 1994.

Neimeyer, Robert, ed. *Death Anxiety Handbook: Research, Instrumentation, and Application.* Washington, DC: Taylor & Francis, 1994.

Oaks, Judy. *Leaders Guide for Grief Recovery Support Groups.* 2d ed. Center for Personal Recovery, 1994. P.O. Box 125, Berea, KY 40403.

Osmont, Kelly, and Marilyn McFarlane. *What Can I Say? How to Help Someone Who Is Grieving.* Portland, OR: Nobility Press, 1988.

Osterweis, Marian, Fredric Solomon, and Morris Green, eds. *Bereavement: Reactions, Consequences, and Care.* Washington, DC: National Academy Press, 1984.

Pacholski, Richard A. *Re-searching Death: Selected Essays in Death Education and Counseling.* West Hartford, CT: Association for Death Education and Counseling, 1986.

Rando, Therese A. *Treatment of Complicated Mourning.* Champaign, IL: Research Press, 1993.

Ray, M. Catherine. *I'm Here to Help: A Hospice Worker's Guide to Communicating with Dying People and Their Loved Ones.* Mound, MN: McRay, 1992.

Sankar, Andrea. *Dying at Home: A Family Guide for Caregiving.* New York: Johns Hopkins University Press, 1991.

Schoeneck, Therese S. *How to Form Support Groups and Services for Grieving People.* Hope for Bereaved, 1989. 1342 Lancaster Avenue, Syracuse, NY 13210.

Silverman, Phyllis R. *Helping Women Cope with Grief.* Beverly Hills, CA: Sage, 1981.

Staudacher, Carol. *Men and Grief: A Guide for Men Surviving the Death of a Loved One; a Resource for Caregivers and Mental Health Professionals.* Oakland, CA: New Harbinger, 1991.

Strong, Maggie. *Mainstay: For the Well Spouse of the Chronically Ill.* Boston: Little, Brown, 1988.

Sturkie, Joan. *Listening with Love: True Stories from Peer Counseling.* San Jose, CA: Resource, 1987.

Sturkie, Joan, and Valerie Gibson. *The Peer Counselor's Pocket Book.* San Jose, CA: Resource, 1989.

Vachon, Mary L. S. *Occupational Stress in the Care of the Critically Ill, the Dying, and the Bereaved.* Washington, DC: Hemisphere, 1987.

Worden, J. William. *Grief Counseling and Grief Therapy: A Handbook for the Mental Health Practitioner.* New York: Springer, 1991.

Death and Dying

Berger, Arthur, and Joyce Berger. *Fear of the Unknown: Enlightened Aid-in-Dying.* Westport, CT: Praeger, 1995.

Berger, Arthur, and others, eds. *Perspectives on Death and Dying: Cross-Cultural and Multidisciplinary Views.* Philadelphia: Charles Press, 1989.

Bertman, Sandra L. *Facing Death: Images, Insights and Interventions.* Bristol, PA: Hemisphere, 1991.

Carlson, Lisa. *Caring for Your Own Dead.* Hinesburg, VT: Upper Access, 1987.

Carroll, David. *Living with Dying: A Loving Guide for Family and Close Friends.* New York: McGraw-Hill, 1985.

Corr, Charles A., and Richard A. Pacholski, eds. *Death: Completion and Discovery.* West Hartford, CT: Association for Death Education and Counseling, 1987.

Davidson, Glen W. *Living with Dying: A Guide for Relatives and Friends.* Minneapolis: Augsburg Press, 1990.

DeSpelder, Lynne Ann, and Albert Lee Strickland. *The Last Dance: Encountering Death and Dying.* Mountain View, CA: Mayfield, 1992.

DiGiulio, Robert, and Rachel Kranz. *Straight Talk About Death and Dying.* New York: Facts on File, 1995.

Doka, Kenneth J., ed., with John D. Morgan. *Death and Spirituality.* Amityville, NY: Baywood, 1993.

Duda, Deborah. *Coming Home: A Guide to Dying at Home with Dignity.* New York: Aurora Press, 1987.

Fulton, Robert, and Robert Bendiksen, eds. *Death and Identity.* Philadelphia: Charles Press, 1994.

Kalish, Richard A., ed. *Death and Dying: Views from Many Cultures.* Amityville, NY: Baywood, 1980.

Kapleau, Philip. *The Wheel of Life and Death: A Practical and Spiritual Guide.* New York: Anchor Books/Doubleday, 1989.

Kastenbaum, Robert. *Death, Society, and Human Experience.* 5th ed. Boston: Allyn & Bacon, 1995.

Kastenbaum, Robert. *The Psychology of Death.* New York: Springer, 1992.

Kastenbaum, Robert, and Beatrice Kastenbaum. *Encyclopedia of Death.* New York: Avon Books, 1992.

Kearl, Michael. *Endings: A Sociology of Death and Dying.* New York: Oxford Univ. Press, 1989.

Kramer, Kenneth Paul. *The Sacred Art of Dying: How World Religions Understand Death.* New York: Paulist Press, 1988.

Kübler-Ross, Elisabeth. *On Death and Dying.* New York: Macmillan, 1969.

Morgan, Ernest. *Dealing Creatively with Death: A Manual of Death Education and Simple Burial.* Bayside, NY: Zion Communications, 1993.

Oaks, Judy, and Gene Ezell. *Dying and Death: Coping, Caring, Understanding.* Scottsdale, AZ: Gorsuch Scarisbrick, 1993.

Rohr, Janell, ed. *Death and Dying: Opposing Viewpoints.* San Diego: Greenhaven, 1987.

Saynor, John Kennedy. *Dead Is a Four Letter Word.* Ajar, Ontario, Canada: W. L. Smith, 1990.

Shaw, Eva. *What to Do When a Loved One Dies: A Practical Guide to Dealing with Death on Life's Terms.* Irvine, CA: Dickens Press, 1994.

Sheikh, Anees A., ed. *Death Imagery: Confronting Death Brings Us to a New Threshold of Life.* New York: Human Sciences Press/Plenum, 1991.

Shepard, Martin. *Someone You Love Is Dying.* New York: Harmony Books/Random House, 1976.

Wass, Hannelore, and Robert A. Neimeyer, eds. *Dying: Facing the Facts.* Washington, DC: Taylor & Francis, 1994.

Loss of a Child

Allen, Marie, and Shelly Marks. *Miscarriage: Women Sharing from the Heart.* New York: Wiley, 1993.

Bereaved Parents of Boulder County. *We Care.* Boulder, CO: Boulder County Hospice.

Bereaved Parents of Boulder County. *When Your Baby Dies.* Boulder, CO: Boulder County Hospice.

Bernstein, Judith. *When the Bough Breaks: Forever After the Death of a Son or Daughter.* Kansas City, MO: Andrews & McMeel, 1997.

Borg, Susan, and Judith Lasker. *When Pregnancy Fails: Families Coping with Miscarriage, Ectopic Pregnancy, Stillbirth, and Infant Death.* New York: Bantam Books, 1989.

Bramblett, John. *When Good-bye Is Forever: Learning to Live Again After the Loss of a Child.* New York: Ballantine Books, 1991.

Chilstrom, Corinne. *Andrew, You Died Too Soon.* Minneapolis: Augsburg Press, 1993.

Connelly, Maureen. *Given in Love: Releasing a Child for Adoption.* Omaha: Centering Corp., 1990.

Corr, Charles A., and others, eds. *Sudden Infant Death Syndrome: Who Can Help and How.* New York: Springer, 1991.

Crider, Tom. *Give Sorrow Words: A Father's Passage Through Grief.* Chapel Hill, NC: Algonquin Books, 1996.

Crouthamel, Thomas G., Sr. *When the Unthinkable Happens: A Father's Journey Through Grief.* Bradenton, FL: Keystone Press, 1994.

Davidson, Glen W. *Stillbirth, Neonatal Death, and Sudden Infant Death Syndrome.* Washington, DC: Hemisphere, 1984.

Davis, Deborah L. *Empty Cradle, Broken Heart: Surviving the Death of Your Baby.* Golden, CO: Fulcrum, 1991.

DeFrain John. *Sudden Infant Death: Enduring the Loss.* Lexington, MA: Lexington Books, 1991.

DeFrain, John, Leona Martens, Jan Stork, and Warren Stork. *Stillborn: The Invisible Death.* Lexington, MA: Lexington Books, 1986.

DeFrain, John, Jacque Taylor, and Linda Ernst. *Coping with Sudden Infant Death.* Lexington, MA: Lexington Books, 1982.

Delgadillo, David, and Peter Davis. *When the Bough Breaks.* San Diego: Desktop Creations, 1990.

Dick, Harold M., and others, eds. *Dying and Disabled Children: Dealing with Loss and Grief.* New York: Haworth Press, 1988.

Donnelly, Katherine Fair. *Recovering from the Loss of a Child.* New York: Macmillan, 1982.

Edelstein, Linda. *Maternal Bereavement: Coping with the Unexpected Death of a Child.* New York: Praeger, 1984.

Ewy, Donna, and Rodger Ewy. *Death of a Dream: Miscarriage, Stillbirth, and Newborn Loss.* Boulder, CO: Boulder County Hospice; New York: Dutton, 1984.

Fischoff, Joseph, and Noreen O'Brien Brohl. *Before and After My Child Dies.* Detroit: Emmons-Fairfields, 1981.

Fritsch, Julie, with Sherokee Ilse. *The Anguish of Loss: For the Love of Justin.* Wintergreen Press, 1988. 3630 Eileen Street, Long Lake, MN 55359.

Gerner, Margaret H. *For Bereaved Grandparents.* Omaha: Centering Corp., 1990.

Gilbert, Kathleen R., and Laura S. Smart. *Coping with Infant and Fetal Loss.* New York: Brunner Mazel, 1992.

Gustaitis, Rasa, and Emle W. D. Young. *A Time to Be Born, A Time to Die: Conflicts and Ethics in an Intensive Care Nursery.* Reading, MA: Addison-Wesley, 1986.

Huber, Terri. *No Time Out from Grief: Surviving the Death of My Son.* Writers Club Press/iUniverse.com, 2000.

Ilse, Sherokee. *Empty Arms: Coping with Miscarriage, Stillbirth and Infant Death.* Wintergreen Press, 1990. 3630 Eileen Street, Maple Plain, MN 55359.

Ilse, Sherokee. *Precious Lives, Painful Choices: A Prenatal Decision-Making Guide.* Wintergreen Press, 1993. 3630 Eileen Street, Maple Plain, MN 55359.

Ilse, Sherokee. *Single Parent Grief.* Wintergreen Press, 1994. 3630 Eileen Street, Maple Plain, MN 55359.

Ilse, Sherokee, and Linda Hammer Burns. *Miscarriage: A Shattered Dream.* Wintergreen Press, 1985. 3630 Eileen Street, Maple Plain, MN 55359.

Ilse, Sherokee, Linda Hammer Burns, and Susan Erling. *When the Bough Breaks: Sudden Infant Death.* Wintergreen Press, 1985. 3630 Eileen Street, Maple Plain, MN 55359.

Johnson, Joy, and Marvin Johnson. *Fathers Grieve, Too.* Omaha: Centering Corp., 1985.

Johnson, Joy, and Marvin Johnson. *Miscarriage.* Omaha: Centering Corp., 1992.

Johnson, Joy, and others. *Newborn Death: A Book for Parents Experiencing the Death of a Very Small Infant.* Omaha: Centering Corp., 1987.

Johnson, Sherry E. *After a Child Dies: Counseling Bereaved Families.* New York: Springer, 1987.

Klass, Dennis. *Parental Grief: Solace and Resolution.* New York: Springer, 1988.

Klass, Dennis. *The Spiritual Lives of Bereaved Parents.* New York: Springer, 1999.

Knapp, Ronald J. *Beyond Endurance: When a Child Dies.* New York: Schocken, 1986.

Kohn, Ingrid, and Peny-Lynn Moffitt, with Isabelle A. Wilkins. *A Silent Sorrow, Pregnancy Loss: Guidance and Support for You and Your Family.* New York: Delacorte Press, 1993.

Kolf, June Cerza. *Grandma's Tears: Comfort for Grieving Grandparents.* Grand Rapids, MI: Baker Books, 1995.

Leon, Irving G. *When a Baby Dies: Psychotherapy for Pregnancy and Newborn Loss.* New Haven: Yale Univ. Press, 1990.

Limbo, Rana K., and Sam Rich Wheeler, with Susan T. Hessel. *When a Baby Dies: A Handbook for Healing and Helping.* LaCrosse, WI: Resolve Through Sharing Bereavement Services, 1986.

Livingston, Gordon. *Only Spring: On Mourning the Death of My Child.* San Francisco: HarperSanFrancisco, 1995.

Margolis, Otto S., and others, eds. *Grief and the Loss of an Adult Child.* New York: Praeger, 1988.

Munday, John. *Surviving the Death of a Child.* Louisville, KY: Westminster/John Knox Press, 1995.

Musser, Linda. *God Is a Birdwatcher.* Omaha: Centering Corp., 1991. (Parental grief.)

National Sudden Infant Death Syndrome Clearinghouse Staff. *Sudden Infant Death Syndrome (SIDS) and Other Infant Losses Among Adolescent Parents.* McLean, VA: National SIDS Clearinghouse, 1988. (Annotated bibliography and resource guide.)

Nelson, Timothy. *A Father's Story.* A Place to Remember, 1994. 1885 University Avenue #110, St. Paul, MN 55104.

Osgood, Judy, ed. *Meditations for Bereaved Parents.* Sunriver, OR: Gilgal, 1983.

Peppers, Larry G. *How to Go on Living After the Death of a Baby.* Atlanta: Peachtree, 1985.

Peppers, Larry G., and Ronald J. Knapp. *Motherhood and Mourning: Perinatal Death.* New York: Praeger, 1980.

Pine, Vanderlyn R., ed. *Unrecognized and Unsanctioned Grief: The Nature and Counseling of Unacknowledged Loss.* Chicago: Thomas, 1990.

Rando, Therese A., ed. *Parental Loss of a Child.* Champaign, IL: Research Press, 1986.

Sanders, Catherine M. *How to Survive the Loss of a Child: Filling the Emptiness and Rebuilding Your Life.* Rocklin, CA: Prima, 1992.

Schiff, Harriet Sarnoff. *The Bereaved Parent.* New York: Penguin Books, 1978.

Seiden, Othniel J., and M. J. Timmons. *Coping with Miscarriage.* Blue Ridge Summit, PA: Tab Books, 1984.

Snyder, Wendy K. *Sudden Infant Death Syndrome Self-Help Support Groups: An Annotated Bibliography.* McLean, VA: National SIDS Clearinghouse, 1988.

Stillwell, Elaine. *Forever Angels.* Omaha: Centering Corp., 2000.

Stillwell, Elaine. *Sweet Memories: For Children and Adults to Create Healing and Loving Memories for Holidays and Other Special Days.* Omaha: Centering Corp., 1998.

Wolterstorff, Nicholas. *Lament for a Son.* Grand Rapids, MI: Eerdmans, 1987.

Loss of a Parent

Akner, Lois, and Catherine Whitney. *How to Survive the Loss of a Parent: A Guide for Adults.* New York: Morrow, 1993.

Angel, Marc D. *The Orphaned Adult.* New York: Human Sciences Press, 1987.

Arnold, Joan Hagan, and Penelope Buschman Gemma. *A Child Dies: A Portrait of Family Grief.* Philadelphia: Charles Press, 1994.

Bratman, Fred. *Everything You Need to Know When a Parent Dies.* New York: Rosen Group, 1992.

Decker, Roberta. "A Daughter's Response to Her Mother's Death: Write Down Your Feelings." In *That Helped Me When My Loved One Died,* edited by Earl A. Grollman, pp. 99–103. Boston: Beacon Press, 1981.

Donnelly, Katherine Fair. *Recovering from the Loss of a Parent.* New York: Dodd, 1987.

Gire, Ken. *The Gift of Remembrance: The Greatest Legacy a Father Can Leave.* Grand Rapids, MI: Zondervan, 1990.

LeShan, Eda. *Learning to Say Good-bye: When a Parent Dies.* New York: Macmillan, 1976.

Myers, Edward. *When Parents Die: A Guide for Adults.* New York: Viking Penguin, 1986.

Wakerman, Elyce. *Father Loss.* New York: Doubleday, 1984.

Loss of a Spouse or Partner

Caine, Lynn. *Being a Widow.* New York: Arbor House, 1988.

Caine, Lynn. *Widow.* New York: Morrow, 1974.

Campbell, Scott, and Phyllis R. Silverman. *Widower: What Happens When Men Are Left Alone.* New York: Prentice-Hall, 1987.

Colgrove, Melba, Harold H. Bloomfield, and Peter McWilliams. *How to Survive the Loss of a Love.* Boston: G. K. Hall, 1992.

DiGiulio, Robert C. *Beyond Widowhood: From Bereavement to Emergence and Hope.* New York: Free Press, 1989.

Elmer, Lon. *Why Her? Why Now? A Man's Journey Through Love and Death and Grief.* New York: Bantam Books, 1990.

Feinberg, Linda. *I'm Grieving as Fast as I Can: How Young Widows and Widowers Can Cope and Heal.* New Horizon Press, 1994. P.O. Box 669, Far Hills, NJ 07931.

Ferguson, Tamara, Austin H. Kutscher, and Lillian G. Kutscher. *The Young Widow: Conflicts and Guidelines.* New York: Amo Press, 1981.

Gates, Philomene. *Suddenly Alone: A Woman's Guide to Widowhood.* New York: HarperCollins, 1990.

Ginsburg, Genevieve Davis. *When You've Become a Widow: A Compassionate Guide to Rebuilding Your Life.* Los Angeles: Tarcher, 1991.

Kahn, Wiliard K., and Jane Burgess Kahn. *The Widower.* Boston: Beacon Press, 1978.

Larson, Hal, and Susan Larson. *Suddenly Single: A Lifeline for Anyone Who Has Lost a Love.* San Francisco: Halo, 1990.

Lewis, C. S. *A Grief Observed.* New York: Bantam Books, 1961.

Loewinsohn, Ruth Jean. *Survival Handbook for Widows and for Relatives and Friends Who Want to Understand.* Glenview, IL: Scott Foresman, 1984.

Lopata, Helena. *Women as Widows: Support Systems.* New York: Elsevier, 1979.

Lund, Dale A., ed. *Older Bereaved Spouses: Research with Practical Applications.* New York: Hemisphere, 1989.

Nudel, Adele Rice. *Starting Over: Help for Young Widows and Widowers.* New York: Dodd, 1986.

Osgood, Judy, ed. *Meditations for the Widowed.* Sunriver, OR: Gilgal, 1985.

Robertson, John, and Betty Utterback. *Suddenly Single: Learning to Start Over Through the Experience of Others.* New York: Simon & Schuster, 1986.

Shuchter, Stephen R. *Dimensions of Grief: Adjusting to the Death of a Spouse.* San Francisco: Jossey-Bass, 1986.

Silverman, Phyllis R. *Widow-to-Widow.* New York: Springer, 1986.

Stroebe, Wolfgang, and Margaret S. Stroebe. *Bereavement and Health: The Psychological and Physical Consequences of Partner Loss.* Cambridge: Cambridge Univ. Press, 1987.

Truman, Jill. *Letter to My Husband: Notes About Mourning and Recovery.* New York: Viking Penguin, 1987.

Murder and Violent Death

Caffell, Colin. *In Search of the Rainbow's End: The Inside Story of the Bamber Murders.* London: Hodder & Stoughton, 1994.

Gilliam, Gwendolyn, and Barbara Chesser. *Fatal Moments: The Tragedy of the Accidental Killer.* Lexington, MA: Lexington Books, 1991.

Henry-Jenkins, Wanda. *Just Us.* Omaha: Centering Corp., 1993. (For survivors of murdered loved ones.)

Hoard, Richard G. *Alone Among the Living.* Athens: Univ. of Georgia Press, 1994. (For survivors of murdered loved ones.)

Lord, Janice Harris. *No Time for Goodbyes: Coping with Sorrow, Anger, and Injustice After a Tragic Death.* Ventura, CA: Pathfinder, 1991.

Overly, Fay. *Missing: A Family's Triumph in the Tragedy No Parent Ever Wants to Face.* Denver: Accent Books, 1985.

Redmond, Lula M. *Surviving When Someone You Love Was Murdered: A Professional's Guide to Group Grief Therapy for Families and Friends of Murder Victims.* Clearwater, FL: Psychological Consultation and Education Services, 1989.

Walsh, John. *Tears of Rage: From Grieving Father to Crusader for Justice—the Untold Story of the Adam Walsh Case.* New York: Pocket Books, 1997.

Suicide

Alexander, Victoria. *Words I Never Thought to Speak: Stories of Life in the Wake of Suicide.* New York: Lexington Books, 1991.

American Association of Suicidology. *Directory of Survivors Support Groups.* Washington, DC: AAS. Published annually.

Beisser, Arnold R. *A Graceful Passage: Notes on the Freedom to Live or Die.* New York: Bantam Books, 1990.

Bloom, Lois A. *Mourning After Suicide.* Cleveland: United Church Press, Pilgrim, 1986.

Bolton, Iris, with Curtis Mitchell. *My Son, My Son: A Guide to Healing After a Suicide in the Family.* Bolton Press, 1984. 1325 Belmore Way NE, Atlanta, GA 30338.

Carr, G. Lloyd, and Gwendolyn C. Carr. *The Fierce Goodbye: Hope in the Wake of Suicide.* Downers Grove, IL: InterVarsity Press, 1990.

Colt, George Howe. *The Enigma of Suicide.* New York: Summit Books, 1991.

Dunne Edward J., John McIntosh, and Karen Dunne-Maxim. *Suicide and Its Aftermath: Understanding and Counseling the Survivors.* New York: Norton, 1987.

Freeman, Arthur, and Mark Reinecke. *Cognitive Therapy of Suicidal Behavior: A Manual for Treatment.* New York: Springer, 1993.

Grollman, Earl A. *Suicide: Prevention, Intervention, Postvention.* Boston: Beacon Press, 1988.

Harper, Jeannie, with Eugene Oliveto. *Hurting Yourself.* Omaha: Centering Corp., 1993.

Heckler, Richard A. *Waking Up Alive: The Descent, the Suicide Attempt, and the Return to Life.* New York: Putnam, 1994.

Hewett, John H. *After Suicide.* Philadelphia: Westminster Press, 1980.

Johnson, Joy, and Marvin Johnson. *Suicide of a Child.* Omaha: Centering Corp., 1993.

Leenaars, A. A., ed. *Life Span Perspectives of Suicide: Time-Lines in the Suicide Process.* New York: Plenum Press, 1991.

Lester, David. *The Cruelest Death: The Enigma of Adolescent Suicide.* Philadelphia: Charles Press, 1993.

Lester, David. *Suicide Prevention: Resources for the New Millennium.* Philadelphia: Charles Press, 2000.

Linzer, N., ed. *Suicide: The Will to Live Versus the Will to Die.* New York: Human Sciences Press, 1984.

Lukas, Christopher, and Henry M. Seiden. *Silent Grief: Living in the Wake of Suicide.* New York: Scribner, 1987.

Morgan, John D., ed. *Suicide: Helping Those at Risk.* King's College, 1987. 266 Epworth Avenue, London, Ontario, Canada N6A 2M3.

Quinnett, Paul G. *Suicide, the Forever Decision: A Book for Those Thinking About Suicide, and for Those Who Know, Love, or Counsel Them.* New York: Crossroads, 1997.

Rickgarn, Ralph L. V. *Perspectives on College Student Suicide.* Amityville, NY: Baywood, 1994.

Ross, Eleanora. *After Suicide: A Ray of Hope. A Guide for the Bereaved, the Professional Caregiver, and Anyone Whose Life Has Been Touched by Suicide, Loss or Grief.* Iowa City, IA: Lynn, 1990.

Stillion, Judith M., Eugene E. McDowell, and Jacque H. May. *Suicide Across the Life Span: Premature Exits.* New York: Hemisphere, 1989.

Wrobleski, Adina. *Suicide Survivors: A Guide for Those Left Behind.* Minneapolis: Afterwords, 1991.

Survival Beyond Bodily Death

Cook, Emily Williams, Bruce Greyson, and Ian Stevenson. "Do Any Near-Death Experiences Provide Evidence for the Survival of Human Personality After Death? Relevant Features and Illustrative Case Reports." *Journal of Scientific Exploration* 12 (1998): 377–406.

Greyson, Bruce. "Near-Death Experiences." In *Varieties of Anomalous Experience: Examining the Scientific Evidence*, edited by Etzel Cardena, Steven Jay Lynn, and Stanley Krippner, pp. 315–52. Washington, DC: American Psychological Association, 2000.

Greyson, Bruce, and Chuck Flynn, eds. *The Near-Death Experience: Problems, Prospects, Perspectives.* Springfield, IL: Charles C. Thomas, 1984.

Johnson, Christopher Jay, and Marsha G. McGee, eds. *How Different Religions View Death and Afterlife.* Philadelphia: Charles Press, 1991.

Kircher, Pamela. *Love Is the Link: A Hospice Doctor Shares Her Experience of Near-Death and Dying.* New York: Larson Publications, 1995.

Lawson, Lee. *Visitations from the Afterlife: True Stories of Love and Healing.* San Francisco: HarperSanFrancisco, 2000.

Lindstrom, Bonnie. "Exploring Paranormal Experiences of the Bereaved." In *Creativity in Death Education and Counseling*, edited by Charles A. Corr and others, pp. 117–43. West Hartford, CT: Association for Death Education and Counseling.

Linn, Erin. *Premonitions, Visitations and Dreams of the Bereaved.* Incline Village, NV: Publisher's Mark, 1991.

Lundahl, Craig R., ed. *A Collection of Near-Death Research Readings: Scientific Inquiries into the Experiences of Persons Near Physical Death.* Chicago: Nelson-Hall, 1982. (Compilation of work by Grosso, Haraldsson, Moody, Noyes, Osis, Ring, and others.)

Moody, R. *Life After Life.* New York: Bantam Books, 1975.

Morse, Melvin, and Paul Perry. *Closer to the Light: Learning from the Near-Death Experiences of Children.* New York: Random House, 1991.

Morse, Melvin, and Paul Perry. *Transformed by the Light: The Powerful Effect of Near-Death Experiences on People's Lives.* New York: Villard, 1992.

Osis, Karl, and Erlander Haraldsson. *At the Hour of Death.* Mamaronek, NY: Hastings House, 1990.

Oyler, Chris, Laurie Becklund, and Beth Poison. *Go Toward the Light.* New York: HarperCollins, 1988.

Palmer, Greg. *Death: The Trip of a Lifetime.* San Francisco: HarperSan-Francisco, 1993.

Ring, Kenneth. *Heading Toward Omega: In Search of the Meaning of Near-Death Experience.* New York: Morrow, 1984.

Ring, Kenneth. *Life at Death: A Scientific Investigation of the Near-Death Experience.* New York: Morrow, 1982.

Ring, Kenneth, Sharon Cooper, and Charles Tart. *Mindsight: Near-Death and Out of Body Experiences in the Blind.* Palo Alto, CA: William James Center for Consciousness Studies at the Institute of Transpersonal Psychology, 1999.

Ring, Kenneth, and Evelyn Valarino. *Lessons from the Light: What We Can Learn from the Near-Death Experience.* Portsmouth, NH: Moment Point Press, 2000.

Ritchie, George. *Ordered to Return: My Life After Dying.* Charlottesville, VA: Hampton Roads, 1998.

Sabom, Michael. *Light and Death: One Doctor's Fascinating Account of Near-Death Experiences.* Grand Rapids, MI: Zondervan, 1998.

Sharp, Kimberly Clark. *After the Light: The Spiritual Path to Purpose.* New York: Avon, 1995.

Sheldrake, Rupert. *Dogs That Know When Their Owners Are Coming Home and Other Unexplained Powers of Animals.* New York: Crown, 1999.

Wiitala, Geri Colozzi. *Heather's Return: The Amazing Story of Communications from Beyond the Grave.* Virginia Beach, VA: A.R.E. Press, 1996.

JOURNALS, MAGAZINES, AND NEWSLETTERS

Bereavement: A Magazine of Hope and Healing. Helpful for mourners and professionals alike. Bereavement Publishing, Inc., 5125 North Union Boulevard, Suite 4, Colorado Springs, CO 80918-2056. Telephone: 719.266.0006. grief@bereavementmag.com.

Death Studies. Journal aimed at professionals, but some survivors find it beneficial as well. Covers counseling, research, education, care, and ethics. Dr. Robert Neimeyer, editor-in-chief. Taylor & Francis subscription office: Frost Road, Suite 101, Bristol, PA 19007. Telephone: 215.785.5800 or 1.800.634.7064.

The Forum. Newsletter of the Association for Death Education and Counseling (ADEC), 342 North Main Street, West Hartford, CT 06117-2507. Telephone: 860.586.7503. www.adec.org.

Illness, Crisis, and Loss. Robert Bendiksen, Ph.D., editor-in-chief, Center for Death Education and Bioethics, University of Wisconsin–La Crosse, La Crosse, WI 54601. Telephone: 608.785.6781. For information, e-mail cdeb@uwlax.edu, or visit Sage Publications at www.sagepub.com.

Journal of Loss and Trauma (formerly the *Journal of Personal and Interpersonal Loss*). Presents issues surrounding traumatic loss and how survivors cope, as well as many other forms of loss. Taylor & Francis subscription office: Frost Road, Suite 101, Bristol, PA 19007. Telephone: 215.785.5800 or 1.800.634.7064.

The Journey: A Newsletter for Survivors of Suicide. Offers conference, grief-support group meetings, and workshop information, as well as articles, stories, artwork, and poems. Published by The Link Counseling Center's National Resource Center for Suicide Prevention and Aftercare, 348 Mount Vernon Highway, Atlanta, GA 30328-4139. Telephone: 404.256.9797. www.thelink.org.

MADDVOCATE. Newsletter published by Mothers Against Drunk Driving (MADD). P.O. Box 541688, Dallas, TX 75354-1688. Telephone: 800.get.madd. www.madd.org.

Mortality. For professionals and laypersons alike. Taylor & Francis subscription office: Frost Road, Suite 101, Bristol, PA 19007. Telephone: 1.800.634.7064 or 215.785.5800.

NewsLink. Quarterly magazine of the American Association of Suicidology (see associations), 4201 Connecticut Avenue NW, Suite 310, Washington, DC 20008. Telephone: 202.237.2280.

Omega—Journal of Death and Dying. Robert Kastenbaum, Ph.D., serves as editor, and Kenneth J. Doka, Ph.D., as the associate editor. *Omega* is a reliable guide for professionals in the field of bereavement and is an excellent resource for laypersons as well. Published by Baywood Publishing Company, Inc., 26 Austin Avenue, P.O. Box 337, Amityville, New York 11701.

Suicide and Life-Threatening Behavior. Official journal of the American Association of Suicidology, 4201 Connecticut Avenue NW, Suite 310, Washington, DC 20008. Telephone: 202.237.2280. Journal is published quarterly by the Guilford Press, 72 Spring Street, New York, NY 10012. Telephone: 1.800.365.7006 or 212.431.9800. E-mail: Staff@guilford.com.

Survival Beyond Bodily Death

Journal of the American Society for Psychical Research. Houses a wealth of information surrounding the concept of life after death and other parapsychological phenomena. American Society for Psychical Research, 5 West Seventy-third Street, New York, NY 10023. Telephone: 212.799.5050. www.aspr.com.

Journal of Near-Death Studies. Foremost journal in the field. Human Sciences Press, Inc., 233 Spring Street, New York, NY 10013-1578. Telephone: 212.807.1047.

Journal of the Society for Psychical Research. The most established journal for paranormal investigations. Society for Psychical Research, 49 Marloes Road, London, W8 6LA. Telephone (from the U.S.): 44.204.0171.937.8984.

INTERNET

1000Deaths.Com. www.1000deaths.com. This is an outstanding Internet site for those bereaved by suicide. It offers "Link for Lights" memorial, supportive resources, and meaningful material.

American Association of Retired Persons (AARP). www.aarp.com. Click on "Coping with Grief and Loss" for articles and bereavement support.

American Association of Suicidology (AAS). www.suicidology.org. Provides a full range of services for survivors and professionals. 4201 Connecticut Avenue NW, Suite 310, Washington, DC 20008. Telephone: 202.237.2280.

American Foundation for Suicide Prevention (AFSP). www.afsp.org. Provides a listing of programs and services for survivors. Telephone: 888.333.AFSP.

American Psychiatric Association. www.apa.org. Offers information on AIDS, suicide, death, dying, grief, healthcare professionals in the field, conferences, and much more. 1400 K Street NW, Washington, DC 20005. Telephone: 888.357.7924.

American Psychological Association. www.apa.org. Offers resources and original online literature related to stress, grief, and counseling.

American Suicide Foundation (ASF). www.asfnet.org. Focuses on suicide prevention. Includes frequently updated state-by-state directory of support groups. 120 Wall Street, New York, NY 10005. Telephone: 800.ASF.4042.

America's Most Wanted. www.amw.com. Official site for television show hosted by John Walsh and aired on the Fox network. Offers resource center, archives, FBI's most wanted, news, education, and information for victims and survivors. Contact site for John Walsh.

Angel Babies. www.angels4ever.com. This touching site specializes in resources for miscarriages, stillbirth, SIDS, and other infant deaths. Information, message boards, support, and a respectful memorial page free of charge.

Association for Death Education and Counseling (ADEC). www.adec.org. This site provides a directory of bereavement and online links to other resources.

Australian Institute for Suicide Research and Prevention (AISRAP). www.gu.edu.au/school/psy/aisrap/. The center is an international clearinghouse for suicide information and research. The website offers an extensive e-library (international references, journal articles, books, proceedings, manuals, theses, audiovisuals, and other packages) upon request and under the direction of Diego De Leo, M.D., Ph.D., Professor of Psychopathology and Suicidology. AISRAP, at Griffith University, Mount Gravatt Campus, 4111 Queensland, Australia. Telephone: 0061.7.3875.3366.

Bereavement and Hospice Support Netline. www.ubalt.edu/www/bereavement. Site provides online directory of bereavement and hospice services throughout the United States.

Bereavement Magazine. www.bereavementmag.com. Offers magazine, bereavement resources, electronic sympathy cards, memorials, and more.

The British Medical Journal (BMJ). www.bmj.com, then click on "Coping with Loss" in the search box. Editors Colin Murray Parkes and Andrew Markus offer grief-related articles online.

Center for Loss and Life Transition. www.centerforloss.com. Lists available classes, bereavement resources, books, Dr. Alan Wolfelt's lecture schedule, and more. Telephone: 970.226.6050.

Center for Renewal Personal Recovery. www.renew.com. Educational site that focuses primarily on stress and crisis management.

Centering Corporation. www.centering.org. Houses a large selection of grief books.

Children with AIDS Project. www.aidskids.org. Provides services for children living with AIDS, such as online support among children who are affected. It also offers information about adoptions.

Compassionate Friends, Inc. www.compassionatefriends.org. An international not-for-profit association that offers online support to families who have experienced the death of a child. Lists books and resource sites and offers helpful online articles. (Highly recommended for bereaved parents.)

Crisis, Grief, and Healing. www.webhealing.com. This international site offers online information and support. Designed by grief therapist Tom Golden in honor of his father.

Death and Dying Grief Support. www.death-dying.com. Expansive site that offers grief support via a free memorial page, angels online, near-death experience articles, message boards, newsletter, and various other departments.

Dignity Memorial. www.dignitymemorial.com. International organization that provides information about funeral services available in over 1,500 funeral homes nationwide. Their Children's Care and other programs respectfully help families in any situation.

Free Mind Generation (FMG). www.geocities.com. A nonprofit organization aimed at preventing suicide among African Americans. National newsletter: *Black Men Don't Commit Suicide.* Based in Atlanta. Telephone: 404. 755.3955.

Grief Healing. www.griefhealing.com. This site is slow but worth the wait. Constructed by Martha "Marty" Tousley in honor of her parents and pets. She offers a premium site for those bereaved by pet loss.

GriefNet. www.griefnet.com. Provides a great deal of support for the bereaved, including e-group support, a beautiful memorial page (free), a bookstore, suicide prevention, bereavement information, and more. Site is supervised by clinical grief psychologist Cendra Lynn.

Griefwork Center. www.griefworkcenter.com. Center based in Kendall Park, NJ.

Growth House. www.growthhouse.org. Expansive and wonderful site for end-of-life care and mourning. Provides directory of resources related to caring for the terminally ill, AIDS, HIV, suicide, and funeral planning, plus a book list, chat rooms, and more. Telephone: 415.255.9045.

Hospice Cares. www.hospice-cares.com. Offers books, online links, original articles, and other information.

Hospice Foundation of America. www.hospicefoundation.org. Multireference source.

International Association for Hospice and Palliative Care. www.hospicecare.com. This interactive web site provides access to information regarding palliative care worldwide, including an international directory of associations, books at discount prices, online newsletters, links, and more. P.O. Box 131639, Ann Arbor, MI 48113.

Library of Congress. lcweb.loc.gov. Provides access to the Library of Congress catalogs and other library databases.

The Link Counseling Center. www.thelink.org. The Link is a nonprofit center founded by Iris Bolton and funded by United Way. The website offers information on grief counseling, crisis numbers, telephone counseling, survivors packet, library, newsletter, and other supportive information for the bereaved, especially survivors of suicide. Provides training, workshops, and conferences. 348 Mount Vernon Highway, Atlanta, GA 30328-4139. Telephone: 404.256.9797.

Mothers Against Drunk Driving (MADD). www.madd.org. Founded in 1980, MADD now has more than six hundred chapters nationwide. The website offers online pamphlets and brochures at no cost, as well as victim assistance, a chat room, and more. P.O. Box 541688, Dallas, TX 75354-1688. Telephone: 800.GET.MADD.

National Organization of Parents of Murdered Children. www.POMC.com. Founded by Robert and Charlotte Hullinger, this organization hosts a National Day of Remembrance for Victims of Homicide each year on September 25. 100 East Eighth Street B 41, Cincinnati, OH 45202. Telephone: 888.818.POMC.

National Public Radio. www.npr.org/programs/death. Provides transcripts from the broadcasts of "The End of Life—Exploring Death in America" program. Covers bereavement issues along with investigations into survival of bodily death.

OncoLink. www.oncolink.upenn.edu. The University of Pennsylvania Cancer Center offers this excellent global resource, with information on most aspects of cancer, including support groups.

A Place to Remember. www.aplacetoremember.com. Specializes in resources for miscarriages, stillbirth, or the death of a baby two years old or younger. Products, chatroom, etc. Offers a beautiful memorial page (free of charge).

QPR Institute (Question, Persuade, Prefer, the three steps that can save a life). www.qprinstitute.org. Provides suicide-prevention training programs, as well as educational and clinical materials for the public, professionals, and institutions. P.O. Box 2867, Spokane, WA 99220. Telephone: 888.726.7926.

Robert Wood Johnson Foundation. www.lastacts.org. Services for chronic illness and palliative-care patients and families.

SAVE (Suicide Awareness/Voices of Education). www.save.org. Provides information about suicide and suicide prevention, as well as grief support for survivors of suicide.

StillGrieving.com. www.StillGrieving.com. Focuses on bereaved parents and grandparents who are no longer in the acute states of grief ("later mourning"; six months or more after the loss). The website houses chat rooms, information, e-groups, and more.

Suicide Information and Education Centre (SIEC). www.sptp@siec.ca. (also known as Suicide Prevention Training Programs, SPTP). Site offers information about suicide and bereavement. Based in Alberta, Canada. Telephone: 403.245.3900.

Suicide Prevention Advocacy Network (SPAN). www.spanusa.org. Offers suicide-prevention programs; seeks to build bridges between suicide-prevention organizations (both public and private) to government agencies and the media. Telephone: 888.649.1366 or 770.642.1419.

Transformations. www.transformations.com. Offers free memorials, gallery, library, and articles online.

Webster's Death, Dying, and Grief Guide. www.katsden.com/death/index.htm. This site provides a great deal of information and resources related to death, dying, and bereavement.

Widownet. www.widownet.com. Information, books, chat rooms, bereavement news, and online support for widows and widowers.

Wills and Estate Planning. www.nolo.com/ChunkEP/EP.inde.htm. Nolo Press's website provides information on funeral planning, probate, death taxes, and other funcral and estate concerns.

Survival Beyond Bodily Death

American Society for Psychical Research. www.aspr.com. First American parapsychological research organization, begun in 1885. Its journal offers information about the concept of life after death and other phenomena. 5 West Seventy-third Street, New York, NY 10023. Telephone: 212.799.5050.

Exceptional Human Experiences. www.ehe.org. EHE is a forum for ideas, research, and personal accounts on topics such as near-death experiences, apparitional encounters, and events that lead to transformation. Founded by Rhea White, EHE Network offers journals and other publications. Original articles are available via their website. EHE Network, 414 Rockledge Road, New Bern, NC 28562.

International Association for Near Death Studies (IANDS). www.iands.org. Resources for those interested in near-death experiences as well as support for experiencers.

Reincarnation International. www.dircon.co.uk/reincarn. The full scope of reincarnation is covered on this website.

Associations, Organizations, and Services

American Academy of Bereavement. A hospital-based organization offering a wide range of services geared toward professionals. 2090 North Kolb Road, Suite 100, Tucson, AZ 85715. Telephone: 800.726.3888.

American Association of Suicidology. With a goal of understanding and preventing suicide, the association serves as a national clearinghouse for information, research, public awareness programs, and training. Publishes an annual *Directory of Survivors Support Groups.* 4201 Connecticut Avenue NW, Suite 310, Washington, DC 20008. Telephone: 202.237.2280.

American Cancer Society. Offers free bereavement support groups throughout the United States. 1599 Clifton Road NE, Atlanta, GA 30329.

American Foundation for Suicide Prevention (AFSP). Specializes in prevention and provides a listing of programs and services for survivors as well. Hosts annual Survivors of Suicide Day, November 18, with participation across the United States and Canada. Telephone: 888.333.AFSP. www.afsp.org.

American Psychiatric Association. National resource for issues surrounding AIDS, suicide, death, dying, grief, depression, anxiety disorders, and panic attacks. Provides resources such as conferences for healthcare professionals. Offers video rentals and much more. 1400 K Street NW, Washington, DC 20005. Telephone: 888.357.7924. www.apa.org.

American Psychological Association. Houses education and information on bereavement, mostly aimed at professionals. Resource for news, articles (online included), and conferences. 750 First Street NE, Washington, DC 20002-4242. Telephone: 202.336.5500. www.apa.org.

American Suicide Foundation (ASF). Focuses on suicide prevention and aftercare. Updated state-by-state directory of support groups. 120 Wall Street, New York, NY 10005. Telephone: 800.ASF.4042 or 212.410.1111. www.asfnet.org.

Animals in Our Hearts. Offers international workshops related to pet loss. Call 916.454.4301 or visit www.animalsinourhearts.com for workshop site locations and other information.

Anxiety Disorders Association of America. Provides information and education on anxiety and panic disorders. 11900 Parklawn Drive, Suite 100, Rockville, MD 20852-2624. www.adaa.org.

Association for Death Education and Counseling (ADEC). The principal association for healthcare professionals and volunteers in the field of bereavement. It offers a full range of education and resources for professionals, as well as resources for the bereaved. 342 North Main Street, West Hartford, CT 06117-2507. Telephone: 860.586.7503. www.adec.org.

Australian Institute for Suicide Research and Prevention (AISRAP). International clearinghouse for suicide information and research. Offers conferences, training, research, and an extensive library of material under the direction of Diego De Leo, M.D., Ph.D., Professor of Psychopathology and Suicidology. AISRAP, at Griffith University, Mount Gravatt Campus, 4111 Queensland, Australia. Telephone: 0061.7.3875.3366. www.gu.edu.au/school/psy/aisrap/.

Befrienders International. Services for the bereaved and professionals. 23 Elysium Gate, 126 New Kings Road, London SW6 4LZ. E-mail: admin@befrienders.org.

Bereaved Parents of the USA. Group that developed from Compassionate Friends; offers similar support. P.O. Box 95, Park Forest, IL 60466. Telephone: 708.748.9184 or 708.748.7672.

Canadian Association for Suicide Prevention (CASP). Focus on prevention and resources for those bereaved by suicide. 201–1615 Tenth Avenue SW, Calgary, Alberta, Canada T3C OJ7. Telephone: 403.245.3900. E-mail: siec@nucleus.com.

Center for Death Education and Bioethics. Research and information center; Dept. 435NH, University of Wisconsin–La Crosse, La Crosse, WI 54601. Telephone: 608.785.6781.

Center for Death Education and Research. A research and information center that houses publications and audiovisual resources for professionals and the bereaved. 1167 Social Science Building, University of Minnesota, Minneapolis, MN 55455.

Center for Living with Loss. Offers books, videos, audiotapes, and other material for the field of bereavement. 990 Seventh North Street, Liverpool, NY 13088.

Center for Loss and Life Transition. Specializes in bereavement education, training, and grief therapy. Under the directorship of Dr. Alan Wolfelt. We highly recommend his training for professionals and volunteers, and his clinical services to all ages, especially children. 3735 Broken Bow Road, Fort Collins, CO 80526. Telephone: 970.226.6050. www.centerforloss.com

Centering Corporation. 1531 North Saddle Creek Road, Omaha, NE 68104. Telephone: 402.553.1200.

Compassion Books. Official book service of the Association for Death Education and Counseling (ADEC). Offers more than four hundred books, audios, and videos related to death, dying, grief, and education. Catalog available. 477 Hannah Branch, Burnsville, NC 28714. Telephone: 828.675.5909.

Compassionate Friends, Inc. International not-for-profit association whose mission is to assist families in the positive resolution of grief following the death of a child, and to provide information to help others be supportive. Bereavement support-group meetings are available in most areas. Association hosts an annual international candle-lighting ceremony on National Children's Memorial Day, December 7. P.O. Box 3696, Oakbrook, IL 60522-3696. Telephone: 630.990.0010. www.compassionatefriends.org.

DEPRESSION/Awareness, Recognition, and Treatment (D/ART) (*see* National Institute of Mental Health).

Dougy Center (*see* National Center for Grieving Children and Families).

Family Services America. Organization helps families deal with stress and grief via counseling services and education. 11700 West Lake Park Drive, Park Place, Milwaukee, WI 53224.

Foundation of Thanatology. Offers conferences and material surrounding death, dying, and mourning. 630 West 168th Street, New York, NY 10032.

Free Mind Generation (FMG). A nonprofit organization based in Atlanta whose aim is to prevent suicide among African Americans. National newsletter: *Black Men Don't Commit Suicide.* Telephone: 404.755.3955. www.geocities.com.

Gateway Center. Conducts international grief workshops, lectures, and training. Grants allow it to provide scholarships for people living with AIDS and for their caregivers. 54 Park Avenue, Bay Shore, NY 11706-7309. Telephone: 516.968.4677.

Griefwork Center. Offers education and professional training, specializing in suicide and sudden death. P.O. Box 5104, Kendall Park, NJ 08824. Telephone: 732.422.0400. www.griefworkcenter.com.

International Association for Suicide Prevention (IASP). St. Luke's Medical Center, Rush University, 1725 West Harrison Street, Suite 955, Chicago, IL 60612-3824. Telephone: 312.942.728. E-mail: iasp@aol.com.

International Association of Pet Cemeteries. Can provide a list of locations of pet cemeteries and crematoriums throughout the United States. 2845 Oakcrest Place, Land O'Lakes, FL 34639. Telephone: 800.952.5541.

International Order of the Golden Rule. Offers materials on funerals, death, dying, and grief. 1000 Churchhill Road, Springfield, IL 62702.

International Work Group on Death, Dying and Bereavement (King's College Centre for Education about Death and Bereavement). Began its death education program in 1976. It offers classes, certification, and outstanding annual conferences for nonprofessionals and professionals interested in furthering their education. 266 Epworth Avenue, London, Ontario, Canada N6A 2M3. Telephone: 519.432.7946. www.wwdc.com/death/resources.

The Link Counseling Center. The Link is a nonprofit center founded by Iris Bolton and funded by United Way. It offers counseling, crisis intervention, training, newsletter, information, networking, and a support system for survivors of suicide. 348 Mount Vernon Highway, Atlanta, GA 30328-4139. Telephone: 404.256.9797. www.thelink.org.

Living Works Education, Inc. Not-for-profit organization seeking prevention of suicide. Offers research and training. 201–1615 Tenth Avenue SW, Calgary, Alberta, Canada T3C 0J7. Telephone: 403.209.0242. E-mail: living@nucleus.com.

Mothers Against Drunk Driving (MADD). Organization founded in 1980 that now has more than six hundred chapters nationwide. Offers victim-assistance programs, pamphlets, brochures, conferences, newsletter, and much more. P.O. Box 541688, Dallas, TX 75354-1688. Telephone: 800.GET.MADD. www.madd.org.

National Association for People with AIDS. Full range of services for patients and caregivers. 1413 K Street NW, Washington, DC 20005.

National Center for Grieving Children and Families (The Dougy Center). Offers national and international training in assisting bereaved children and teens. P.O. Box 86852, Portland, OR 97286. Telephone: 503.775.5683. www.dougy.org.

National Council of Family Relations. Education and referral resource. 1219 University Avenue SE, Minneapolis, MN 55415.

National Depression Screening. This organization's toll-free, year-round number can be called for a list of research and clinics where free depression screening is provided in most local communities. Telephone: 1.800.573.4433.

National Depressive and Manic-Depressive Association. Offers information, education, and resources on depressive states. 730 Franklin, Suite 501, Chicago, IL 60616. Telephone: 312.642.0049. www.ndmda.org.

National Foundation for Depressive Disorders. Provides information and resources on the topic of depression. P.O. Box 2257, New York, NY 10016. Telephone: 800.248.4344.

National Funeral Directors Association. Provides booklets on the subjects of funerals, death, and bereavement. 11121 West Oklahoma Avenue, Milwaukee, WI 53227.

National Hospice Organization. Offers information on palliative care for the terminally ill and bereavement support for their survivors. 1901 North Fort Myers Drive, Suite 307, Arlington, VA 22209.

National Institute of Mental Health. Source for information and resources covering most areas of mental health, including stress, anxiety, panic disorders, death, dying, and bereavement. Houses DEPRESSION/Awareness, Recognition, and Treatment (D/ART), a service program specializing in the topic of depression. 5600 Fishers Lane, Room 7C-02, Rockville, MD 20875. Telephone: 301.443.5158. www.nimh.hih.gov.

National Organization for Victim Assistance. Offers information for survivors. www.nova.com.

National Organization of Parents of Murdered Children, Inc. Offers ongoing support to parents and other survivors as they deal with their grief and the criminal justice system. Support is provided via artwork, audiotapes, books, articles, online service, support-group meetings, and crisis intervention. The organization also offers training to professionals in the field. 100 East Eighth Street, Suite B-41, Cincinnati, OH 45202. Telephone: 888.818.POMC or 513.721.5683. www.pomc.com.

National Resource Center for Suicide Prevention and Aftercare, provided by The Link Counseling Center, supported by United Way and private donations. This organization offers quality aftercare for those bereaved by suicide as well as suicide-prevention services via support groups, telephone counseling, grief counseling, resource materials, library, lectures, workshops, and training. 348 Mount Vernon Highway, Atlanta, GA 30328. Telephone: 404.256.9797.

National Sudden Infant Death Syndrome Foundation. Provides support-group information and educational materials. 2 Metro Plaza, Suite 205, 8320 Professional Place, Landover, MD 20785.

National Suicide Hot Line. Suicide prevention crisis line; also provides local referral information. Telephone: 888.suicide.

Organization for Attempters and Survivors of Suicide in Interfaith Services (OASSIS). Organization supports religious leaders, suicidologists, attempters, and those bereaved by suicide. Holds conferences on religion and suicide. 4541 Burlington Place NW, Washington, DC 20016. Telephone: 202.363.4224. E-mail: jamestclemons@aol.com.

Pregnancy and Infant Loss Center. Provides services for those affected by miscarriage, stillbirth, and infant death. 1421 West Wayzata Boulevard, Wayzata, MN 55391.

QPR Institute (Question, Persuade, Prefer—the three steps that can save a life). Suicide prevention training programs, as well as educational and clinical materials for the public, professionals, and institutions. P.O. Box 2867, Spokane, WA 99220. Telephone: 888.726.7926. www.qprinstitute.org.

SAFER. (Suicide Counselling Service of the Greater Vancouver Mental Health Service Society.) Offers full range of services, especially in the areas of suicide prevention and bereavement. 300–2425 Quebec Street, Vancouver, British Columbia, Canada, V5T 4L6. Telephone: 604.879.9251.

Scott and White Hospice, affiliated with the acclaimed Scott and White Memorial Hospital and Clinic in Temple, Texas. Offers ongoing grief-support groups. Scott and White Hospital teams with the Texas A&M University System Health Science Center College of Medicine to present outstanding conferences under the directorship of Louis A. Gamino, Ph.D. 2401 South Thirty-first Street, Temple, TX 76508. Telephone: 254.727.4090 or 254.724.7609. www.sw.org.

Suicide Information and Education Centre (SIEC), also known as Suicide Prevention Training Programs (SPTP). Offers group workshops and training specializing in suicide intervention, bereavement counseling, and education. 201–1615 Tenth Avenue SW, Calgary, Alberta, Canada T3C 0J7. Telephone: 403.245.3900. www.sptp@siec.ca.

Suicide Prevention Advocacy Network (SPAN). Offers suicide-prevention programs. It also seeks to build bridges between suicide-prevention organizations (both public and private) to government agencies and the media. Telephone: 888.649.1366 or 770.642.1419. www.spanusa.org.

Suicide Prevention Center. Provides crisis services as well as resources for prevention. 4760 South Sepulveda Boulevard, Culver City, CA 90230. Office telephone: 310.751.5324. Crisis number: 310.391.1253.

University of North Carolina Continuing Education. Offers Living Through Loss programs facilitated by Linda Goldman and Tom Golden. www.uncc.edu/conteduc.

Widowed Persons Service. Provides referral service, educational literature, programs, and financial and legal counseling for widows and widowers. 1909 K Street NW, Room 580, Washington, DC 20049.

World Health Organization (WHO). Worldwide organization that connects the public with the field's leading authorities on health-related topics, including suicide. Provides international technical support, produces and disseminates information, and helps with bereavement-support groups. International office: Avenue Appia 20, 1211 Geneva 27, Switzerland. www.who.org.

Survival Beyond Bodily Death

Bigelow Chair of Consciousness Studies, University of Nevada–Las Vegas. Presents a yearly series of public lectures on human consciousness and the possibility of its persistence after death. Guest speakers are international authorities from the fields of thanatology, bereavement, and parapsychology. All lectures are free and open to the public. Telephone: 702.895.1970. www.unlv.edu.

Division of Personality Studies, University of Virginia Health System. Under the direction of Ian Stevenson, M.D., and Bruce Greyson, M.D. Conducts premier studies on near-death experiences and reincarnation. P.O. Box 800152, Charlottesville, VA 22908-0152. Telephone: 804.924.2281. www.med.virginia.edu.

International Association for Near-Death Studies (IANDS). Hosts annual conferences on the topic and is an excellent resource for education, information, and research. www.iands.org.

Parapsychology Foundation. Founded in 1951 by Eileen Garrett. It houses one of the world's largest parapsychological libraries open to the public. The *Parapsychology Foundation Review* can be received online. 228 East Seventy-first Street, New York, NY 10021. Telephone: 212.628.1550. www.parapsychology.org.

Rhine Research Center. Founded by J. B. Rhine, the center is successor to the Duke University Parapsychology Laboratory. Publishes the *Journal of Parapsychology;* offers study opportunities, research, and library to those dedicated to the field of consciousness and parapsychology. 402 North Buchanan Boulevard, Durham, NC 27701-1728. Telephone: 919.688.8421. www.rhine.org.

Society for Psychical Research. Founded in 1882 for the scientific investigation of life after death; publishes one of the most respected journals in the field. 49 Marloes Road, London, W8 6LA. Telephone (from the U.S.): 44.204.937.8984.

Glossary

alarm phase first stage of stress; the initial impact of crisis or change.

anticipatory grief grief that occurs before the actual loss, as in the case of the elderly or terminally ill.

attachment the innate need to bond with another; a sense of connection between loved ones.

bereavement adaptation period following the death of a loved one.

closure loose ends are gathered, the initial devastation or a certain aspect of the loss is resolved.

complicated grief grief that has remained intense, prolonged, or both; grief that interrupts or prevents normal daily activities.

coping grief behavior; a learned response; the manner in which someone contends with grief.

dissociate when part of consciousness separates from the whole; thoughts or consciousness departs from the body.

dysfunctional grief grief that prohibits growth by prolonged suffering, interrupts normal activities, or causes life not to be lived to the fullest.

exhaustion phase last and final phase of stress; total breakdown develops when intense stress is prolonged.

grief a process that carries a number of feelings and behaviors; carries an underlying sense of sorrow and longing.

innate inborn; biological; present from birth; not acquired or learned. (Attachment and grief are inborn; they are products of nature as opposed to being learned.)

mourning expressing or externalizing grief; adapting to loss.

projection judging others by one's own thoughts and feelings; putting one's internal feelings, thoughts, beliefs, or values onto another person.

religious a member of a religious order, or one who faithfully practices a doctrine.

resistance phase second phase of stress; resisting change results in breakdown.

spirituality believing in a divine being or a power higher than self; life practiced with compassion, reverence, conscientiousness, serenity, and joy; trusting that the world is evolving as it should.

stressor any circumstance that creates stress.

thanatology the study of death and dying.

transcendence moving beyond one point to another; elevated above the former; survivors grow beyond the person they were at the time of the loss.

Works Consulted

Adler, Jerry. "There's Just the Three of Us." In *His Life and the Kennedy Legacy*, p. 36. *Newsweek* Memorial Issue, 1999.

Adler, Ronald B., and Neil Towne. *Looking Out/Looking In: Interpersonal Communication*. New York: Holt, Rinehart & Winston, 1987.

American Association of Suicidology, prepared by John L. McIntosh. *Survivors of Suicide Fact Sheet*. Washington, D.C. 1998.

American Cancer Society. *Life After Loss Facilitator's Handbook*, Atlanta, GA, 1999.

American Psychiatric Association. *Let's Talk About Panic Disorder* Washington, DC: APA, 1992.

Arcangel, Dianne. "Heather's Return." *Journal of the American Society for Psychical Research* 93 (1999): 226–31.

———. "Tribute to Karlis Osis." *Journal of the American Society for Psychical Research* 90 (1996): 228–30.

———. "The Wheel of Life Review." *Journal of the American Society for Psychical Research* 91 (1997): 353–56.

Astin, J. A., E. Harkness, and E. Ernst. "The Efficacy of 'Distant Healing': A Systematic Review of Randomized Trials." *Annals of Internal Medicine* 132 (2000): 903–10.

Bowlby, John. *Attachment and Loss, Vol. 1: Attachment*. New York: Basic Books, 1982.

Bowlby, John. *Attachment and Loss, Vol. 3: Loss: Sadness and Depression*. New York: Basic Books, 1980.

"A Boy Says Good Bye to His Dad." *Texas Magazine*, November 22, 1964, p. 1.

Cantor, Christopher, and Penelope J. Slater. "Marital Breakdown, Parenthood, and Suicide." *Journal of Family Studies* 1 (October 1995): 91–102.

Carlson, Margaret. "Farewell, John." *Time*, August 2, 1999, p. 33.

Compassionate Friends. "New Statistics on Death of a Child Available," *We Need Not Walk Alone*, Anniversary Issue, Oakbrook, IL, 1999.

Connally, Nellie, with Michael Druary. "Texas' First Lady Relives the Day the President Died." *Texas Magazine*, November 22, 1964. Originally published by *McCall's* magazine, 1964.

Cook, Emily Williams, Bruce Greyson, and Ian Stevenson. "Do Any Near-Death Experiences Provide Evidence for the Survival of Human Personality

After Death? Relevant Features and Illustrative Case Reports." *Journal of Scientific Exploration* 12 (1998): 377–406.

DeSpelder, Lynne Ann, and Albert Lee Strickland. *The Last Dance: Encountering Death and Dying.* Mountain View, CA: Mayfield, 1992.

Doka, Kenneth J. *Disenfranchised Grief.* Lexington, MA: Lexington Books, 1989.

Dossey, L. *Healing Beyond the Body.* Boston: Shambhala, 2001.

———. "Immortality." *Alternative Therapies in Health and Medicine* 6 (2000): 12.

———. *Reinventing Medicine.* San Francisco: HarperSanFrancisco, 1999.

Erikson, Erik H. *Identity: Youth and Crisis.* New York: Norton, 1968.

Erikson, Erik H. *Insight and Responsibility.* New York: Norton, 1968.

Fitzgerald, Helen. *The Grieving Child: A Parent's Guide.* New York: Simon & Schuster, 1992.

Fodor, J. "The Big Idea." *(New York) Times Literary Supplement,* July 3, 1992, p. 20.

Gamino, Louis A. "Why 'Just Get Over It' Doesn't Work: Lessons from the Scott and White Grief Study [1994–97]." Paper presented at Clinical Challenges in Bereavement: Beyond Supportive Care, Austin, TX, October 6, 2000.

Greeley, Andrew M. *Religious Change in America.* Cambridge: First Harvard University Press, 1996.

Greyson, Bruce. "Near-Death Experiences." In *Varieties of Anomalous Experience: Examining the Scientific Evidence,* edited by Etzel Cardena, Steven Jay Lynn, and Stanley Krippner, pp. 315–52. Washington, DC: American Psychological Association, 2000.

Greyson, Bruce, and Chuck Flynn, eds. *The Near-Death Experience: Problems, Prospects, Perspectives.* Springfield, IL: Charles C. Thomas, 1984.

Hirsh, S. *Using the Myers-Briggs Type Indicator in Organizations: A Resource Book.* Palo Alto, CA: Consulting Psychologists Press, 1985.

Holmes, T. S., and R. H. Rahe. "The Social Readjustment Rating Scale." *Journal of Psychosomatic Research* 11 (1967): 213–18.

Huber, Terri. *No Time Out from Grief: Surviving the Death of My Son.* Writers Club Press/iUniverse.com, 2000.

Jonas, W. B. "The Middle Way: Realistic Randomized Controlled Trials for the Evaluation of Spiritual Healing." *Journal of Alternative and Complementary Medicine* 7 (2001): 5–7.

Jowett, Benjamin, trans. *The Works of Plato.* 1945.

Jung, C. *Psychological Types.* New York: Princeton University Press, 1971.

Kastenbaum, Robert. *Psychology of Death.* New York: Springer, 1992.

Keirsey, D., and Marilyn Bates. *Please Understand Me.* Del Mar, CA: Gnosology Books, 1984.

Kircher, Pamela. *Love Is the Link: A Hospice Doctor Shares Her Experience of Near-Death and Dying.* New York: Larson, 1995.

Kroeger, O., and J. Thuesen. *Type Talk.* New York: Dell, 1988.

Kübler-Ross, Elisabeth. *Death, the Final Stage of Growth.* Englewood Cliffs, NJ: Prentice-Hall, 1975.

———. *On Death and Dying.* New York: Macmillan, 1969.

Lawrence, G. *Descriptions of the Sixteen Types.* Gainesville, FL: Center for Applications of Psychological Type, 1993.

Lundahl, Craig R., ed. *A Collection of Near-Death Research Readings: Scientific Inquiries into the Experiences of Persons Near Physical Death.* Chicago: Nelson-Hall, 1982. Compilation of work by Osis, Haraldsson, Ring, Moody, Noyes, Grosso, and others.

Maddox, J. "The Unexpected Science to Come." *Scientific American,* December 1999, pp. 62–67.

Martin, Terry L., and Kenneth J. Doka. *Men Don't Cry . . . Women Do: Transcending Gender Stereotypes of Grief.* Philadelphia: Brunner/Mazel, 2000.

Matthews, Jim. *Four Dark Days in History: November 22, 23, 24, 25.* Los Angeles: Special Publications, 1963.

McCaulley, M. *The Myers-Briggs Type Indicator and Leadership.* Gainesville, FL: Center for Applications of Psychological Type, 1988.

Miller, L. "Boomers Hire Consultants to Help Go from Good Life to 'Good Death.'" *Wall Street Journal,* February 25, 2000, p. 1

Miller, Lyle H., and Alma Dell Smith. *The Stress Solution.* New York: Pocket Books, 1993.

Moody, R. *Life After Life.* New York: Bantam Books, 1975.

Morse, Melvin, and Paul Perry. *Closer to the Light: Learning from the Near-Death Experiences of Children.* New York: Random House, 1991.

———. *Transformed by the Light: The Powerful Effect of Near-Death Experiences on People's Lives.* New York: Villard, 1992.

Myers, I. *Introduction to Type.* Palo Alto, CA: Consulting Psychologists Press, 1962.

Myers, I., and M. McCaulley. *A Guide to the Development and Use of the MBTI: A Manual.* Gainesville, FL: Center for Applications of Psychological Type, 1985.

Neimeyer, Robert. *Lessons of Loss: A Guide to Coping.* Philadelphia: Brunner Routledge, 2001.

———, ed. *Death Anxiety Handbook: Research, Instrumentation, and Application.* Washington, DC: Taylor & Francis, 1994.

Noyes, R., Jr., and R. Kletti. "Depersonalization in the Face of Life-Threatening Danger: An Interpretation." *Omega* 7 (1976): 103–14.

Parma, S., D. G. Waller, R. Yeates, and P. Fenwick. "A Qualitative and Quantitative Study of the Incidence, Features and Aetiology of Near Death Experiences in Cardiac Arrest Survivors." *Resuscitation* 48 (2001): 149–56.

Piaget, Jean. *The Child's Construction of the World.* London: Routledge & Kegan Paul, 1929.

Radin, Dean, and Jannine Rebman. "Are Phantasms Fact or Fantasy? A Preliminary Investigation of Apparitions Evoked in the Laboratory." *Journal of the Society for Psychical Research* 61 (1996): 843.

Rando, Therese A. *Treatment of Complicated Mourning.* Champaign, IL: Research Press, 1993.

Ring, Kenneth. *Heading Toward Omega: In Search of the Meaning of Near-Death Experience.* New York: Morrow, 1984.

———. *Life at Death: A Scientific Investigation of the Near-Death Experience.* New York: Morrow, 1982.

Ring, Kenneth, Sharon Cooper, and Charles Tart. *Mindsight: Near-Death and Out of Body Experiences in the Blind.* Palo Alto, CA: William James Center for Consciousness Studies at the Institute of Transpersonal Psychology, 1999.

Ring, Kenneth, and Evelyn Valarino. *Lessons from the Light: What We Can Learn from the Near-Death Experience.* Portsmouth, NH: Moment Point Press, 2000.

Sabom, Michael. *Light and Death: One Doctor's Fascinating Account of Near-Death Experiences.* Grand Rapids, MI: Zondervan, 1998.

Sanders, Catherine M. *Grief: The Mourning After, Dealing with Adult Bereavement.* New York: Wiley, 1989.

Selye, Hans. *Selye's Guide to Stress Research.* 3 vols. New York: Van Nostrand Reinhold, 1983.

———. *Stress Without Distress.* New York: Signet Books, 1974.

Sife, Wallace. *The Loss of a Pet, the Human-Animal Bond.* New York: Macmillan, 1993.

Somé, Malidoma Patrice. *Of Water and the Spirit.* New York: Putnam, 1994.

Stephenson, John S. *Death, Grief, and Mourning: Individual and Social Realities.* New York: Free Press, 1985.

Stroebe, Margaret, Wolfgang Stroebe, and Robert O. Hansson, eds. *Handbook of Bereavement: Theory, Research, and Intervention.* New York: Cambridge Univ. Press, 1999.

Tubesing, Nancy, and Donald Tubesing. *Structured Exercises in Stress Management*, vol. 1. Duluth, MN: Whole Person Press, 1983.

Walsh, John. *Tears of Rage: From Grieving Father to Crusader for Justice—The Untold Story of the Adam Walsh Case.* New York: Pocket Books, 1997.

Weenolsen, Patricia. *Transcendence of Loss over the Life Span.* New York: Hemisphere, 1988.

Weiss, Brian. *Messages from the Masters: Tapping into the Power of Love.* New York: Warner Books, 2000.

Wiitala, Geri Colozzi. *Heather's Return: The Amazing Story of Communications from Beyond the Grave.* Virginia Beach, VA: A.R.E. Press, 1996.

Wolfelt, Alan D. *Death and Grief: A Guide for Clergy.* Levittown, PA: Accelerated Development, 1988.

Worden, William. *Grief Counseling and Grief Therapy: A Handbook for the Mental Health Practitioner.* New York: Springer, 1991.

Zalaznik, Patricia. *Bibliography on Grief.* Minneapolis, MN: Abundant Resources, 1995.

Notes

Foreword

1. L. Miller, "Boomers Hire Consultants to Help Go from Good Life to 'Good Death,'" *Wall Street Journal*, February 25, 2000, p. 1.

2. L. Dossey, *Healing Beyond the Body* (Boston: Shambhala, 2001).

3. S. Parma and others, "A Qualitative and Quantitative Study of the Incidence, Features and Aetiology of Near Death Experiences in Cardiac Arrest Survivors," *Resuscitation* 48 (2001): 149–56.

4. J. Searle, Quotation on front cover of *Journal of Consciousness Studies*, vol. 2, issue 1, 1995.

5. J. Fodor, "The Big Idea," *(New York) Times Literary Supplement*, July 3, 1992, p. 20.

6. J. Maddox, "The Unexpected Science to Come," *Scientific American*, December 1999, pp. 62–67.

7. L. Dossey, *Reinventing Medicine* (San Francisco: HarperSanFrancisco, 1999).

8. J. A. Astin, E. Harkness, and E. Ernst, "The Efficacy of 'Distant Healing': A Systematic Review of Randomized Trials," *Annals of Internal Medicine* 132 (2000): 903–10; W. B. Jonas, "The Middle Way: Realistic Randomized Controlled Trials for the Evaluation of Spiritual Healing," *Journal of Alternative and Complementary Medicine* 7 (2001): 5–7.

9. L. Dossey, "Immortality," Alternative Therapies in Health and Medicine 6 (2000): 12.

Chapter 1

1. John Bowlby, psychiatrist and former president of the International Association for Child Psychiatry, conducted extensive research and published the most significant findings on human attachment and grief. For further reading, see, especially, his *Attachment and Loss*, vol. 1: *Attachment* (2d ed., 1982) and vol. 3: *Loss: Sadness and Depression* (1980).

Chapter 2

1. The Institute of Medicine released a 223-page report in November 1999 indicating that 98,000 Americans die unnecessarily each year from medical

mistakes, most of which are medication errors. "People get the wrong drug or the wrong dose, or they get it at the wrong time, or it's given to the wrong patient," explains Donald M. Berwick, a Harvard professor of healthcare policy, president of the Institute for Healthcare Improvement, and an investigator from the committee of nineteen experts. More Americans die from medical mistakes than from breast cancer, highway accidents, or AIDS.

2. Adapted from T. S. Holmes and R. H. Rahe, "The Social Readjustment Rating Scale," *Journal of Psychosomatic Research* 11 (1967): 213–18.

3. Hans Selye, former president of the International Institute of Stress, published significant findings on stress, including *Selye's Guide to Stress Research*, 3 vols. (New York: Van Nostrand Reinhold, 1983), and *Stress Without Distress* (New York: Signet Books, 1974).

4. Similar to a muscle, the brain itself can actually feel overexerted.

5. Louis A. Gamino, "Why 'Just Get Over It' Doesn't Work: Lessons from the Scott and White Grief Study" (Paper presented at Clinical Challenges in Bereavement: Beyond Supportive Care, Austin, TX, October 6, 2000).

6. American Psychiatric Association, 1997. Adapted from Lyle H. Miller and Alma Dell Smith, *The Stress Solution* (New York: Pocket Books, 1993).

7. Adapted from American Cancer Society, *Life After Loss Facilitator's Handbook* (1999), and Nancy Tubesing and Donald Tubesing, *Structured Exercises in Stress Management*, vol. 1 (Duluth, MN: Whole Person Press, 1983).

8. Robert A. Neimeyer, ed., *Death Anxiety Handbook: Research, Instrumentation, and Application* (Washington, DC: Taylor & Francis, 1994); Margaret Stroebe, Wolfgang Stroebe, and Robert O. Hansson, eds., *Handbook of Bereavement: Theory, Research, and Intervention* (New York: Cambridge Univ. Press, 1999); J. William Worden, *Grief Counseling and Grief Therapy: A Handbook for the Mental Health Practitioner* (New York: Springer, 1991).

9. American Psychiatric Association, 1997. Adapted from Miller and Smith, *The Stress Solution.*

Chapter 3

1. American Psychiatric Association, *Let's Talk About Panic Disorder* (Washington, DC: APA, 1992).

2. Ronald B. Adler and Neil Towne, *Looking Out/Looking In: Interpersonal Communication* (New York: Holt, Rinehart & Winston, 1987).

Chapter 4

1. For further reading, we recommend Malidoma Patrice Somé's *Of Water and the Spirit* (New York: Putnam, 1994).

2. "New Statistics on Death of a Child Available," *We Need Not Walk Alone* (magazine of The Compassionate Friends), Anniversary issue, 1999, p. 14.

3. *Survivors of Suicide Fact Sheet* (Washington, DC: American Association of Suicidology) 1998.

4. Data provided by the World Health Organization.

5. The Australian Institute for Suicide Research and Prevention, under the directorship of Dr. Diego De Leo, a professor of psychopathology and suicidology, is continuing research begun by Christopher Cantor and Penelope Slater. Cantor and Slater's study of 1,375 cases of suicide examined the association of marital disruption and parenthood as predictors of suicide (Cantor and Slater, "Marital Breakdown, Parenthood, and Suicide," *Journal of Family Studies* 1 (October 1995): 91–102.

6. Dianne Arcangel, "Tribute to Karlis Osis," *Journal of the American Society for Psychical Research* 90 (1996): 228–30.

7. Geri Colozzi Wiitala chronicled her story in *Heather's Return: The Amazing Story of Communications from Beyond the Grave* (Virginia Beach, VA: A.R.E. Press, 1996).

8. Gamino, "Why 'Just Get Over It' Doesn't Work (2000)."

Chapter 6

1. Adapted from Arcangel, "Tribute to Karlis Osis," p. 228.

Chapter 7

1. Margaret Carlson, "Farewell, John," *Time*, August 2, 1999, p. 33.

2. Jerry Adler, "There's Just the Three of Us," in *His Life and the Kennedy Legacy*, p. 36 (*Newsweek* Memorial Issue, 1999).

3. We have substituted "Elisabeth" for the more formal "Kübler-Ross" because she preferred the former.

4. Adapted from Arcangel, "The Wheel of Life Review," *Journal of the American Society for Psychical Research* 91 (1997): 353–56.

5. Neimeyer, *Death Anxiety Handbook*.

6. Worden, *Grief Counseling and Grief Therapy*. Worden was a professor of psychology at Harvard Medical School. Although he wrote this book for healthcare professionals, it can also benefit laypeople who want to take a more active and cognitive approach after the death of a loved one.

7. Monica McCormick, personal communication, 2000. Dr. Everett McCormick, a Florida physician, created and developed the activity. Website: www.BIRAKIT.com.

8. Terri Huber, *No Time Out from Grief: Surviving the Death of My Son* (Writers Club Press/iUniverse.com, 2000).

Chapter 8

1. An enormous body of work suggests that many men recover from loss by intellectualizing, mastering their emotions, and taking action (exercising, washing the car, repairing the house, working overtime, etc.). For further reading,

refer to Terry L. Martin and Kenneth J. Doka, *Men Don't Cry . . . Women Do: Transcending Gender Stereotypes of Grief* (Philadelphia: Brunner/Mazel, 2000).

Chapter 9

1. Nellie Connally, "Texas' First Lady Relives the Day the President Died," *Texas Magazine*, November 22, 1964.

Chapter 10

1. Benjamin Jowett, trans., *The Works of Plato* (1945), 614b.
2. Emily Williams Cook, Bruce Greyson, and Ian Stevenson, "Do Any Near-Death Experiences Provide Evidence for the Survival of Human Personality After Death? Relevant Features and Illustrative Case Reports," *Journal of Scientific Exploration* 12 (1998): 377–406.
3. R. Noyes, Jr., and R. Kletti, "Depersonalization in the Face of Life-Threatening Danger: An Interpretation," *Omega* 7 (1976): 103–14.
4. Kenneth Ring, *Mindsight: Near-Death and Out of Body Experiences in the Blind* (Palo Alto, CA: William James Center for Consciousness Studies at the Institute of Transpersonal Psychology, 1999).
5. Melvin Morse and Paul Perry, *Closer to the Light: Learning from the Near-Death Experiences of Children* (New York: Random House, 1991).
6. Bruce Greyson, "Near-Death Experiences," in *Varieties of Anomalous Experience: Examining the Scientific Evidence*, edited by Etzel Cardena, Steven Jay Lynn, and Stanley Krippner, pp. 315–52 (Washington, DC: American Psychological Association, 2000).
7. While working as director of psychiatric emergency services at the Universities of Virginia, Michigan, and Connecticut, as clinical director of psychiatry at the University of Connecticut Medical Center, and as professor of personality studies in the Department of Psychiatric Medicine, University of Virginia.
8. Pamela Kircher referred to death coincidents as shared near-death experiences in her 1995 book *Love Is the Link: A Hospice Doctor Shares Her Experience of Near-Death and Dying* (New York: Larson), p. 141.
9. Kenneth Ring, *Heading Toward Omega: In Search of the Meaning of Near-Death Experience* (New York: Morrow, 1984).
10. Neimeyer, *Death Anxiety Handbook.* Robert Neimeyer, Ph.D., professor in the Department of Psychology at the University of Memphis, editor of *Death Studies,* and former president of the Association for Death Education and Counseling, is among the most published and respected clinicians and researchers in the field. For further reading, please see the resources section at the end of this book.

Index